WHAT
THE RAILWAYS
DID FOR US

WHAT
THE RAILWAYS
DID FOR US

Stuart Hylton

AMBERLEY

Front Cover: Stanier 8F 2-8-0 No. 48151 scurries across Dandry Mire viaduct with the 'Fellsmen' charter, 10 July 2013. (Gordon Edgar)

Back Cover: A Southern Railway poster celebrating the centenary of Waterloo Station in 1948. (John Christopher Collection)

First published 2015
This edition published 2016

Amberley Publishing
The Hill, Stroud
Gloucestershire, GL5 4EP

www.amberley-books.com

British Library Cataloguing in Publication Data.
A catalogue record for this book is available from the British Library.

ISBN 978 1 4456 5952 7 (paperback)
ISBN 978 1 4456 4135 5 (ebook)

Typeset in 10pt on 13pt Sabon.
Typesetting and Origination by Amberley Publishing.
Printed in the UK.

CONTENTS

Introduction and Acknowledgements

It is hard, from a distance of nearly two centuries, to imagine the impact the coming of the railways must have had at the start of the nineteenth century. The understanding of time and distance that everybody had had from beyond living memory was suddenly turned upside down. Journeys that would have appeared impossible were suddenly not just feasible, but also affordable for all but the poorest in society.

The railways' immediate physical impact was dramatic enough – great mechanical horses, breathing fire and smoke and drawing impossibly heavy trains at unimaginable speeds across a landscape transformed by the embankments and cuttings, viaducts and tunnels their passage demanded. No feats of civil engineering had been seen to match them for scale since Roman times – or possibly ever.

But the wider changes to the world in which our forebears lived were to be more dramatic still. They would transform the way war was conducted and peace was maintained; prove to be one of the drivers of the dramatic industrial growth of the nineteenth century; create opportunities for many to become enormously wealthy, but impoverish many more, who invested unwisely; cause the state to think again about the policy of laissez-faire that was its default position; transform our leisure; radically reshape our towns and cities and change our very notions of time and how we measured it.

I have tried in these pages to give a summary of some of these huge impacts, but I realised early on the enormity of the task I had undertaken. To complete it in a single volume, rather than a whole shelf of books, requires me at times to be more anecdotal than encyclopaedic. But I hope at least you will be encouraged to look further into any aspects that particularly interest you. I have been greatly assisted by the wealth of excellent material that has been written on the subject. I hope I have done it justice and, here and there, managed to add to it in some small way. I have listed my main published sources in the bibliography. Much more material exists on the internet, for access to which you need only put your topic of interest into a search engine.

I make no apologies for concentrating mainly on the first century of the railway era, for this was the time that their greatest impact was being felt. Nor have I tried to look at impacts beyond the British Isles, for that would have required not one shelf of books, but several. Those looking to learn more about the international dimension can do no better than to start with the books by Christian Wolmar and Nicholas Faith, listed in the bibliography. I also feel a particular debt of gratitude to the late Professor Jack Simmons, whose books have been a valued guide throughout my work. Any merit in my book owes a great deal to all my sources; any shortcomings are my responsibility alone.

Particular thanks for the illustrations go to the Great Western Society and their archivist, Laurence Waters; to David Porter, the custodian of the Clayton Tunnel, for his picture of the remarkable north portal of the tunnel; and to Manchester City Council for the use of their illustrative material. I have tried to identify these main sources in the book. I have also tried to obtain permissions to use any copyrighted material. If I have inadvertently missed any, please accept my apologies and tell me about it via the publisher. If I, and the book, survive to a second edition, I will try to ensure that any oversights are addressed.

On a matter of detail, at various points in the book I started out trying to give a modern cash equivalent for historic costs, but one thing I learned in the course of trying to do so is that these figures can vary enormously, depending on the basis that one uses for inflating the figures. In the end, I decided to commend the very simple approximation adopted by White in his book *London in the Nineteenth Century*. This says that the Victorian pound, from whichever part of the Victorian period we are looking at, is worth roughly £100 in modern money.

CHAPTER 1

The Shock of the First Railways

Railways Before Steam

[The stones were guided] in a very clever manner down to ye town upon carriages with low broad wheels, covered with iron, which run upon a wooden frame made ye length of ye hill, so that when ye machine is sett agoing it runs down ye hill without any help, only one man behind to steer it, & in this manner above three hundred Tunn of stones are carried down at one load.

(John Evelyn, great-grandson of the diarist, describes a railway he saw in 1738)

Railways existed long before the days of George Stephenson. The earliest record of one appears in a stained-glass window in the minster of Freiburg im Breisgau in Germany, and dates from around 1350, and there are even suggestions that the Romans and Greeks used grooved stones as a kind of primitive railway to guide wagons. In Britain, some of the first references are in 1597 and 1598, to a line carrying coal from the mines of Sir Francis Willoughby at Woollaton and Strelley to the River Trent. The one John Evelyn was describing above was built in 1731 by Ralph Allen, to carry stone from a quarry near his home at Prior Park to barges on the River Avon. Railways (or tramways) were often used in conjunction with canals (sometimes providing a lower-cost alternative to extensions to a canal where the case for the waterway was marginal).

However, these differed from modern railways in a number of important respects. The early ones ran on wooden rails, and generally carried coal or minerals – but not passengers – from the point of extraction to the nearest navigable water. The land on which the railways were built was often in a single ownership and they relied upon humans or horses – or in Evelyn's example, gravity – for their motive power. Their impact on their environment was therefore much more limited than what was to follow – what actress Fanny Kemble called 'the magical machine with the flying white breath'.

Some early views on the steam railway:

What can be more palpably absurd than the prospect held out of locomotives travelling twice as fast as stagecoaches?

(The Conservative journal *The Quarterly Review*, 1825)

We see, in this magnificent creation, the well-spring of intellectual, moral and political benefits beyond all measurement and all price.

(*The Quarterly Review*, now taking a very different line at the opening of the Liverpool & Manchester Railway in 1830)

No one will pay good money to get from Berlin to Potsdam in one hour when he can ride his horse there in one day for free.

(King William I of Prussia (1864))

Rail travel at high speed is not possible because passengers, unable to breathe, would die of asphyxia.

(Dionysius Lardner, *The Steam Engine Familiarly Explained and Illustrated* (1824))

The Duke … could not see the necessity for these branch lines; it was well enough for through lines, they might be desirable for the country, but branch lines were uncalled for. If a place was within 20 miles of a railway it was all that could be wished or desired.

(The Duke of Cleveland, petitioned in 1844 to allow a branch line to cross his estate)

Public opinion is, as might be expected, much divided on the question, whether the prosperity of the Borough [Reading] will eventually be increased or diminished by the facility of communication with London, which the railway will produce; much uncertainty on this subject must necessarily prevail. But it is generally remarked that the greatest advocates for the railway are much less sanguine of success than formerly.

(*Berkshire Chronicle*, 1840)

That was a sight to have seen, but one I never care to see again! How much longer shall knowledge be allowed to go on increasing?

(Parish clerk William Hinton, on seeing his first locomotive in 1841)

Nothing quite prepared Britain for the coming of the first railways. The golden age of the canals had seen the countryside affected by some major engineering works, but again the canal boats themselves were man- or horse-drawn, and any carriage of passengers was a small-scale afterthought to their major function, delivering goods. There had even been a few tentative experiments with steam propulsion – taken furthest on boats, rather than on rail, once the stranglehold of James Watt's patents on the technology had expired – but steam locomotion on land did not have a secure future until it proved itself in the Rainhill trials of 1829. In the rest of this chapter, we look at the things – mostly bad – that the first railways were expected by the doom-mongers to do for early nineteenth-century Britain.

Suddenly the human race was confronted by a whole new set of ideas about time and space. Man, whose boundaries for thousands of years had been limited by the speed at which a horse could gallop, suddenly found himself the master of an infinitely wider universe. Within a handful of years, the maximum speed at which a man could travel went from about 15 miles an hour (albeit briefly), to rail services averaging 60 or more miles an hour over much longer distances. The public – and in particular that segment of the public that was supposed to be informed about these matters – did not know what to make of it. As we saw from one of the quotes above, they did not even believe the human body was capable of withstanding such unnatural velocity and early objectors to the railways on health grounds made some extravagant claims:

Boiling and maiming ... were destined to be everyday occurrences. Tunnels ... would expose healthy people to colds, catarrhs and consumptions, while the 'carbonic acid' generated by locomotive fuel in tunnels would cause suffocation by the destruction of the atmosphere. Not only was immense velocity fraught with danger to respiration but head and brain would be weakened by successive journeys (leading to premature ageing).

(Blythe, p. 25)

Pioneers like George Stephenson and Brunel knew early on what the potential for speed of this new mode of travel was, but deliberately tended to underplay it, for fear of terrifying both the general public and, in particular, their parliamentary masters, who had the power to withhold approval for their schemes. They had quite enough public anxiety to worry about:

> A distinguished man of science 'evoked the spectre [of] pleurisy that would certainly attack passengers when going through tunnels, always provided that they escaped the catastrophes resulting from the explosion of locomotive boilers'. And French doctors predicted that every conceivable disease would inevitably result from travelling by railway, since 'the too rapid transition from one climate to another would have a deadly effect upon the respiratory passages', while the brusque change of diet would give birth to dyspepsia or dysentery.
>
> (mikes.railhistory.railfan.net)

Wiser medical counsel dismissed these fears, but for a time they had considerable influence until they could be proven wrong. A particular 'scientific' thorn in Brunel's side was one Dionysius Lardner, the Professor of Natural Philosophy and Astronomy at the newly established London University (now UCL). Lardner was well-known as a populariser of science of his day, and engaged in a series of public disputes with Brunel over various aspects of his work. Lardner seemed to want it both ways. On the one hand, he argued that Brunel's broad gauge locomotives would be very limited in the loads they could pull and the speed at which they could pull them, due to their wind resistance (Brunel was able to demonstrate that any shortcoming Lardner had witnessed was due instead to a problem with a particular locomotive's blast pipe, which they were quickly able to fix). At the same time, Lardner argued that, if a train's brakes failed while going downhill through the Box Tunnel, its speed would quickly build to 120 mph, at which point all the passengers would be suffocated. Again, Brunel was able to show that friction and wind resistance (the latter a commodity Lardner said Brunel's locomotives possessed in such abundance) would regulate its speed.

For some – such as the merchants in Manchester and Bristol – the issue was simple. The railway would bring them far closer to their source of raw materials or to their main market, which would reduce costs and was to be wholeheartedly welcomed. Many communities up and down the country saw it the same way, and actively campaigned for the new railway to come to their town or city.

For others, such a radical shake-up of the established order was less straightforward. For those who would be in direct competition with the railways – the canals, the turnpike roads and the stagecoach operators – outright opposition on commercial grounds was the order of the day. The worst fears of the canal and turnpike interests would, in many cases, prove to be well founded and they faced a bleak future in the longer term. But, for the stagecoach operators, the future was far less grim. Long-distance inter-city stagecoach traffic may have been killed off by the railways but, at the same time, a whole new market of shorter, feeder services linked to the railway network grew up. The overall volume of business actually grew, if the total number of horses employed is anything to go by. However many people, perhaps understandably, found it hard to understand how a scheme that (it was claimed in some quarters) would supersede the horse could lead to an increase in its use, and assumed the figures being reported from pioneer areas like Manchester were simply wrong.

Wealthy landowners were among the most implacable opponents of the first railways, not least because they would bring the common herd within sight of their estates. The earls of Derby and Sefton, faced with the Liverpool & Manchester Railway crossing their land, expressed their opposition to their fellow lords:

> The sanctity of their domains would be invaded, and the privacy of their residences destroyed, by thus bringing into their neighbourhood a public highway, with all the varied traffic of coals and merchandise and passengers, that would be the consequence of such an establishment.

> (Booth, p. 15)

They further sought to argue that 'the locomotive engine was an unsightly object', and that the cost of the railway would be three or four times the original estimate, making it a 'wild and impracticable scheme'. These aristocratic concerns were reinforced by the canal interests, who sought to nip this railway nonsense in the bud: 'The railway, as a conveyance, would be neither cheap nor expeditious; … it would be a grievous injury to the landowners on the line, and at the same time ruinous to the projectors themselves.' (Ibid., p. 32)

However, much of this opposition carried little weight in the House of Lords. With regard to the nuisance value of the steam locomotive: 'so poor a case was made, and so little objectionable did the Engine appear to be, even from the testimony of the opponents, that their Lordships did not think it necessary to hear any evidence on the other side.' (Ibid., p. 33)

Landowners might have other objections to a railway nearby. They may not want it to interfere with their hunting (the Earl of Darlington was an early and vehement opponent of the Stockton & Darlington Railway on hunting grounds, and the railway had to be diverted around his estate). In the event, hunting benefited greatly from the railways. Whereas hunts were previously purely local affairs, the railways opened up prime hunting country to a much wider clientele. Special carriages were laid on to transport horses and other hunting paraphernalia to meets. What previously required a commitment for the entire season could now be done as a day trip: 'During the hunting season, gentlemen may have their horses forwarded to Swindon by the morning express.' (Great Western advertisement in the *Berkshire Chronicle*, 1855)

Others simply did not want the railway to interfere with their view, so some railway companies were forced to spend large sums crafting elaborate and stately tunnel entrances, bridges and stations on large estates, in an effort to overcome their railway's assault on the landowner's delicate sensibilities (more on these later).

For the working farmer, a more practical objection to the railway might be that it would interfere with land drainage and the flow of water. There were concerns about fragmentation of landholdings, and some farmers might fear losing their near monopoly in supplying food to the nearby urban area, which they held only so long as everyone's mobility was limited. The railway would open up the market to competition from much further afield – in the case of the Great Western Railway serving London, even from Wales or Ireland. One Welsh merchant, arguing in support of the railway, cited the case of a consignment of butter that he supplied to interests in London in pre-railway (and pre-refrigeration) days. The order was despatched in November but only arrived in February, by which time it had allegedly lost 50 per cent of its value (the real surprise was that the loss in value was as little as 50 per cent).

Merely trying to investigate a route for a railway could attract violent opposition, as William James found out in 1822 when he tried to carry out a survey between Liverpool and Manchester. They were stoned and threatened with being thrown down a mineshaft. A prizefighter, specially hired by James to protect his theodolite, got into a bout of fisticuffs with a collier hired to break it. The prizefighter won but, meanwhile, the collier's friends drove off the rest of the survey team with stones and were able to smash the equipment. Similar obstruction was one of the reasons given for Stephenson's initial survey of the Liverpool–Manchester route being so flawed, since part of it had to be conducted surreptitiously, by night, and sometimes in the face of gunfire.

For some opponents of the railways, the objection centred around pollution, of the moral as well as the environmental kind. William Wordsworth, the Poet Laureate, made a number of representations (some in verse, naturally) expressing his fear of the working classes coming on holiday to vulgarise his beloved Lakeland by their presence, once the railway enabled them to do so. This is from Wordsworth's 'On the projected Kendal and Windermere Railway of 1844', published in the *Morning Post*:

> Is then no nook of English ground secure
> From rash assault? Schemes of retirement sown
> In youth, and mid the busy world kept pure
> As when their earliest flowers of hope were blown,
> Must perish; – how can they this blight endure?

He added (this time in plain prose): 'We have too much hurrying about in these islands; much for idle pleasure, and more from over-activity in the pursuit of wealth, without regard for the good and happiness of others.' (Quoted in Hoskins, p. 210.)

But Wordsworth's objections were nothing if not elitist. The democratic argument, that the railway would enable more people to enjoy the beauty of the Lakes, cut absolutely no ice with him, for in his view the great unwashed were incapable of appreciating natural beauty. As he told the *Morning Post*:

> Such an appreciation was 'so far from being intuitive, that it can be produced only by a slow and gradual process of culture...' Better to leave it to 'those who have been in the habit of observing and studying the peculiar character of such scenes'. Instead of invading the Lake District, 'artisans and labourers, and the humblest classes of shopkeepers' should be content with 'little excursions ... after having attended divine worship'.
>
> (Quoted in Faith, p. 54)

Wordsworth's objections were naturally extremely unpopular, and the report recommending that the railway go ahead dismissed them as 'wholly untenable'. Just to add to Wordsworth's chagrin, he himself would become a tourist attraction for the rail-borne visitors to gawp at.

The loss of tranquillity and privacy were two charges often levelled at the first railways. Dr Johnson had said the same about the canals in the eighteenth century. Art critic John Ruskin, by no means a fan of the railways, had complained that they would simply mean that 'now every fool in Buxton can be in Bakewell in half an hour, and every fool in Bakewell at Buxton; which you think a lucrative process of exchange – you Fools Everywhere.' (Quoted in Morgan (ed.), p. 219)

One stage beyond an influx of fools was the fear, which existed in many more 'desirable' communities, of undesirables travelling out to them from the cities by railway. Not surprisingly, it was one raised by the residents of Windsor to oppose a branch line from the Great Western to their town:

> We shall not fail to have a daily importation of all the ladies from St Giles's, and the thieves from the Seven Dials ... [Within three years] the whole line would be occupied by teams of navigators and persons of the worst description, and that it would be impossible for any decent female to walk out alone, and we should be subject to all sorts of depredations, added to which the facility it would afford to the passage of the hordes of Irish and other casual paupers from Bristol to London and the accidents to which all railways are liable, would all enhance the burdens of agricultural parishes.
>
> (*Berkshire Chronicle*, 23 November 1833)

But, even before the completed railway could start exporting urban undesirables, there was another problem, as this opponent of the Great Western Railway pointed out:

> The time which the projectors of the railway calculated on for completing the line between London and Reading was three or four years; and, during that time, the country would be disturbed by great numbers of workmen, a great part of whose earnings would be spent in drunkenness and disorderly conduct.
>
> (*Berkshire Chronicle*, 14 December 1833)

A Middlesex parson in the 1830s recorded the dire effects the navvies building the Great Western Railway had had on what was then the village of Southall, some of which appear to have been more than transitory:

> A remarkable change for the worse took place about this time in the hitherto retired neighbourhood of Southall Green. The railway spread dissatisfaction and immorality among the poor, the place being inundated with worthless and overpaid navigators ('navvies'); the very appearance of the country was altered, some families left, and the rusticity of the village gave place to a London-out-of-town character. Moss-grown cottages were retired before new ones with bright red tiles, picturesque hedgerows were succeeded by prim iron railings, and the village inn, once a pretty cottage with a swinging sign, is transmogrified to the

'Railway Tavern' with an intimation gaudily set forth that 'London porter' and other luxuries hitherto unknown to the aborigines were to be procured within.

(Quoted in Hoskins, p. 213)

For John Keate, the headmaster of Eton, the problem was not so much that undesirables would be brought into his locality, but rather that his pupils would get themselves transported out of it, in order to become undesirables. He feared the railway would corrupt the morals of Eton boys by giving them easy access to the dissipations of London. He appealed to William Gladstone, no less, to stop the railways serving Windsor and Eton, and putting them in danger of 'interfering with the discipline of the school, the studies and amusements of the boys, affecting the healthiness of the place, from the increase of floods and endangering even the lives of boys'. In similar vein, criminals, having committed a felony in rural England, could quickly jump on board a train and soon be back in the metropolis, beyond the reach of such country law enforcement agencies as there were (in this connection, it is worth noting that the Metropolitan Police – the world's first professional police force – was only established in 1829, the year of the Rainhill trials on the Liverpool & Manchester Railway).

Eton naturally had a number of influential people among its alumni, which meant its objections had to be expensively bought off when the second Great Western Railway Bill went before Parliament in 1835. These safeguards included 'a good and sufficient [that is, 10-foot] fence on each side' of a 4-mile stretch of the line nearest the College, complete with guards to patrol it 'for the purpose of preventing or restricting all access to the said railway by the scholars of Eton College'. As a further deterrent to scholarly travel, the Company was not allowed to build a station at nearby Slough. The railway got round this by renting some rooms at the nearby Crown Inn to serve as an office and waiting room, and letting the passengers walk down onto the track to board the trains. Later they bought their own pub, the New Inn, most of which they turned over to railway activities. An irate College took the matter to court, but were told by the Lord Chancellor that the railway could do anything which was not expressly forbidden in the Act (which this was not). By 1848 the railway even secured a branch line to Windsor, running even closer to the College (however, this required further policing of the line, which was not allowed to be withdrawn until 1886).

Similar opposition came from another educational institution, the University of Oxford, whose Chancellor was none other than one-time war hero and Prime Minister the Duke of Wellington. He disapproved of railways on the grounds that they encouraged the lower classes to travel about and would promote the development of subversive ideas among them. He used his influence to ensure that the railway initially came no nearer the City of Oxford than Steventon, 10 miles away. For years, passengers (77,567 of them in 1842) had to endure the additional three-shilling coach trip that added an hour and a half to their journey time, to or from Oxford.

Another literary entrant into the debate was Charles Dickens. Here he details the chaos caused to the community by the digging up of Camden town for the London & Birmingham Railway:

The first shock of a giant earthquake had, just at that period, rent the whole neighbourhood to its centre. Traces of its course were visible on every side. Houses were knocked down; streets broken through and stopped; deep pits and trenches dug in the ground; enormous heaps of earth and clay thrown up; buildings that were undermined and shaking, propped up by great beams of wood. Here, a chaos of carts, overthrown and jumbled together at the bottom of a steep unnatural hill; there, confused treasures of iron, soaked and rusted in something that had accidentally become a pond. Everywhere were bridges that led nowhere; thoroughfares that were wholly impassable; Babel towers of chimneys, wanting half their height; temporary wooden houses and enclosures, in the most unlikely situations; carcasses of ragged tenements and fragments of unfinished walls and arches, and piles of scaffolding, and wildernesses of bricks, and giant forms of cranes, and tripods straddling above nothing. There were a hundred thousand shapes and substances of incompleteness, wildly mingled out of their places, upside down, burrowing in the earth, aspiring in the air, mouldering in the water, and unintelligible as any dream. Hot springs and fiery eruptions, the usual attendants on earthquakes, lent their contributions of confusion to the scene. Boiling water hissed and heaved within dilapidated walls; whence also the glare and roar of flames came issuing forth; and mounds of ashes blocked up rights of way, and wholly changed the law and custom of the neighbourhood.

(*Dombey and Son*, 1846)

Outside the urban areas, one of the reasons the early railways had such a dramatic impact on the landscape was that the limited performance of the early locomotives required a very level trackbed. The eastern part of the Great Western line to Bristol – known for its flatness as 'Brunel's billiard table' – had no gradients of more than 1 in 660, and none of the early engineers generally exceeded 1 in

250. To accommodate this within the confines of the real world required some extravagant cuttings, embankments and viaducts. Raw as these must have seemed when being built, nature has now reclaimed them as things of beauty in their own right, as well as giving travellers new prospects of unaltered nature, looking out from the railway.

Public concerns about railways were not helped by the (relatively frequent) accidents that occurred during the early days. As I record later, Charles Dickens himself was involved in one in 1865. These were graphically (not to say luridly) reported by such journals as the *Illustrated London News* and *Punch* and, if the actual details of the accident were not gruesome enough for their readers' tastes, they would speculate on how things might have been even worse.

The activities of protesters at the parliamentary stage could result in some oddities in the drafting of the final Act. In the case of the Whitby & Pickering Railway, their approval included clauses both permitting and forbidding the use of locomotives on the line, and the fourth version of the Liverpool & Manchester Railway Act (the one that finally let the railway into Manchester itself) forbad the use of locomotives anywhere but on their approved tracks – as if they were going to jump off them and run amok through the streets like ravening beasts.

Partly as a result of all this protest, Britain became the most expensive country in the world in which to get consent for a railway. Sometimes the parliamentary process alone could cost thousands of pounds a mile, added to which some landowners might extract quite exorbitant payments for their land as the price for removing their objections (though, as Biddle shows, direct comparisons with the cost of overseas railways are not necessarily as straightforward as they might appear).

We can follow the debate over one – not untypical – railway proposal. Battle lines began to form from the moment in August 1833 that an advertisement appeared in the *Berkshire Chronicle* and other local newspapers, inviting investors to put their money into something called the Great Western Railway. It promised to:

Multiply the number of travellers, improve the conveyance of goods, encourage manufactures, diffuse the advantages of the vicinity of towns over the country intersected by the railway, improve the supply of provisions to the metropolis and extend the market for agricultural produce, give employment to the labouring classes, both during construction and by its subsequent effects, and increase the prosperity of the neighbourhood.

(Quoted in Phillips, p. 4)

The prospectus for the Great Western Railway between London and Bristol had been published and investors were being sought. They were trying to raise £3 million in £100 shares, for each of which a £5 deposit was initially required. The promoters spoke highly of the scheme:

> The Directors are encouraged in this great National Undertaking by the support of the Landowners and Occupiers, whose Property will thereby become closely and advantageously connected with the Metropolis, as well as with the remote Western Districts of England.
>
> (*Berkshire Chronicle*, 7 September 1833)

The one achievement they were coy about was the improvement in journey times that would be achieved. They talked of reducing the time for travelling from Reading to London from the 4½–5 hours taken by the stagecoaches to 1½–2 hours. The reality was that, from the earliest days, the journey could be done in about an hour, but the promoters were not about to alarm the public by forecasting such a dramatic increase in speeds.

Editorial coverage in this local newspaper was – initially – supportive:

> We learn that the Bristol people are enthusiastic in the plan, and we have the authority of gentlemen thoroughly competent to pronounce an opinion for saying that there is every reason to believe the Great Western Railway will be completed in no very great space of time.
>
> (*Berkshire Chronicle*, 7 September 1833)

But their optimism was premature, for public meetings were arranged along the projected line of the railway. Ostensibly, these were to discuss the merits of the scheme, but in reality their purpose was to mobilise opposition to it. In vain did Charles Saunders, the secretary to the Railway, attend one such meeting at Slough and try to argue in its favour. There was also one aristocratic landowner who at least arrived at the meeting as a supporter of the scheme. Lord Orkney owned some mills in the village of Woburn. They were, he said, being put out of business by steam mills in London undercutting them. Their only hope was the provision of cheaper, rail-hauled coal. But he was apparently so taken aback by the strength of opposition to the railway that he subsequently withdrew his support. The meeting resolved that: 'The said railways are not called for by any public necessity and would be highly prejudicial to the parts of the county of

Bucks through which it is proposed they will pass.' (*Berkshire Chronicle*, 23 November 1833)

An alternative public subscription was launched to fund opposition to the proposal. Opponents were quick to deny any suggestion of widespread landowner support for the railway, poured scorn on the promoters' estimated cost of the scheme (with good reason, as it would turn out) and claimed that it had failed to raise more than a tiny fraction of the necessary investment.

But the landowning interests did not have it all their own way. In March 1834 a large public meeting was held in Reading town hall, where the secretary of the railway company was given the opportunity to present their scheme. The meeting decided to start a petition to support the scheme, and to get their local MP to present it to Parliament.

Landowners and rival commercial interests continued to be opposed to the railway. The Commissioners of the Thames Navigation (whose interests were closely allied to those of the canals) were particularly vociferous, claiming that the scheme would lead to 'the destruction of land, the asseverance of enclosures, the inundation of foreign labourers and the increased Poor Rate'. They said that 'no case of public utility had been made out to justify such an uncalled-for encroachment on the rights of private property' and their general committee was 'instructed and empowered to take all such steps as they shall deem advisable for effectually opposing the progress of this useless and mischievous project'. The local press was similarly divided. The pro-Whig *Reading Mercury* was a keen supporter of the scheme, while the Conservative *Berkshire Chronicle* – after its initial enthusiasm – became the mouthpiece of its opponents.

Ever more ingenious arguments were found against the railway. It was claimed that Bristol and London, as rival seaports, could have no community of interest in the project (this argument was used to counter evidence of the commercial success of the Liverpool–Manchester and London–Birmingham railways. These, it was claimed, linked a seaport and a manufacturing town, for which the business case was very different); it was also claimed that Reading could not benefit from the scheme as it had no potential for developing manufacturing industry; that disuse of the Thames would cause it to silt up; and that the scheme would fail, leaving nobody with the obligation to reinstate the landscape to its previous condition. For good measure, it would also absorb capital that could be better employed elsewhere, impoverish estates and drive landowners from their land.

In case all else failed, the opponents tried appealing to the nobler instincts of the ruling classes: 'We show you a positive evil; an evil to which no English gentleman can be insensible. Woe be to the land, whenever the love of their own green fields, their avenues, their trees, their cottages becomes cold in the breast of our nobles and our chiefs.' (*Berkshire Chronicle*, 23 November 1833)

The cause of the scheme was not helped by the Great Western promoters initially submitting a botched partial scheme to Parliament (covering the sections from London to Reading and Bath to Bristol only) in early 1834. This, its detractors claimed, was neither 'Great' nor 'Western', and it was thrown out. A second Bill, this time for the whole scheme, was finally approved on 31 August 1835.

As we saw, some opposition stemmed purely from rival commercial interests and, sure enough, the impact of the railways on at least some of their competitors was found to be as dramatic as the doom-mongers had predicted. The inns at Hounslow had been home to 2,000 post horses, but:

> As early as April 1842, a daily paper reports: 'At the formerly flourishing village of Hounslow, so great is now the general depreciation of property on account of the transfer of traffic to the railway, that at one of the chief inns there is an inscription, "new milk and cream sold here"; while another announces the profession of the chief occupier as "mending boots and shoes".'
>
> (Acworth, quoted in Morgan (ed.), p. 90)

The forty coaches that ran daily through Northampton had all closed within six months of the opening of the railway. While at another formerly important coaching centre:

> Maidenhead is now in miserable plight. The glories of 'The Bear', where a good twenty minutes were allowed to the traveller to stow away three or four shillings' worth of boiled fowls and ham to support his inner man during the night are fast fading away forever. This celebrated hostelry is about to be closed as a public inn.
>
> (Ibid.)

(Not all forecasts of doom were correct. Your author had occasion to visit 'The Bear' – purely for research purposes – and can report that his inner man was still being catered for in 2014.)

Patterns of shopping also changed. Shopkeepers in the small towns around Manchester all complained that their former customers now travelled into Manchester to make their purchases. The canals also suffered as railways came into direct competition with them. The Manchester & Leeds Railway caused the value of Rochdale Canal shares to fall from £150 to £40 within two years, while those of the Calder & Hebble Navigation fell from 500 guineas (£525) to £180.

One fear of the new railways was perhaps less well articulated than some of these other concerns, largely because those who held it had no organised voice, no political power. The new technology of the railways should not be seen in isolation; it was developing at the same time as many other industrial technologies were being introduced. The net effect of them was all too often to replace human labour with machines, creating hardship for those who were displaced. The early nineteenth century was the time of Captain Swing and the Luddites, opponents of new technology and, more particularly, the misery it brought in its wake. Henry Booth was aware that the same charge might be levelled at the railways, but in their case he thought the fears were unfounded:

It has frequently been [a] matter of regret, that in the progress of mechanical science, as applicable to trade and manufactures, the great stages of improvement are too often accompanied with severe suffering to the industrious classes of society … as the substitute of mechanism for manual labour is the object generally aimed at, immediate deprivation to the labouring community seems the inevitable result … The Liverpool & Manchester Railway presents one great object for our admiration, almost unalloyed by any counteracting or painful consideration. We behold, at once, a new theatre of activity and employment presented to an industrious population, with all the indications of health and energy and cheerfulness which flow from such a scene.

(Booth, pages 85–6)

Booth went on to imagine a hundred railway projects equivalent to the Liverpool & Manchester Railway, generating a capital expenditure of £50 million–60 million: 'What a source of occupation to the labouring community! What a change in the facility of giving employment to capital, and consequently in the value of money!' (Ibid., p. 89)

And what a change it turned out to be, and how swiftly it happened! By 1842, within just twelve years of the Liverpool & Manchester Railway opening, Britain would have a rail network nearly 2,000 miles in length. In the following chapters, we look at the consequences of this for Victorian England – and how they still affect us today.

CHAPTER 2

The Railways and Class

If there is one part of my public life on which I look back with more satisfaction, it is with reference to the boon we have conferred on third-class travellers.

(Sir James Allport, General Manager of the Midland Railway)

By universal admission, there are, roughly speaking, three classes in all societies, and the existing arrangement of railway carriages appears to correspond very closely with the ordinary habits of life.

(*Times* leader, 12 October 1874, opposing the Midland Railway's decision to abolish second-class travel)

In first class, the passengers insult the railway staff, whereas in the third class the railway staff insult the passengers. Now I learn that in second class, the passengers insult each other.

(Quoted in Faith, p. 237)

How far did the railways perpetuate established Victorian ideas of class distinction, or did they help to break them down or change them? Before the railways, public transport on the roads fell into one of four categories (not then referred to as 'classes'), according to the speed and comfort they offered. Top of the pile (and most expensive) were the mail coaches (then the fastest things on the road). Next came the ordinary stagecoaches, whose passengers were differentiated by whether they rode inside or outside. The poorest travellers went by slow goods wagons, for whom there was no inside option, or they walked. Similarly, steamships divided their passengers into 'cabin' or 'deck'.

But class would proliferate on the railway network with, at one time, as many as seven different classes of travel available. For the very rich, like the Duke of Wellington, there was the option of having your private carriage loaded onto a flat truck, avoiding all contact with the lower classes. When the Liverpool & Manchester Railway opened in 1830, it at first used class just to differentiate between slower and faster trains, though they had separate first- and second-class booking offices and waiting rooms at their Liverpool Road station from the outset. But the Grand Junction Railway used 'first-' and 'second-class' to differentiate between individual passengers from its opening in 1837. On some early railways, the distinction between first and second class truly mirrored that in the earlier stagecoaches – giving passengers the choice of travelling under cover or exposed to the elements.

At the opening of the Sheffield & Rotherham line in 1838, a reporter suggested that the outdoor option would be preferred by a wider clientele in fine weather, and this was borne out by a report to the President of the Board of Trade in February 1842:

> In fine weather respectable tradespeople, clerks, etc., avail themselves of the third-class carriages to a considerable extent; but the bulk of the half million third-class passengers who are carried on this railway in the course of the year are strictly the working classes, weavers, masons, bricklayers, carpenters, mechanics and labourers of every description, some of whom formerly used to travel by carts, but the great number by foot.
>
> (Parliamentary Papers, XLI. pp 25 seq.)

But what was the railway companies' attitude to the carriage of 'persons in the lower stations of life'? A third class had made its appearance on parts of the Stockton & Darlington line by the mid-1830s, again using open wagons. The early railways did not anticipate – and in many cases, did not welcome – the volume of third-class custom they would attract. Perhaps the most extreme expression of this comes from the Great Western Railway. Their third class originated from an initiative by one of their independent carriers – a Mr Dibbin – who announced that he was going to carry passengers in open trucks, mixed in with his goods trains.

Normally, the instruction to the Great Western staff was to offer no assistance whatsoever to third-class travellers. The one exception was in extremely cold weather, when the third-class traveller in his open carriage faced the risk of literally freezing to death on a long journey. This fate was by no means unknown to outside passengers on stagecoaches, but the higher speed of trains made the risk greater. On at least one occasion when Great Western Railway staff found a third-class passenger close to death by hypothermia, they removed him from his seat in the open wagon and dumped him in the street outside the station, to avoid the inconvenience and paperwork of a death on railway premises. Few concessions to creature comfort were made in third-class travel, though this railway at least offered a roof (if not glazed windows):

> There was a general feeling of bare boards and cheerlessness as you entered them … even the windows were but small apertures [and] the seats were cushionless … Trains stopped at every little place on the way; you were shunted here and shunted there, or found yourself resting in some lonely siding for what seemed an age.

> (Quoted in Briggs, p. 237)

But the wrath of the railway companies was directed most at those wealthy merchants who could well afford to travel first class, but who saved money by travelling third class. There were even calls for one company to employ chimney sweeps to make a point of sitting next to these cheapskates and making sure they went home with an authentically grimy experience of the proletarian class of travel.

George Hudson, the 'Railway King', had a similarly dismissive attitude towards third-class passengers. Asked by a parliamentary commission what the capacity of his third-class accommodation was, he replied as if he were tinning sardines: 'I do not know what number of passengers are put into the third-class trucks, because there is a great difference in the way of packing them!'

One of the first government interventions in the operation of the railways and, in particular, in relation to third-class passengers, resulted from a fatal accident. On Christmas Eve 1841 a Great Western train ran into a landslip at Sonning, near Reading. Eight third-class passengers, travelling in low-sided open wagons, were killed – either thrown out or crushed between the locomotive and the heavy goods wagons behind them. This led to an investigation into the conditions in which third-class passengers were carried, and to the 1844 Railway Act, which introduced 'parliamentary trains'. This law required railway companies to provide at least one service a day at a maximum fare of one penny a mile, and meeting minimum standards of safety and comfort. (However, the law did not prevent these trains from being – in some cases – extremely slow (the Act only required them to average 12 miles an hour) or inconveniently timed for passengers.) This was a rare and early example of a government interfering in the operation of private companies. Moreover, trains which met these requirements were exempt from passenger duty, the government tax on most rail travellers, meaning that the state was subsidising a 'social good'.

The Railway Department of the Board of Trade specified the standards with which they expected the 'parliamentary carriage' to comply:

Free admission of light and air.
Protection against wind, wet and cold.
Lamps for night journeys.
Seats with backs, and of sufficient depth to permit all persons to sit with ease.
Windows for 'look outs'.
Doors in sufficient numbers on each side to prevent confusion in getting in and out and to provide means of ready escape in case of accidents.
Moderate proportion in the size of the carriages.
'Acceleration of speed' [whatever that means].

They produced a report, describing (with illustrations) the carriage designs by which the different railway companies proposed to comply with these standards. What is clear from it is that none of the companies complied fully, and some fell woefully short of them in almost every particular. Moreover, the parliamentary train rules did not prevent rail companies also continuing to operate ordinary third-class services to lower standards, outside of the legislation. Some companies, such as the Manchester & Leeds and the Edinburgh & Glasgow, even managed to put on fourth-class services which undercut the rates charged by parliamentary trains. Some of the worst examples of these were the so-called stanhopes, run by the Manchester & Leeds among others, where all the passengers were obliged to stand in order to pack more people in, and the Great Western's continuing use of open wagons for third-class travel, which did not cease entirely until the 1870s. Even the *Railway Times* of the day took the view that third-class customers should be thankful for whatever they got: 'We do not feel disposed to attach much weight to the argument in favour of third-class carriages with seats. On a short line, little physical inconvenience can result from their absence.' (Quoted in Hylton (2007), p. 91)

Punch begged to differ, and compared the treatment of third-class passengers unfavourably with that meted out to animals:

The mode in which our third-class travellers are treated is a scandal to an age which legislates for the comfort of a cab-horse and places water-troughs along the Strand for the benefit of any lost sheep or idle dog that may feel disposed to take to drinking in that crowded locality ... It is, certainly, as cruel to expose a number of thinly-clad women and children to rain and wind for several hours on a railway train, as it is to exact from an unhappy donkey more than a fair day's work for a fair day's thistles.

(Punch 26 (1854), p.133)

None the less, third class quickly became a major part of railways' income. By 1843, third-class travel represented 60 per cent of the passenger traffic between Edinburgh and Glasgow, and 35 per cent of that company's passenger revenues. Nationally, they soon made up a majority of all railways' fare-paying customers and a sizeable part of their income.

As we see elsewhere in the book, the demolition of whole urban neighbourhoods by the railways led to some serious social problems and, from 1864 onwards, some railways were compelled to lay on ultra-cheap 'workmen's trains' to get 'persons of the labouring classes' back into town, to enable them to continue in their jobs – and thus provided a seventh class of travel. Both the hours of running of these trains and the question of who might ride in them were regulated by the government (in some cases, conditions could be applied, requiring the passengers to give evidence of their employment as workmen to qualify for travel).

One of the fears expressed by some railway operators at the time was that, if conditions aboard third class ever approached the tolerable, the operators would experience a loss of revenue as travellers switched from second to third class. But the Midland Railway, under their General Manager James Allport, challenged this orthodoxy. Allport had travelled extensively in America and had been impressed with the standard of accommodation provided by George Pullman in his railway carriages (which was all the more necessary, since American railway journeys could take two or three days). The Midland became the first of the major railway companies to do away with second class altogether. They did so in 1875, for reasons that were solely business-related:

Based on the realisation that the three-class system was uneconomical and that larger returns were to be derived from stimulating than from discouraging third-class travel. Though unconvinced and indignant, the other companies had no alternative but to follow the example set by the Midland ... Soon third-class accommodation equalled the old second; soon it was much better.

(J. A. R. Pimlott, *The Englishman's Holiday* (London, 1947))

By the middle of the nineteenth century there was the start of a rapid decline nationally in the second-class travel market. In 1859 32.23 per cent of railway travellers bought second-class tickets, but by 1874 this had fallen to just 15.12 per cent. In the Midland's case, the proportion fell from 23.37 per cent to 11.24 per cent over the same period. These lower levels of take-up, combined with the higher cost of providing second-class carriages, made that part of the business much less profitable. At the same time, third-class travel was booming; again, between 1859 and 1874 the proportion of national ticket sales that were third class rose from 49.93 per cent to 76.66 per cent. So the Midland closed down its second-class business, and upgraded its third-class accommodation by reclassifying its second-class carriages as third, at the same time as reducing third-class fares, as a means of saving operating costs and of poaching some of the growing third-class market from its rivals. Nationally, the railways generally could not ignore the growing importance of third-class travel to their finances. By 1888 88 per cent of ticket sales and 77 per cent of railway revenues nationally came from third-class passengers.

Passenger Numbers by Class

Year	1st Class	2nd Class	3rd and Parliamentary
1851–2	11.9%	36.3%	52.7%
1870	9.6%	22.4%	67.9%

Passenger Receipts by Class

Year	1st Class	2nd Class	3rd and Parliamentary
1851–2	32.0%	38.7%	30.3%
1870	24.2%	30.1%	45.7%

(Quoted in Evans, p. 398)

There were naturally complaints from the dwindling numbers of passengers who could not afford first class, but travelled second to avoid what they saw as the rowdiness of third class. Other objectors were the adherents to the 'All Things Bright and Beautiful' view of social order. As the hymn says:

> The rich man at his castle,
> The poor man at his gate;
> God made them high and lowly
> And ordered their estate.

They took the view that, by scrapping second class, the company was bringing the lower orders nearer to equality with their betters and giving them ideas above their station. Some of the Midland's rival companies also shouted foul, but most were forced to follow the Midland's lead over the next twenty-five years, as second-class ticket sales continued to fall, reaching just 6 per cent of national sales by 1899. Those companies that specialised in passenger traffic were among the last to abolish second-class travel. The Great Western did away with theirs in 1910 and, in 1938, the London & North Eastern scrapped it on their suburban services, becoming the last of the mainstream providers to do so. First and third remained the two ticket categories after nationalisation until 1956, when third class was rebranded 'Standard', to remove at least part of the class distinction on the nation's railways.

Moving towards the luxury end of the market, in 1844–5 express trains started to appear on the London–Brighton and London–Exeter lines. These were first and second class only, but charged a supplement for the express service, effectively making them another couple of classes. However, they were not popular, started to be withdrawn from 1859 and were mostly gone by 1890. Pullman saloon cars, (pioneered, naturally, by the Midland and priced to exclude the riff-raff – apart from the very rich riff-raff) were also introduced on the London–Brighton and other lines, conveying 'over three hundred merchant princes and others to their marine villas at Brighton'. Other railways also had a pricing structure that differentiated both by standard of accommodation and by speed of the service, though these were again gradually phased out by the 1870s. As a further mark of distinction, some northern railways, linking Manchester with places like Blackpool, Windermere and Llandudno, had special carriages available only to members of a club.

But for some, no matter how luxurious the accommodation in first class, the social stigma of travelling (or at least being seen to travel) by rail was too much to be borne. Augustus Hare, writing in around 1850, describes how his family came to terms with the opprobrium of public transport, and of having to sit opposite complete strangers in the same carriage: 'At last we came to use the ordinary rail carriage, but then for a long time we used to have post horses to meet us at some station near London. My mother would not be known to enter London in a railway carriage – "it was so excessively improper".' (Quoted in Robbins – p. 41)

The Class Make-Up of Cities

The railways could also influence the social composition and even (indirectly) the form of governance of towns and cities. In the early days of the Industrial Revolution, before the revolution in personal mobility, entrepreneurs and their workforces lived cheek by jowl, in the same streets and sometimes even the same buildings. It was to these entrepreneurs that the industrial towns often looked for civic leadership, for example as Boroughreeve (an ancient form of elected official, rather like a mayor, who oversaw the running of the town).

The introduction of horse buses first created the opportunity for those who could afford it to live at a distance from their place of work, in a rather more salubrious suburb. However, the limited range of the horse buses meant that most of these suburbs still lay within, or close to, the administrative area of the town. So, for example, desirable residential areas (of the day) like Cheetham and Ardwick abutted the ancient township of Manchester and actually formed part of the 1838 borough.

The railways played their part in enabling those who could afford it to flee the squalor of the growing industrial inner city (and the more you could afford, the further out and more salubrious the suburb to which you could flee). This has to be qualified by the comments elsewhere in the book about the extent to which the early suburbanisation of some of our major cities was driven by buses and trams (and, in some cases, boats) as well as rail. But, whatever the relative importance of different modes of transport, one consequence of suburbanisation was that it deprived the industrial towns and cities of much of their traditional pool of civic leaders. This lack of civic leadership created a crisis in 1837 for Manchester's Court Leet (a medieval survival, part of the chaotic governance of Manchester in the early nineteenth century).

Unable to find a suitable candidate for Boroughreeve from within the local membership of the established Church, they tried to press-gang one William Nield into taking the job, threatening him with a huge fine if he did not. However, Nield was a Quaker, debarred by his religion from swearing oaths (a prerequisite for holding public office). More to the point, he was supported by Richard Cobden (who would later demonstrate his genius as a polemicist with the Anti-Corn Law League). The battle which followed exposed the severe shortcomings of

Manchester's traditional form of governance and helped lay the ground for the incorporation of Manchester as a municipal borough in 1838.

But it was just not the loss of political leadership in the industrial cities that gave rise to concern. Some felt the outflow of potential civic leaders left nobody to set the proletariat a good moral example. Evans cites the comment of one observer in 1856, that the main working class area in Leeds, south of the River Aire, 'is deprived of all those civilising influences and mutually respectful feelings which are exercised when rich and poor – employer and employed – know more of each other than they possibly can under present arrangements'.

But how far were these 'mutually respectful feelings' born of closer contact the product of wishful thinking? A Manchester newspaper, writing in 1819 (before the process of suburbanisation had really got under way), said: 'Here there seems to be no sympathy between the upper and lower classes of society, there is no mutual confidence, no bond of attachment.' (Quoted in Evans, p. 172)

In London, the railways affected the class structure of the city in a rather more fine-grained way. Broadly speaking, areas served by the Metropolitan or District Underground lines tended to attract housing for more affluent groups than those areas served purely by horse trams, which were seen as catering for the lower orders. Trams were actually banned from the West End and all but the fringes of the City, since they were felt to lower the tone of these exclusive parts of London.

One exception was Paddington, which was served by rail but tainted by its proximity to the slums of North Kensington and the lower-class housing along the Harrow Road, which served (among others) lower-paid railway workers employed at the Great Western terminus. The status of Paddington took a further nose-dive when the construction of the Metropolitan line created a demand in the area (at least temporarily) for cheap lodgings for the navvies digging the tunnels. 'Respectable' working-class families fled.

Workmen's Trains and the Twopenny Tube

Another exception to the general rule of railways serving more affluent areas was the group served by railways offering very cheap (hence affordable) workmen's fares. The parliamentary trains required by the Railway Act of 1844 were the first such services, albeit limited. But the first real workmen's services were introduced on the Eastern Counties Railway in 1847, linking Canning Town with North Woolwich to enable dock workers to catch the Woolwich ferry across the Thames. Another was on the London, Chatham & Dover Railway, who in 1860 accepted the principle of running workmen's trains, even though their Act did not require it of them when they were allowed to enter the City of London at Blackfriars.

Yet another area of growth in working-class housing was the north-east quadrant of London, where the Great Eastern Railway had been required to lay on workmen's services for as little as 2*d* for a journey of up to 22 miles. This was a quid pro quo for them knocking down large areas of working-class housing to build their Liverpool Street terminus, and made areas like Leytonstone, Walthamstow and Tottenham affordable. Developers responded by building large areas of low-rent housing there. The Great Eastern Railway's workmen's trains were credited with the rapid growth of Walthamstow, from 7,137 in 1861 to 95,131 in 1901.

From 1864, the House of Lords required all new rail Bills for services into London to include provision for workmen's trains. By 1899 there were 104 workmen's trains serving London, carrying some 23,000 passengers daily. Their impact on the fabric of the city was mixed. While on the one hand they removed one of the barriers that stopped working people living in more healthy environments, they were felt to accelerate the decay of the areas in the centre that were being depopulated. Nor, as we shall see in a later chapter, did they liberate everyone from the inner-city slums. The workmen's train was not unique to London; other cities, such as Birmingham and Glasgow, also had them and in Liverpool 23.8 per cent of the total passenger revenue of the Overhead Railway in 1913 came from workmen's services. Workmen's trains tended to be phased out after the Second World War.

The first electric services appeared on the Underground in 1890, and that year also marked the total abolition of different classes of travel. A flat-rate fare of 2*d* was charged for all journeys, giving the world the 'Twopenny Tube'. The *Railway Times* doubted whether Londoners were ready for such a seismic change in their travelling arrangements: 'We have scarcely yet been educated up to that condition of social equality when lords and ladies will be content to ride side by side with Billingsgate "fish fags" and Smithfield butchers.' (*Railway Times*, 8 November 1890)

The Trimmings: Railways, Class and Waiting Rooms

Refreshment room manageress to waitress: 'These tarts are quite stale. They've been on the counter a fortnight. Would you mind taking them through into the third-class refreshment room?'

(*Aye*, pages 147–8 – joke, *c.* 1931)

If passengers were travelling in a style which befitted their position in life, what more natural than that they should also await their train in the appropriate style? The stations potentially created some rare opportunities for the different classes to come into unregulated contact – where the poor could sell goods and services to the rich, or simply beg from them – but the railways did their best to minimise the opportunity for this, by providing separate waiting, dining and toilet facilities for the different classes (overseas, the class distinctions were often compounded by those of race).

On the Liverpool & Manchester, as elsewhere in the early days, the volume of passenger travel had not been anticipated, and only the line's two termini had waiting rooms at first. The intermediate stops along the line did not even have recognisable stations for the first ten or fifteen years. The termini made up for it, however; by 1836 Liverpool Lime Street had no fewer than five waiting rooms – separate first- and second-class rooms for men, the same for women and something labelled simply 'Ladies' Waiting Room', presumably for those females of any class, or none. Edinburgh had something similar. The main line of the Caledonian Railway still retained separate first- and second-class dining and waiting rooms some forty-five years after the railway had dispensed with second-class travel. A rare departure from these distinctions came in the redevelopment of Waterloo station, opened in 1922. This had the customary first- and third-class toilets for ladies, but just a single facility for men, with marble floors, white tiles and every facility (described by *Railway Magazine* as 'perhaps the finest in England').

At Bath Spa Brunel went one stage further and had not just separate waiting rooms but separate holding areas (he called them by the unfortunate name of 'pens') on the platform for first- and second-class passengers. No mention was made of how third-class passengers were to be dealt with, and Great Western historians seem to assume they were loaded in the goods depot or marshalled on some unspecified part of the platform when there were no 'respectable' people around.

Although some of the great Victorian railway termini are regarded today as national monuments, as 'the nineteenth century's distinctive contribution to architectural form', railway companies do not generally appear to have invested much money or thought in the waiting rooms themselves. Samuel Sidney describes even the first-class facilities at Euston in 1851 as 'dull to a fearful degree and furnished in the dowdiest style of economy'. As for the second class, he dismisses it as 'a dark cavern'. Anthony Trollope found the facilities at Taunton even worse – 'Everything is hideous, dirty and disagreeable.' But art critic John Ruskin thought it entirely appropriate that railway stations should be devoid of ornament:

Now, if there be any place in the world in which people are deprived of that portion of temper and discretion which are necessary to the contemplation of beauty, it is there. It is the very temple of discomfort, and the only charity that the builder can extend to us is to show us, plainly as may be, how soonest to escape from it. The whole system of railroad travelling is addressed to people, who, being in a hurry, are therefore, for the time being, miserable ... The railroad is in all its relations a matter of earnest business, to be got through as soon as possible. It transmutes a man from a traveller to a living parcel. For the time he has parted from the nobler characteristics of his humanity for the sake of a planetary power of locomotion. Do not ask him to admire anything. You might as well ask the wind ... Better bury gold in the embankments than put it in ornaments at the stations.

(John Ruskin, *The Seven Lamps of Architecture*, 1849)

The architect Augustus Pugin mocked the pretention of the London and Birmingham termini of the London & Birmingham Railway, including Euston's 'colossal Greek portico', which provided an overblown gateway to some very utilitarian station buildings:

This piece of Brobdingnagian absurdity must have cost the company a sum which would have built a first-rate station, replete with convenience, and which would have been really grand from its simplicity ... The London gateway could not shelter a porter ... These two gigantic piles of unmeaning masonry, raised at an enormous cost, are a striking proof of the utter disregard paid by architects to the purposes of the building they are called upon to design.

(Quoted in Morgan, p. 228)

While Ruskin and Pugin may have wanted less ornament in their railway buildings, some railways went well beyond the unadorned. As we saw, the intermediate stops on the Liverpool & Manchester were at first undifferentiated from the rest of the line, had no facilities whatsoever and were simply points at which it had been agreed trains would stop. Passengers at these stopping points stood in the midst of nature until the train arrived (presumably it was thought that nobody of importance would board or leave a train there). At Moreton-on-Lugg, on the Shrewsbury & Hereford line, the station amenities consisted of a hollow tree.

And for the Very Rich...

> Lord de Mowbray: 'Equality is not our metier. If we nobles do not make a stand
> against the levelling spirit of the age, I am at a loss to know who will fight the
> battle. You may depend upon it that these railroads are very dangerous things.'
>
> (Disraeli, from his novel *Sybil*)

While 'plain', or even 'hideous, dirty and disagreeable' may have been the order of
the day for the common traveller, the nobility played by different rules. Some, as
we saw, preferred not to mix with the hoi polloi at all, and would travel in their
own private coach loaded onto a specially designed railway wagon. For others,
you had to visit the station serving their ancestral home to sample real grandeur.
The Duke of Rutland travelled to and from Belvoir Castle via Redmile station, the
waiting room to which had a huge carved oak fireplace, depicting Belvoir Castle
and the hunt in full chase. The Duke of Westminster had his own waiting room
at Waverton and Earl Brownlow an entire suite at Berkhamsted. The first-class
waiting accommodation at Rowsley had 'superior furniture' for the delectation of
visitors to nearby Chatsworth House.

Of course, the queen had the most sumptuous waiting facilities laid on wherever
she went, be it at Euston, Paddington, either of the two Windsor stations, Wolferton
(for Sandringham, which was built in the style of the stable and coach block of a
great stately home) and Ballater (for Balmoral, with its lengthened platforms to
take royal trains and its royal waiting room, complete with regal blue porcelain).
She even had sumptuous facilities she did not use. Originally the Great Western line
went no nearer to Windsor than Slough. The railway, anxious to gain her majesty's
patronage, built a suitably palatial hotel, the Royal, by Slough station, with private
facilities in which she could freshen up before the final stage of her journey between
Windsor Castle and London. Unfortunately, in 1849 permission was granted for a
spur off the main line to serve Windsor, and the hotel was bypassed. In the absence
of any distinguished visitors to Slough, it closed four years later.

But the queen did not stop at private waiting rooms. She also had private stations
– four of them – Nine Elms in London; St Margaret's, Edinburgh; Gosport (for the
Isle of Wight ferry); and Whippingham, the station serving Osborne on the Isle of
Wight. She was not unique in this; a number of railway directors had their own
private stations, as did some factories and mine-owners, and the Army.

But that other monarch – the Railway King, George Hudson – capped them all.
Having paid £500,000 for the Duke of Devonshire's estate at Londesborough,

he had his own private branch line installed, and brought the railway right into his own back yard (if 'back yard' can be a suitable description for a 12,000-acre estate).

If you could have your own station, why not your own personal train as well?

It was a not uncommon custom, if any important person missed his train, to charter a 'special' and start in pursuit. With good luck he might count on overtaking a train which had only had half an hour's 'law', before it had got much more than half the distance between London and Brighton. On one occasion, the Secretary of the London & Greenwich Railway, having missed the train, mounted an engine, and started in such hot pursuit, that he ran into the tail carriage with sufficient violence to break the legs of one or two passengers.

(Acworth, quoted in Morgan, p. 93)

Sherlock Holmes may have chartered special trains to get to the scene of the crime speedily but it was not always considered quite proper. When Winston Churchill did it during an election campaign, for example, opponents seized upon it as evidence of his flashiness.

The Ultimate in First-Class Travel

Her Majesty travels at the rate of 40 miles an hour … I am desired to intimate Her Majesty's wish that the speed of the Royal Train … should on no account be increased at any one part of the line in order to make up for the time lost by an unforeseen delay at another.

(Instructions from Queen Victoria's private secretary to the railway companies, 30 August 1854 and 26 August 1852)

Having touched on the subject of royal travel, it might be worth saying a word about some of the protocols that surrounded the monarch's journeys. Queen Victoria's predecessor, William IV, was a rooted opponent of the railway and had to be persuaded out of using his influence to block the building of the Great Western (in the event he did not live to see the benefit from it). But Victoria – and, more particularly, her progressive husband – found it a great boon. Her road-going coaches used to throw her about violently (they tended to travel quickly, to prevent the common herd getting too up-close and personal) but on the railway the ride was smooth enough for her to carry on working on her state papers.

The queen did not make her first trip by train until 13 June 1842. She had been preceded by her consort (a train man since November 1839) and by the Dowager Queen Adelaide, who was already a frequent and enthusiastic patron of the London & Birmingham Railway. Victoria was not even the first reigning monarch to travel on the British railways – that honour fell to Frederick IV of Prussia, who took time out from a visit to Windsor to celebrate the christening of the future Prince of Wales to go sightseeing in London by rail.

Victoria was a nervous passenger and, as we saw above, the driver was not supposed to exceed 40 miles an hour (even Prince Albert was known to say to the railway staff, 'Not quite so fast next time, Mr Conductor, if you please.' Ironically, the queen's funeral train in 1901 was delayed, and touched speeds of 80 mph as it tried to make up time on her final journey back to London). But in life, the stately royal progress had to be timetabled into whatever other users of the line had planned (the queen taking precedence, naturally). This was made more complicated by them having to send a pilot train along the route fifteen minutes before her, to ensure the line was safe. Once she was on her way, no train (except a mail train) was allowed to pass her on the opposite line, and any ones parked had to be checked for overhanging loads. Before the day, all the carriages to be used in the royal train had to be identified, taken out of service and thoroughly overhauled. The whole length of the track had to be checked and patrolled on the day, with men being placed at any point where evil-doers might trespass on the line. All gates onto the railway had to be securely padlocked. The detailed estimated times of arrival at every station along the route also had to be agreed and the platforms cleared of the public beforehand. There were other constraints. Any siding in which the royal train parked had to be level, so as not to cause the royal bathwater to tilt. Should any of these safeguards fail, the royal train carried the means to make an emergency connection to the lineside telegraph wires. A small army of telegraph men, fitters, electricians and other repair men, under a Royal Train Foreman, were also carried.

It was the queen who forced the unenthusiastic Duke of Wellington to travel by train, in August 1843, when he was made to accompany her to Southampton. But one group who were not yet ready for conversion were the French royal family. In July 1843, King Louis Philippe announced the intention of the French royal family to travel to their chateau at Bizy by train. But his Council of Ministers, no doubt mindful of a disastrous railway fire at Versailles in 1842, when fifty passengers were burned to death, ruled that 'this mode of travelling by railway was not sufficiently secure to admit of its being used by the King' and he was made to travel by horse-drawn carriage.

So, while the railways did not fundamentally challenge society's attitudes towards class and status, they did help modify the class structure of our cities, and made some important changes to the way our poorest travellers were treated. Finally, if we wanted evidence of the social mobility that the railways could confer as the nineteenth century progressed, we need look no further than the passing of three of the pioneers of the railway. Richard Trevithick, the original genius behind steam locomotion, died a pauper in 1833; George Stephenson, the uneducated engine minder turned railway builder, died in his substantial country home in Derbyshire in 1848; his son, the university-trained railway and locomotive builder Robert Stephenson, became Member of Parliament for Whitby and, after his death in 1859, was buried in Westminster Abbey.

CHAPTER 3

The Railways as Town Planners

The direct effects of railway building are, after all, considerable enough in themselves to require no exaggeration. They profoundly influenced the internal flows of traffic, the choices of site and the patterns of land use, the residential densities and development prospects of the central and inner districts of the Victorian city.

(Kellett, p. 419)

In the previous chapter, we began to see how the railways could influence the social class structure of our cities. Now we look in more detail at the profound ways in which the railways, acting as unofficial town planners, helped determine the shape of our towns, cities and countryside. To begin with, the railways transformed the established inner cities of Victorian Britain.

Simon Jenkins argued that the coming of the railways to London had a more profound effect than anything since the Great Fire of 1666. They effectively destroyed large areas of the city centre and forced a considerable part of the population out of the central districts. Goods yards, coal yards, locomotive depots, sidings, engineering works and other railway works swept away what were sometimes entire urban communities:

Areas like Holbeck in Leeds, Saltley in Birmingham, Battersea and New Cross in South London, Willesden in North London, Edgehill in Liverpool and Ardwick in Manchester were totally dominated by railways ... At Gorton in Manchester were the works of the Manchester, Sheffield and Lincoln Railway, and those of Messrs Beyer Peacock.

(Trinder, p. 228)

In most provincial city centres, it is estimated that the railways at their height directly controlled the use of between 8 and 10 per cent of the land and influenced the functioning of up to 20 per cent (in terms of attracting rail-related activities). According to Kellett, by 1890 the main railways had spent over £100 million (about one-eighth of all their capital expenditure) on the provision of termini and the approaches to them.

The railways were not the first developers to displace large numbers of people. Leaving aside the accidental clearance programme of the Great Fire of 1666, referred to by Jenkins, the building of St Katherine's Docks in London in 1827–8 rendered over 11,000 people homeless. If any of them complained, it does not appear to have influenced the decision-making process in any way. Their suffering was at least observed and recorded by Charles Dickens' brother-in-law, Henry Austin, who saw how they were forced to double up with other families in squalid and overcrowded conditions. As we will see, by no means all Londoners could enjoy the 'higher standards of space and cleanliness in their housing' that the suburbs offered.

The earliest railways suffered from a lack of capital and a lack of influence over landowners, which made it difficult to enter the heart of major towns and cities and provide a satisfactory terminus. All too often, their approach was therefore to terminate their railway near the edge of the built-up area, using the simplest possible line of approach and going through areas involving the minimum disturbance of property (or, more to the point, the minimum of expensive objection from landowners and occupiers).

Thus it was that Manchester's first Liverpool Road station was built on the edge of the then built-up area, so far out that the railway felt it necessary to lay on a coach between the station and their office in the town centre. The Great Western Railway terminated at a somewhat down-at-heel village called Paddington, just outside the metropolis, after attempts to share Euston station came to nothing. Satirists of the day had a couplet whose primary purpose was to contrast the charismatic Prime Minister William Pitt with his inept successor Henry Addington, but which also spoke volumes about the village:

Pitt is to Addington
As London is to Paddington.

As a result of this approach, many major towns and cities had duplicate stations and/or lacked through running of services. By 1880, twelve of the fifteen largest towns in Britain even had competing routes to London to choose from. Viewed in strategic terms, this duplication increased the cost of providing these communities with railway services, as not just stations but also approach lines, depots, engine sheds and other facilities all had to be duplicated. It reduced the overall dividends for shareholders and, with a town planning hat on, it also unnecessarily increased the proportion of the inner town or city area that was given over to railway-related activities.

Many of the early city centre stations were primitive affairs, some with only the track and not the platforms roofed over. But even without spending on elaborate buildings, some of the earliest railway companies were genuinely shocked at the price of inner urban land. This was especially true when the prospective vendor knew that it was wanted for the railway. For railway building jacked up land prices in the area generally, and the vendors would know that delay was urgently to be avoided by the railway company. William Reed, secretary to the London & Southampton Railway, said: 'I think I may safely say that within our London termini there is nothing extravagant and nothing done for display, but it has cost us a great deal more than we had calculated for the whole of our stations.' (Quoted in Kellett, introduction)

As a general rule of thumb, the first mile of any railway from the terminus would cost them more than any other mile along the route, however difficult conditions may be elsewhere. Where some railway companies indulged in flights of architectural fancy (like the London & Birmingham's grandiose Euston arch), they made the problem worse for themselves. In extreme cases, land costs could be the ruin of the company. The Eastern Counties Railway had spent its entire land purchase budget by the time it had reached Colchester, barely halfway to its intended destination, Great Yarmouth, and other companies had to finish it off.

Railway termini became a 'separate speculation' owing to their cost and complexity and a number of contractors (such as Samuel Peto and the Waring brothers) and engineers (John Hawkshaw and John Fowler) became specialists in their development, carrying out many of the major developments in London and elsewhere.

The Railways and the Poor

> The railway locomotive has a giant's strength but is no better than a blind and undistinguishing Polyphemus when he is called in as a sanitary reformer.
>
> (Evidence by Henry Davies to the House of Commons in 1861, cited in Kellett,
>
> p. 335)

The present railways injure the working class of large towns by the construction of their works, but do not benefit it by their administration, at least not equally or as much as they might. The railway has to go through a poor suburb of a big town, through the working-class quarter: it demolishes the houses, already too full; it increased the compression, already too great. But though it pulls down the old dwellings of labourers, it does not take them to new dwellings. Lord Derby presented a resolution to the House of Lords, compelling railways near large towns to have a cheap working-class train, night and morning, suitable for daily labour. But with the present management we have no such train ... the government, if they owned the railways, might give the working class their share in the benefits of swift locomotion, though they will never get it from others.

(Walter Bagehot in *The Economist*, 7 January 1865)

The railway companies targeted areas of slum housing for their routes into the city as one means of keeping costs down, as the vicar of one such London parish bitterly observed:

The special lure of the capitalist is that the line will pass only through inferior property, that is through a densely peopled district, and will destroy the abode of the powerless and the poor, whilst it will avoid the properties of those whose opposition is to be dreaded, the great employers of labour.

(Revd William Denton of St Bartholemew's, Smithfield, quoted in Wolmer (2012), p. 29)

The generally impoverished residents of these inner areas had little say over what became of their homes and communities. They were generally without the vote and, as renters rather than owners, had no property rights to protect them and got little or no compensation. Often large residential areas would be the freehold property of a single wealthy individual or institution, who would be glad to take the railway's money and be rid of their troublesome slum tenants. Commercial occupiers, by contrast, were more likely to have individual freeholds, which were messier to acquire. Local authorities were also likely to smile upon any scheme which rid their area of unsightly and unhealthy slum dwellings. 'In one case, virtually a whole parish was demolished, using techniques of deception and force which reflected grave discredit on the Midland Company and provided reformers with an example of railway clearances which was cited for twenty years.' (Evidence to the House of Commons, cited in Kellett, p. 322)

A few social reformers railed against the railways cutting a swathe through these areas and, from 1853, railway companies had a requirement placed on them to produce a 'demolition statement', listing the numbers of people displaced by their schemes, whenever thirty or more 'working-class houses' within a single parish were taken for a railway scheme. However, by this time many of the schemes which had taken the largest number of working-class houses had already been completed, for example at London Bridge, Fenchurch Street, Waterloo, Euston and parts of Paddington. In any event, nobody ever seemed to check these figures and they are thought to have been extensively falsified.

One ploy was for the railway company to pay the slum landlord secretly to evict his tenants some time before the properties were actually required by the railway company, so that the eviction could not be directly blamed on the railway. This had the added benefit for the landlord that he could claim any compensation that might otherwise be due to the residents. Another related trick, used by the Midland Railway, was to employ a separate company to acquire the property (in their case, 700 dwellings), evict the occupants and later sell the cleared site to the railway. The 'more than thirty' criterion excluded a good many smaller schemes and the definition of what constituted a 'working-class house' offered considerable scope for interpretation. Some railway companies would pay a premium for housing which came without the complication of occupants – with no questions asked as to how the vacancies had been achieved.

Thus it was that the official figure for the number of people displaced by the underground railway between Paddington and Farringdon Street was just 307; but a contemporary source claimed that the section of the route from King's Cross to Farringdon Street alone took out 1,000 houses that would have been home to some 12,000 people. Similarly, only 135 of the more than 800 houses removed to make way for Liverpool's Central station were caught by these criteria.

A total of sixty-one demolition statements were completed between 1853 and 1900, in which it was claimed that a total of 72,000 people had been displaced by railway developments. However, it is known that, in at least one of these, only the heads of household had been counted, meaning that the impact of the scheme was understated by a factor of about four or five. Simmons suggests that the real number of people affected by railway development was in excess of 120,000, allowing for the known density of housing and its overcrowding in inner-city areas. In Manchester, according to one estimate, around 20,000 Mancunians were displaced by the railways. The new goods depot at London Road required the demolition of some 600 houses and Central station displaced around 1,200 people when it was constructed in the 1870s. The building of the Great Northern goods warehouse of 1898 involved the disappearance of much of the city's ancient quarter of Alport.

As the railway companies came to understand the realities of city centre real estate, they tended to bid for compulsory purchase powers over as much land as they could get away with in their parliamentary bills, secure in the belief that they would be able to sell on any not needed for the railway at a profit later on. What land they did not get included in their bills became of interest to separate rail-related commercial interests, who may have displaced as many people as the railways themselves. Even so, the railways could still be left with odd corners of compulsorily purchased land that were neither needed for railway use nor viable commercial sites. These could end up as a wilderness of unkempt gardens, middens, claypits and scavengers' yards, further blighting the area.

The problem for the inner-city slum dweller was that no one, and certainly not the railway companies, gave much thought to where the displaced population would go. There were pious hopes that they would all be able to move out to the more salubrious suburbs, and requirements were placed upon some railway companies in their parliamentary Acts to lay on workmen's trains, as a means of making this happen. The truth was very different, as even *The Times* recognised:

> The poor are displaced but they are not removed. They are shovelled out of one side of the parish, only to render more overcrowded the stifling apartments in another part ... But the dock and wharf labourer, the porter and the costermonger cannot remove. You may pull down their wretched homes; they must find others and make their new dwellings more crowded and wretched than their old ones. The tailor, shoemaker and other workmen are in much the same position. It is mockery to speak of the suburbs to them.

> (*The Times*, 2 March 1861)

Many of these workers were in casual employment, and had no choice but to live on the doorstep of the factory or dock, to be readily to hand if and when work became available. So, far from helping the cities to expand and create a better environment for its residents, the railways tended to increase the occupancy of what remained of the inner city's residential areas. As if to add insult to injury, the laws of supply and demand ensured that the rents for this ever more crowded and scarce accommodation were driven sharply upwards. St James Clerkenwell adjoined the Farringdon clearance areas (discussed elsewhere in this chapter).

It saw its density of occupation rise from 8.6 persons per house in 1841 to 9.6 in 1851, 9.9 in 1861 and 10.6 in 1871, with 'respectable artisans' being forced to live cheek by jowl with 'some of the worst class'. In overall terms, inner-city populations may have declined, but conditions worsened for a good proportion of those who were left behind. As for most local authorities, they did not even start becoming housing providers until the last years of the century.

On the odd occasion that any railway company showed a hint of social responsibility, it could be no more than a cynical gesture, designed to assuage hostile public opinion. In one instance, the Metropolitan Railway bought up a court of housing, to rehouse at least a few of those being displaced by their development. Two years on, with the railway safely built, the tenants were evicted and the housing became more profitable warehousing. Not until 1874 (by which time the bulk of the railway network was in place) was a requirement placed on the railway companies to rehouse the people their schemes displaced and, even then, this was often evaded or ignored. Only in the twentieth century did the requirement start to get effectively enforced.

The railways fought any such responsibility all the way. Economist George Paish spoke for them: '[It is] the height of unwisdom to increase the cost of transportation by compelling the railways to provide for the re-housing of the working classes. [Where this happened, he argued, the burden should fall on] the community as a whole.' (Quoted in Simmons (1986), p. 34)

The reformer Lord Shaftesbury told Parliament of the chaos occasioned by a railway compulsory purchase order in a poor residential area:

> It is terrific to see the condition of the people before a demolition begins. It is perfectly true that notice is given according to form, but poor working men cannot attend to that sort of thing, and in fact they delay to begin to act because they have no time to lose in looking about for houses, and they rarely act until the men come to pull the roof off their heads, and then I have seen the people like the people in a besieged town, running to and fro, not knowing what on earth to do.
>
> (Parliamentary papers, quoted in Simmons (1986), p. 34)

Nor were the authorities necessarily very interested in what took the place of the slums, provided the slums went. In the 1840s, road improvements in the Farringdon Street area of London swept away a vast swathe of indescribably squalid housing, but left behind large areas on either side of the road which stood undeveloped for years: 'But the object of the new street ... had been as much slum clearance as metropolitan improvement. So rebuilding, as a critic of the City Corporation noted, was of little interest: the poor "had been driven away, and what more could be wanted?"' (William Gilbert, *The City* (1877), pages 18–19, quoted in White p. 43)

The lack of development along this route made it particularly attractive to the first underground railway builders, who therefore did not have to compensate property owners for any subsidence to their properties.

Not all the cheap housing areas in the town and city centres, and on their fringes, may have been devoured by the railways and related commercial development. But the degraded environment the railways created was a strong deterrent to anyone thinking of investing in its improvement or replacement. So much of the housing that was left, often dating from before the 1830s, was left to rot, as owners hung on in the hope of an offer from a commercial developer. Any housing development that did take place was likely to be of a low-grade, jerry-built variety on a short building lease.

In addition to the land they physically took, the railways tended to disrupt lines of communication between communities, and greatly increased the amount of road traffic and congestion around them. Railway lines could constitute a major barrier to mobility in a city and, in order to reduce the need for road closures, many urban railways ran along viaducts. These brought their own form of blight, as one Town Clerk of Manchester noted: 'If you go along a railway with a viaduct, the very quality of the property you look down upon shows it is not the place where improvements may be looked for – a viaduct puts a stop absolutely to any improvement from the time it is constructed.' (Quoted in Kellett, p. 346)

This was reflected in the property values in the areas around Manchester's arches, which showed no increase over a period where prices elsewhere in the city rose by 75 per cent. Even if viaducts did not result in the total closure of a route, their awkward angles and often minimal space standards around the arches meant that they often became pinch points in the road network. Those archways that were enclosed tended to attract the lowest grade of (often offensive) trades. Those archways that were left open attracted 'the more disreputable element of the population', or those who were most desperate – drunks, unsuccessful criminals, those engaged in immoral practices, those looking for somewhere to conceal the bodies of unwanted babies, or who were simply destitute. A few people tried turning these dark and dank spaces into 'houses for the poorer class of people' and some entrepreneurs tried fitting them out as live-work units, despite the difficulty of providing such basic amenities as chimneys, windows and essential services.

Two archways on the line from London Bridge to Greenwich were even fitted out as a chapel and a pub, but generally viaducts were an obstacle to the betterment of any area. But not everybody saw the railways in these terms:

> The railway system ... has largely altered the centre of the town ... In each instance insanitary areas have been cleared, streets abolished, new thoroughfares opened, and leading lines of communication improved. To these railway extensions ... a large part of suburban Birmingham owes its progress.
>
> (J. T. Bunce, *History of the Corporation of Birmingham* volume 2 (1885))

It cannot be denied that railway developments removed some notorious slums. In Birmingham, the authorities welcomed the fact that New Street station removed 'a certain class of the inhabitants living just beyond the principal and best streets' – that is to say, the slums and brothels behind Navigation Street. In similar vein, two extensions of Waterloo station, in 1866/67 and twenty years later, secured the removal of London's notorious Granby Street red-light district. In Manchester, Oxford Road and Central stations removed some of the appalling slums, described by Engels, around parts of the River Medlock (though Oxford Road station also directly overlooked the notorious Little Ireland area). Manchester's Victoria and London Road stations (the latter known today as Piccadilly) both took out large areas of substandard housing.

But railway development could itself have a blighting effect upon a hitherto respectable area, one that that started it on the downward slope towards becoming the next slum:

> Each of these new railway lines became itself the source of new divisions and demarcations ... for every slum destroyed in their construction a new one came into existence around them; they became the new dialect lines of social distinction, having each of them a right and a wrong side, and serving in their finished state to restrict and confine in as much as in their building they cleared out and exposed.
>
> (Quoted in Simmons, p. 33)

But if railways could blight, they could also in some circumstances have a regenerative effect. In London, shops close to an Underground station would advertise the fact and commercial land and premises in these areas attracted a premium. Two of the directors of the Hammersmith & City Railway – Charles

Blake and John Parson – took this a stage further and made a considerable amount of money by buying up land in the vicinity of an existing or proposed Underground station and selling it on, often to their own railway, at a profit.

One man who did have a genuine and socially responsible vision for the railways was Charles Pearson, solicitor to the City Corporation and the man who can be said to be the father of the London Underground. He proposed a huge new central terminus for London's railways, with all the existing stations linked together by an underground railway. All of this would be supplemented by a new town of 10,000 cottages at either Hornsey or Tottenham, let out at affordable rents to artisans who worked in the city. The rail fares from there into the city would also be set at a level that made it viable for them to commute. Needless to say, by no means all of his vision came to fruition.

Railway Towns

In some cases, the railway companies created entire new communities out of virtually nothing, as they acted not just as town planner but also property developer. Swindon was a tiny backwater until the Great Western decided to locate their railway works there. In addition to the works and other railway buildings, they also constructed 300 cottages for railway staff which formed the nucleus of a new part of the town. Schools, churches and recreational facilities followed and, as demand for housing continued to grow, private speculators stepped in to add to the town's growth.

The *Illustrated London News* described the rapid pace of progress in creating the new Swindon, not long after the decision was taken to construct it.

The new town, which has sprung up within the last two years, is principally occupied by the artisans employed by the Railway Company, who make it a sort of depot for their various works. The houses are all neatly built of stone, with slated roofs and arranged in streets. They have already Bristol, Taunton, Exeter and Bath Streets; and others are fast rising.

The church ... is situated at the west end of the town and is a very beautiful structure; and the school-houses attached are built in the same style. Numerous other buildings and villas are in progress; all building of stone, which is very plentiful in this neighbourhood. The old town of Swindon is about a mile and a half from the station, on the crown of a hill to the south. The view from it is very commanding, the country being very flat on all sides, but remarkably rich and finely wooded. The old town has all the characteristics of an English market town. The old picturesque cottages and houses are here beginning to make way for the more modern style of architecture; and, if half the projects now in contemplation are completed, the old and new towns will ere long be amalgamated in one.

(Illustrated London News, 18 October 1845)

Similar town expansions took place in conjunction with the railway works at Crewe, the expansion of Shildon to serve the Stockton & Darlington's railway works and the London & Birmingham Railway's development at Wolverton. The hamlet of Furness became Barrow-in-Furness after the Furness Railway arrived there, and the South Eastern Railway founded the new town of Ashford next door to the old one in 1847. The small textile town of Horwich trebled in size in five years after the Lancashire & Yorkshire Railway based its works there, and in 1889 the small village of Bishopstoke became the railway town of Eastleigh, and had a population of 15,200 by 1904. Some more established towns – such as Peterborough, Carlisle, Boston and Doncaster – also expanded substantially as a result of the railways. Simply being at a junction of two railways could be its own impetus for growth, as was the case for places like Didcot, Redhill, Middlesbrough and Carnforth.

In addition to direct employment on the railways, railway towns could also generate spin-off industries. Thus Crewe had a clothing company producing LNWR uniforms, and a printing works turning out all of its posters and documents.

The railways not only created new settlements, they could also run them. Thus Brunel's colleague Daniel Gooch became the Member of Parliament for Swindon, and F. W. Webb, the Chief Mechanical Engineer of the LNWR, became a rather intimidating Mayor of Crewe.

But the coming of the railway was not an automatic guarantee of growth. Railways could as easily draw trade and industry away from a town as attract it in. Both Bath and Macclesfield declined in population after the railway's arrival when their railways did not generate large-scale local employment and the towns' staple industries went into reverse.

Coastal Ports

Coastal ports faced a mixed future in the railway age. Coastal shipping was all too often in competition with the railways, and was in many cases unable to compete.

Some fishing ports benefited from having the railway to make their catches available to a wider urban market. Others found the railway useful in supplying them with goods and raw materials for onward transportation by sea, often overseas (Cardiff, Barry, Southampton and Fleetwood became what Best describes as 'made or refashioned ports in [the railways'] industrial image') while the north-eastern coal ports found there was enough demand for coal in London to keep their colliers busy. Some ports even found themselves transformed into leisure resorts. But elsewhere ports could find themselves going into a rapid decline, as the railways creamed off trade that used to go by coastal shipping.

The Railways and Suburbia

The role of the railways in promoting suburban growth in our provincial towns and cities varies, according to their individual circumstances, but is less marked than in London, whose Metro-land is described in another chapter. Part of the problem seems to be that the provincial cities were all markedly smaller than the capital; many prime areas for suburban growth in Victorian times lay only 2–3 miles from the centre – not far enough out to make rail a really attractive proposition, compared with the competing modes of transport. Only in later times, as the cities grew and those who could afford it started looking further afield for their semi-rural idylls, did the railways start to come into their own. Some lines – like the Birmingham West Suburban Railway – survived by being both a main line and a suburban service, though long-distance and suburban services could find themselves competing for the available track space. Purely suburban services – like the Nottingham Suburban Railway – often struggled financially.

Other examples can be found as well.

Glasgow's Pollokshields was promoted in 1849 as a high-class residential suburb by the Stirling-Maxwell family, patrons of the arts who had been associated with the city since the year 1270. Strict planning criteria were laid down and many of Glasgow's leading architects were commissioned to design buildings for it. Development took place mostly between 1855 and 1910, but it was only relatively late in that period that the extension to the Cathcart Railway to the area added its impetus to the suburb. However, shortly afterwards Glasgow would begin the electrification of its trams and, with the suburb being only 2 miles from the city centre, railways would have had little competitive advantage over them.

In Glasgow as a whole, the physical barrier of the River Clyde, awkward landowners and fierce competition between railway companies all militated against the development of the local rail network. Much of the development of suburban lines did not take place until the years 1885–1910, some of it making use of the increased platform capacity provided at Central station and St Enochs in the Edwardian period. Meanwhile, in 1902, the Glasgow & South Western Company had withdrawn its suburban services to Govan and Springburn, concentrating on the outer suburbs and the Ayrshire coast. This period also saw the development of some cheap workmen's fares between east and central Glasgow and major employers on Clydebank.

More generally, the trams were serious competition to the railways for suburban traffic in most cities; they had better penetration of their catchments, running along roads and stopping to pick up more frequently than the railway; they were also clean (electric powered) and cheap (often local authority supported). Various railways tried electrifying their own routes and introducing steam railcars (a steam-powered precursor to the modern diesel multiple unit) in an effort to compete, with varying degrees of success.

Trams and buses also featured heavily in the suburbanisation of Manchester. It was the first town in Britain to get a horse-drawn bus service (in 1824) and it linked the centre with what were then the new suburbs of Pendleton, Ardwick and Cheetham Hill. Of the various railway services serving Manchester, only the Manchester South Junction actively sought (and succeeded in attracting) substantial suburban business. The rest tended to be focussed more on strategic inter-city traffic. Even towards the end of the nineteenth century rail had not made great inroads into local travel. For example, the supposed workman's trains between Oldham and Manchester in the 1890s would have cost 3s 6d a week – well beyond the means of most working men of the day.

Meanwhile the city had been active in developing its tram network, which was possibly the most comprehensive in the country. At its height in 1905, Manchester had four times as many trams per head of population as London and twice that of Glasgow, and these served most of the needs of the suburban population. But for those at the very top of Manchester's economic pile, there was always the railway – and Alderley Edge.

When rich and virtuous Mancunians die, they do not go to Heaven, they go to Alderley Edge. The village today is described as being 'famous for its affluence and its expensive houses'. Those house prices are just about the highest in the country, outside the more exclusive parts of London, and it is said that the village's per capita consumption of champagne is also the highest in the land. But Alderley Edge is just an extreme example of the railways' role as a town planner.

Things were very different in the 1830s. Then it was a rundown hamlet known as Chorley, consisting of a few cottages, an inn called the De Trafford Arms, a tollgate and a smithy. All of this changed when the Manchester & Birmingham Railway passed through it in 1842. The railway, for once keen to supplement its long-distance custom with daily commuters, offered a free twenty-one-year season ticket to any Manchester businessman who bought a house with a rateable value in excess of £50 within a mile of the station. The ticket took the form of a silver oval that the owner could wear on his watch-chain (a similar, but more downmarket, scheme was tried to promote suburban development along the Dumbartonshire and Ayrshire coast in Scotland, but without conspicuous success. There, people simply had to rent a house of a given value to get their season ticket).

The railway was even responsible for the village's change of name. It is said that they wanted to avoid confusion with Chorley in Lancashire, which had its own station. The name 'Alderley' was an ancient one for settlements in the area, while the 'Edge' part refers to a sandstone escarpment above the village, affording spectacular views across Greater Manchester.

One of the local landowners, Sir Humphrey de Trafford, knew an opportunity when he saw one. He laid out an estate of new roads, on which he sold plots for individual development. Most had been taken up by 1910. The most desirable of these were snapped up by Manchester cotton barons, and the houses built on them are today worth many millions of pounds each. At the same time the village acquired a church, schools, shops, the Queen's Hotel and all the other appurtenances of civilised living. At the same time, the railways also developed the Edge as a visitor attraction by offering cheap rail excursions from the city. The *Manchester Courier* in 1843 reported that the last train leaving Alderley for Manchester one Sunday evening had 112 carriages, was a quarter of a mile in length, carried over 3,000 people and took two locomotives to draw it.

In Liverpool, travel across water formed a part of the early suburbanisation process. Seaside locations from Southport to Hoylake began to attract aspiring Liverpudlians from the 1820s – about the time that paddle steamers were making their appearance. Many of those living in the affluent southern suburbs near the Mersey chose to travel by road into the city centre, and it is along the roads linking the two that much of the city's upmarket shopping is to be found. Although Liverpool was one of the first settlements to benefit from the railway age, the initial absence of any formal station facilities between there and Manchester suggests that the early management were not particularly interested in attracting suburban commuter custom. Suburban railways only became important to Liverpool from the 1870s.

Modern Birmingham has the biggest network of suburban rail services outside of London. 300 miles of passenger routes serve nineteen towns and cities and 119 stations. But did the railway give us the suburbs or did it just respond to their growth? Sutton Coldfield was just about the first part of Birmingham's hinterland to get its own branch railway, in 1862, but it was by no means a railway creation. The town had an ancient history and by charter had been designated a Royal Town as long ago as 1528. By the time the railway arrived it had its own substantial town hall and an equally impressive list of public houses. Nor did the town grow dramatically after the railway's arrival. Twenty years later, in 1885, its population was still less than 8,000. Although part of the city today, it was at least far enough away from central Birmingham (7 miles) to give the railway a competitive edge over the road-based commuting alternatives of the day.

The Birmingham West Suburban Railway was planned in 1876 with the intention of extending the south-west quadrant of Birmingham into rural Worcestershire. But it was bankrolled by the Midland Railway, who also had a strategic objective for it, in terms of improving their Bristol–Derby main line.

But there was one other impact of the railways on the hierarchy of settlements, one which meant the railways were not an automatic benefit for everyone. Walter Bagehot put it most succinctly: 'Every railway takes trade from the little town to the big town, because it enables the customer to buy in the big town.' (Walter Bagehot, *The English Constitution*, chapter 5)

The Railways and the Canals

One final contribution railways helped to make to the British landscape by the mid-twentieth century was a nationwide network of often abandoned and unnavigable canals, many of which have happily at last been restored. They had been the nation's arteries during the early stages of the Industrial Revolution. The Duke of Bridgewater, the pioneer who built the canal bearing his name, was one of those who foresaw the danger that railways posed to his brainchild. As an old man (he died in 1803), he said of the canals, 'They will last my time, but I see mischief in those damned tramroads.'

For a time, the canals held their own against the railways – in 1848 the canals between Liverpool and Manchester were still handling twice the freight tonnage of their railway rivals (having dropped their freight rates by 30 per cent to compete), and Birmingham's canal network continued to expand until the 1850s. One great advantage they initially had was that a great infrastructure of factories and warehouses had grown up along the banks of the canals, meaning that goods could be delivered door to door. The railways had to factor in the additional cost and delay of transhipping them from railhead to final destination. But gradually industrial development began to congregate around the railways, and the writing was on the wall for the waterways.

Railway Architecture and Railway 'Antiquities'

We trust that now the line has thus nearly approached completion, care will be taken in future to avoid in the construction of stations, that lavish and ridiculous expenditure which must have struck everyone who has passed along the line from Diss to Stowmarket and Ipswich.

(The *Norwich Mercury* on the opening of the Eastern Union Railway
to Norwich,1849)

Turning now from the broad sweep of urban planning to the relative detail of urban design, the railways' influence was not always a negative one. The railways gave us many of the finest examples of Victorian architecture and over 2,000 are now listed as being of historical or architectural interest – only the Church of England has more listed buildings. Some are even Scheduled Ancient Monuments – the oldest (and most august) level of recognition. The preserved structures range from the most monumental, such as the Forth Bridge and the great railway termini of London and other major cities, to buildings more domestic in scale but beautifully detailed, such as country stations and signal boxes.

The fact that they survive to this day is due in part to the fact that many of them were massively over-engineered. One Victorian railway engineer who was not a fan of over-engineering was Thomas Bouch. Unlike some of his contemporaries, he built a reputation for economising on construction costs. But there was also such a thing as under-engineering, as he was to learn when his Tay Bridge collapsed in a storm in 1879, sweeping a trainload of seventy-five people to their deaths. His plans for a crossing of the Firth of Forth were quickly abandoned thereafter.

Not every architectural embellishment was the choice of the railway company. Victorian landowners often objected to a railway crossing their land, and part of the price for removing these objections could involve dressing up some functional part of the railway's architecture as a medieval folly. In this final section, we look at some of the architectural follies the railways (or, rather, the landowners) gave us. One such was the Clayton Tunnel, on the main London–Brighton line. At one end, the portal to the tunnel was quite unremarkable. At the other, the trains issued out of what appeared to be the gate of a medieval castle, with two towers, complete with crenellations, arrow slits and an incongruous cottage peeping out from behind the castle parapet. The tunnel was later the site of a major railway accident in which twenty-three people were killed, and was subsequently thought to be the inspiration for Charles Dickens' ghost story 'The Signalman'. However, it is not entirely clear whether this particular example was built at a landowner's whim; other theories suggest it may have been built in 1841 as a monument to the 6,000 men who spent three years digging the tunnel, or that it was meant to reassure nervous passengers that they were not entering the gates of Hell.

If it was a landowner's whim, he was not alone; at Audley End, Essex, Lord Braywood demanded (and got) a fanciful tunnel entrance of huge semicircular concentric rings in stone and brick. The tunnel itself was completely redundant – a cutting would have served the needs of the railway perfectly well, at less cost. For good measure, his lordship also had a porte cochère added to the station nearest to his mansion, so that he could dismount from his carriage in the dry. One tunnel that perhaps deserved its grandiose treatment was Brunel's masterpiece, the Box Tunnel, at the time the longest ever built. The western portal, visible from the London–Bath road, has an arch that Rolt likens to 'a triumphal gateway to the Roman city'.

The Box Tunnel was central to Brunel's vision for the Great Western, but the tunnel at Kemble, Gloucestershire, was another totally unnecessary structure imposed by a landowner's determination not to have a railway visible on his land. Also unnecessary, but for money-grabbing reasons, was London's Primrose Hill tunnel. Again, a cutting would have sufficed, but the owner of the land above was Eton College (as we see elsewhere in the book, normally doughty opponents of anything to do with railways). On this occasion, they were not above laying out a housing estate on their land, partly to secure maximum compensation from the railway. They did not want a cutting reducing the development potential of their site.

The Duke of Rutland objected to having the railway cross his land in the Peak District at surface level. The railway therefore offered to put it into a cutting. But the good lord was another one not prepared to countenance even the possibility of seeing wisps of steam arising from the cutting. The railway company were therefore obliged to build the totally unnecessary 1,058-yard-long Haddon tunnel, at an average depth of 12 feet below the surface. At the same time, the duke had no qualms about using the railway himself, once it was built. He travelled from Bakewell station, which therefore naturally had to be made rather grander than it would otherwise have been, with his family crest carved into the stonework.

The Guthrie family had lived at Guthrie Castle since 1468, and took objection to the Arbroath & Forfar Railway crossing their land in 1836. As part of the compensation, it was agreed that the railway would bridge the main entrance to their estate (the railway was to be on an embankment) with something disguised as a medieval gateway, containing a porter's lodge. It was paid for by the railway but commissioned by the laird, and looked like Walt Disney's idea of 'ye olde gateway', complete with hexagonal turrets, crenellations and carved corbels. It is not recorded what living conditions would have been like for any resident porter, with what became the Caledonian Railway's main line to Aberdeen thundering over his head, day and night.

In another example, in Wimborne, Somerset, the eminent Victorian architect Sir Charles Barry was giving Canford Manor a makeover between the years 1846 and 1851, just as the Southampton & Dorchester Railway sought to cross the owner's land. As part of the deal, and despite the fact that it was a mile from the house, the railway was required by the landowner to bridge the east drive to the manor with an elaborate Tudor-Gothic structure in yellow stone, to match the house.

At Shugborough, the home of the Earl of Lichfield, the proposed railway would be within sight of the Grecian 'follies' with which his estate was littered. He insisted that the railway bridge over the Lichfield Drive was every bit as fanciful as his other ornaments, topped off as it was with three plinths bearing the family coat of arms, a seahorse and a lion. Shugborough tunnel was given a similar treatment, Egyptian at one end, Norman at the other, generously adorned with family crests, arrow slits, gargoyles and crenellations. Further crenellations and arrowslits may be admired on the Midland Counties Railway's Red Hill tunnels.

But not all of these follies were the product of some dubious aristocratic aesthetic sensibility. Maldon East, on a branch of the Eastern Counties Railway, got a station which was far grander than the line's traffic could justify. According to Biddle, 'the neo-Jacobean frontage would not have disgraced a nobleman's mansion'. The reason for this seems to be that, at the time it was being built, the ECR's Deputy Chairman, David Waddington, was standing as the local parliamentary candidate. He wanted to keep the construction workers in the area, as possible electoral support, and over-specifying the station was one of the means towards his end (it seems to have worked; he got elected, even if the finances of the ECR were dealt a blow in the process).

But if we are looking for megalomania on a grand scale, we can do little better than the small town of Monkwearmouth, across the river from Sunderland. Its station is of a size and grandeur far beyond the importance of the town or its railway, its huge classical portico described by Pevsner as looking like 'a provincial Atheneum ... purest neo-Greek'. It is thought that it was commissioned to celebrate George Hudson's election as Sunderland's Member of Parliament. He also happened to be the chairman of the local railway company.

Examples of where railway architecture provides an unambiguous adornment, rather than a curiosity, to the place in which it sits can be found (incongruously) in the chapter on the railway and vandalism. The railways had another, more subtle impact on the appearance of our built environment. Before the railways (and certainly before the canals), most buildings would have been made of local materials – local stone or brick where these were available, or timber-framed construction elsewhere – and these helped to establish a sense of place. The development of the railway network 'liberated' construction from these 'constraints' and meant that mass-produced materials like harsh red or yellow bricks were widely available. They had the effect of putting many smaller local slate pits, stone quarries and brickworks out of business and imposing a much greater degree of uniformity across the nation. In places like Reading, which were the hub of railway lines to different parts of the country, an architectural vernacular of patterned brickwork developed, using a variety of different coloured bricks brought in from the four corners of the railway network.

The railways are even held responsible in some quarters for Victorian style itself. Glancey cites the prolific architect Augustus Welby Pugin as one who benefited from the railways by spreading his practice around the country, and speculates that the eclecticism of High Victorian architecture may itself have had a lot to do with the railways making it possible for architects to work nationally, rather than locally.

On a more positive note, by 1846 railway interests had acquired the Ashton Canal, one of whose main cargos was stone from the Peak District. The railway took over the trade and this had a marked and positive effect upon the appearance of Victorian Manchester:

The railways have brought excellent stone from the immediate neighbourhood of the quarries, at so low a rate of carriage, that its cost is often exceeded by brickwork, and consequently it is much used for the whole fronts of buildings ... The stone most used is known as 'Yorkshire pierpoints'; it is a sandstone of good yellow colour. And according to one architect, is nearly as cheap as the best red facing bricks, and quite as cheap as what are called in Manchester 'seconds'.

(*Builder* magazine, 15 November 1845, quoted in Parkinson-Bailey, p. 51)

Even today the railways are helping to shape the nation. As this is being written, a long-running battle of words is being fought over the High Speed 2 rail proposal, with claim and counterclaim being made about the impact the scheme would have on the cities served by it (and equally, on those it bypasses). Even more modest railway improvements, for example shortening the journey times to London or other economic magnets, can have a marked impact on housing demand, prices and the pressure for further provincial growth. They can equally have an impact on job creation in the peripheral areas, though improved communications can just as easily suck the economic activity (and labour force) out of a declining area as draw it in.

The Railways as Town Planners – The Verdict

So how good or bad were the railways as the – possibly unwitting – planners of our towns and cities? If one disregards for a moment the grave social hardships consequent upon their actions, the slum clearance bulldozer that was the railway did at least remove the physical blight of unplanned slum chaos from many areas of our towns and cities, creating an order of a kind.

At the same time, they could sow the seeds of the slums of the future. London's Waterloo Road was in 1845 an area teetering on the margins of respectability as a residential quarter. It was then that the South Western Railway announced their plans for an interim terminus near York Road, and the northward trickle of respectable households out of the area turned into a flood. But worse was to come. The temporary station opened in 1848 but, in the meantime, the collapse of railway mania meant the permanent terminus did not materialise, and the temporary terminus became permanent: 'The ruin of Waterloo Road as a street of residential decency was now complete. Its neighbourhood became mid-Victorian London's most lurid and beastly red-light quarter, best known by the name of its main mart, Granby Street.' (Michael Sadlier, *Forlorn Sunset*, p. 237)

But introduce the railways into a town or city that has, up to that point, been planned in some logical fashion and you could have a recipe for chaos, as Best argued in his lament for his native Edinburgh. He saw the tidy and rational principles of development that had been followed up to the 1830s being overwhelmed by a mess of railways and yards that cut through the fabric of the planned city.

But it was not the core business of the railways to plan our towns and cities; they were in business to provide an efficient public transport service and to do so profitably. The main reason they had such a huge impact on planning was that the public authorities of early to mid-Victorian Britain had done so little to make the planning of their urban areas, and dealing with the social consequences of those land-use decisions, part of their own remit. It was an error they would spend the next century and more trying to remedy.

The Railways and Crime

All railways are public frauds and private robberies.

(Colonel Charles Sibthorp, MP for Lincoln 1826–32 and 1835–55, opponent of
railways and of change generally)

The fear of crime has been associated with the railways from its earliest days. Concerns ranged from the very minor – things like fare dodging and trespass, which are mainly the business of the railway companies – through theft, petty and not so petty, to large-scale fraud, by which both the railways and the general public may be affected. There were also the passengers' fears about the new possibilities for murder, robbery and sexual assault that the railways opened up. These fears were no doubt further fuelled by the rich vein of dramatic possibilities for evil-doing discovered in the railways by writers and playwrights, and discussed in another chapter. So did the railways bring with them an epidemic of crime?

Railway Policemen

Railways and their security needs pre-dated the existence of most organised police forces in Britain. The first parliamentary Railway Act dated from 1758, but the first professional police force – the Metropolitan Police – was only formed as the result of legislation in 1829. At the Rainhill trials of that year, the absence of any significant local police force led to 300 railway workers being sworn in as special police constables, to control the crowds and generally keep the peace. They were supplemented by a troop of cavalry, stationed at intervals along the track. Before even this, the records of the Stockton & Darlington Railway for 30 June 1826 speak of the Railway's 'police establishment' of 'one superintendent, four officers and numerous gatekeepers'.

The Liverpool & Manchester Railway set up their own police establishment in November 1830. They did so under (pre-railway) legislation dating from 1673 and their initial duties were to preserve law and order on the construction site of the railway and to control the movement of railway traffic – so they were also signalmen. The first railway to get statutory powers to employ its own policemen was the London & Birmingham in 1833, followed two years later by the Great Western, though a magistrate was still needed to appoint them. At first their jurisdiction related solely to the railway's own land, though the London & Birmingham got this extended in 1837 to half a mile on either side of the track. By 1840 they had powers of arrest for trespass or obstruction. From 1853, the London & North Western even had their own detective force, used primarily to combat widespread pilfering on the railway.

It is not clear how far these early policemen could perform an effective law enforcement function as we would understand it, as well as being signalmen, managing the movement of trains with hand or flag signals in the days before mechanical signalling (which sounds like a full-time job in its own right). They were certainly placed in sentry-box-type structures (called police stations) at intervals along the line and used timed intervals to keep the trains a safe distance apart (or at least that was the theory).

It was not until the Special Constables Act of 1838 that the railways were given a specific duty to keep the peace on and around the railway. This 'Act for the Payment of Constables for Keeping the Peace near Public Works' said that 'great mischiefs have arisen by the outrageous and unlawful behaviour of labourers and others employed on railroads, canals and other public works' and made the railway companies responsible for the cost of appointing special constables to keep the peace. One survival of this early dual role for railway policemen (as distinct from special constables) is that modern signalmen are still known by the police nickname of 'Bobby'. All sorts of other tasks might also be allotted to these earliest policemen – they could be called upon to be ticket sellers or collectors, or even substitute guards.

The Lawless Navvies

> The navigators were the most neglected and spiritually destitute people I ever met; ignorant of Bible religion and Gospel truth, infected with infidelity, and prone to revolutionary principles.
>
> (Quoted in Francis, *A History of the English Railway* (1851))

One of the biggest problems the early railway police had to contend with in their law enforcement role was other employees of the railway. One of the reasons the railways' bad reputations preceded their opening was the lawless behaviour of the armies of navvies that built them. Whatever forces of law and order that were available locally (including the Army) often had to be called upon to suppress the navvies' drunken, riotous behaviour, especially after they got paid (their 'randies', as they called their payday celebrations). On more than one occasion, when the pub in which they were celebrating payday ran out of beer, the navvies responded by demolishing the pub. In 1836 the inhabitants of Slough and Buckinghamshire even called upon the newly formed Metropolitan Police to come and protect them from the Great Western Railway workers.

The railways may have had a duty to keep the peace on and around the railways, but sometimes the problems with the navvies exceeded their capabilities. A four-day battle between English and Irish navvies on the Chester & Birkenhead Railway in 1839 was only ended when the troops were called in. The Army was also brought in when a group of riotous navvies murdered a ganger on the Edinburgh & Glasgow Railway in 1840. The ringleaders were rounded up and hanged on a makeshift trackside gallows. The railway police could even put themselves in mortal danger. When two navvies were arrested for stealing watches near Edinburgh in 1846, a mob of their compatriots marched on the lock-up, freed the prisoners and murdered their gaoler. As bad as their criminality, to the navvies' detractors, was their immorality and its potentially corrosive effect upon impressionable citizens. The sale of wives was said to be commonplace, with the normal going rate at the Woodhead contract held to be a gallon of beer, though others variously fetched a shilling, or just fourpence.

One factor that may have militated against navvies being brought to book for their misdeeds was the fact that they tended to be known only by their nicknames. One engineer, trying to track down three miscreants, demanded that a fellow navvy tell him their names:

> They were the Duke of Wellington, Cat's Meat and Mary Anne; preposterous as it may sound, he knew them by no other names. The nose of the first, the previous profession of the second and the effeminate voice of the third, gained those attractive titles.

> (F. S. Williams, *Our Iron Roads* (5th edition, 1888), p. 141)

Others took a rather more charitable view of the navvies, on the grounds that they were as much sinned against as sinning. This from the House of Commons Select Committee on railway labourers in 1846:

> They are ... crowded into unwholesome dwellings, while scarcely any provision is made for their comfort or decency of living; they are released from the useful influences of domestic ties, and the habits of their former routine of life (influences and habits the more important, in proportion to their want of education); they are hard worked; they are exposed to great risk of life and limb; they are too often hardly treated; and many inducements are presented to them to be thoughtless, thriftless and improvident.
>
> (Quoted in Coleman, p. 22)

Samuel Peto, the great railway contractor turned Member of Parliament, spoke more warmly still about the navvy:

> I know from personal experience that if you pay him well, and show him you care for him, he is the most faithful and hardworking creature in existence ... give him legitimate occupation, and remuneration for his services, show him you appreciate those services, and you may be sure you put an end to all agitation. He will be your faithful servant.
>
> (Debate at the opening of Parliament, 1851, quoted in Coleman, p. 70)

Peto practised what he preached. He provided books and teachers for his navvies, formed sickness clubs and benefit societies and showed them how to use savings banks. He even built them temporary cottages. Well-meaning Christians undertook missionary work among the navvies, in an effort to get them to mend their ways. Attempts were made to establish a Christian Excavators' Union and a Christian Excavators' Temperance Pledge. Neither was conspicuously successful, especially when the few men who were willing to forswear the demon drink were asked to single themselves out by wearing a blue ribbon.

One irony is that there did not need to be such large armies of navvies working on the railways. From as early as 1843 American railway builders (where labour was relatively more scarce and expensive) were using steam shovels as a cheaper (and quicker) alternative to manual labour. There, the term 'navvy' meant a steam shovel. On this side of the Atlantic, the cost benefits were more marginal, and contractors preferred to stick with the old pick and shovel way of doing things.

The Battle of Saxby and Other Disorders

Lest it be thought that it was only the lower orders who were guilty of railway-related violent disorder, it is worth focussing for a moment on the behaviour of some of the landed gentry when their estates were threatened by the railways, and on the railway companies themselves. In 1844 the Midlands County Railway was surveying the route of a proposed branch line between Syston, near Leicester, and Peterborough. One of the major landowners on the route was the Earl of Harborough and the railway offered to buy the necessary land from him. The earl, who was also a major shareholder in the nearby Oakham Canal, not only refused to sell the land, but also forbad the surveyors to enter his Stapleford Park estate. The surveyors nonetheless walked along the canal towpath, where they were accosted by the earl's men, who 'arrested' them, until a policeman pointed out that they were perfectly entitled to walk along a public right of way.

The Midland Railway gathered reinforcements, variously described as 'railway employees' and 'hired thugs', and returned, only to be met by a similarly reinforced body of estate workers, canal employees and their own hired thugs. The local police were powerless to break up the resulting fight, involving up to 300 people, with the earl himself active in the fray (at one stage driving his carriage at full tilt into the railwaymen). The railway's surveying equipment ended up in the canal and members of both sides found themselves before the magistrates. This was what became known as the Battle of Saxby. Despite the earl's best efforts, the railway got parliamentary approval in June 1845.

George Stephenson was the engineer for the Syston & Peterborough Railway and he should by then have been used to violence as part of his conditions of work. As we saw, when surveying the Liverpool & Manchester Railway he had encountered opposition from the earls of Sefton and Derby, and from Robert Bradshaw, representing the Estate of the late Duke of Bridgewater, whose canal interests would be threatened by the railway. The obstacles placed in Stephenson's way were similar to those faced by his predecessor, William James. They had to endure name-calling, stoning, threats of ducking and other bodily violence (some of which came from members of the nobility). When they tried surveying at night – a difficult enough task in itself – guns were fired in their general direction to put them off. Where violence failed, the opposition tried using the law of trespass to remove the surveyors.

Brunel was not above using violence to get his way. He was centrally involved in the Battle of Mickleton in 1851, described as the 'last pitched battle between two private armies on UK soil'. Brunel was engineering the Oxford, Worcester & Wolverhampton Railway, and a key part of the project was the 875-yard Campden Tunnel, which was subcontracted to one Robert Marchant. Brunel grew dissatisfied with Marchant's progress and stopped paying him. When Brunel's arrears reached £34,000, Marchant and his men stopped working and the entire railway was held up. The *Illustrated London News* of the day describes the confrontation that followed (Peto & Betts were the contractors responsible for the other parts of the line, to whom Brunel reassigned Marchant's part of the contract):

At the Worcester end of the tunnel, Mr Cowdery (an agent for Peto & Betts) with 200 men from Evesham and Wyre carrying pickaxes and shovels, met Marchant, who dared them to proceed on pain of being shot. He was carrying several pistols.

Mr Brunel, unable to persuade Marchant to move, told Peto & Betts' men to proceed and take the line. A rush was made and several heads were broken and three men had dislocated shoulders. A Marchant man who drew his pistols was set upon and his head nearly severed from his body.

Marchant and his men left for an hour and returned with three dozen policemen from the Gloucester constabulary and some privates from the Gloucester Artillery and two magistrates who read the Riot Act. Fights had again broken out and several received broken arms and legs.

At 4 Mr Charles Watson, of Warwick, arrived with 200 men and the Great Western Company sent a similar number to expel Marchant. The magistrate told Marchant's men to start work and Peto & Betts' men to stop work.

Marchant gave in and he adjourned with Mr Brunel to come to some amicable agreement. Whilst they were doing so a small number of navvies again started fighting and one had his little finger bitten off. Eventually Messrs Cubitt and Stephenson acted as arbitrators and work suspended for a fortnight.

(*Illustrated London News*, 26 July 1851)

It is estimated that Brunel assembled a force of some 2,000 navvies with which to intimidate Marchant, so talk of private armies is no exaggeration.

Murder

As we saw in the chapter about the fear of the early railways, many people were concerned that the railways would bring the criminal dregs of the inner city to their respectable neighbourhoods (and enable the wrongdoers to make a swift getaway, once their foul deeds had been committed). They felt no easier about travelling with such miscreants in the confined space of a railway compartment, particularly in the days of non-corridor trains. When the French Chief Justice, Poinsot, was murdered in a railway carriage in 1860, one British newspaper confessed that 'a certain feeling of uneasiness has arisen at the idea of the extreme facility with which the crime appears to have been perpetrated'. While in Britain it may have prompted uneasiness, in France it created a lucrative market for publishers and newspaper proprietors, for books and articles about railway crime. But, in almost fifty years, only four killers were convicted of murders actually committed in British railway carriages.

A German named Franz Müller, a twenty-four-year-old tailor, assaulted and robbed elderly banker Thomas Briggs while travelling on the North London Railway. He threw the dying man from the moving train and was eventually hanged for his crime in November 1864. Public concern about Briggs' murder led to the Regulation of Railways Act 1868, requiring the installation of communication cords in all carriages, although you had to lean out of the carriage window to operate some of the early, outside ones. Another consequence of the murder was that some companies put windows – known as 'Müller's lights' – between compartments, so that passengers could at least see what was going on next door. Last, and certainly least, Müller's taste in cut-down hats (which he left at the scene of the crime) prompted a new fashion.

Percy Lefroy Mapleton, a twenty-one-year-old journalist, stabbed and shot coin dealer Isaac Gold (sixty-four) while travelling on the London–Brighton express. He disposed of the body in the Balcombe tunnel, where it was not found immediately, but the fact that Mapleton left the train covered in Gold's blood and was found to have his coin collection in his possession led to his arrest and execution in November 1881.

George Parker murdered and robbed an elderly farmer named Pearson, and wounded his wife, between Surbiton and Vauxhall stations on the London & South Western Railway in 1901. He leapt from the train as it entered Vauxhall station, but was apprehended after 'an exciting chase'.

John Dickman murdered John Nisbet on a train between Newcastle-upon-Tyne and Alnmouth in March 1910. Nisbet had been the cashier to a colliery and had been carrying a bag containing the colliery's wages.

More common were cases involving alleged sexual assault in the privacy of the railway carriage, but some of these could involve an element of blackmail on the part of the woman. It could be left to a jury to choose between two conflicting accounts of events, based upon the impression the key witnesses made on them. One of the most famous of these cases, that of Colonel Valentine Baker, is covered in the chapter about women and the railways.

If the railways helped criminals leave the scene of their crime more quickly, the provision of instant communications along the railway line also proved early on to have major crime-fighting potential. A telegraph link had been installed between Paddington and Slough stations by 1843. On New Year's Day in 1845 a man called John Tawell put prussic acid in the stout of Sarah Hart, his mistress, and then made for nearby Slough station, where he boarded the London train. However, her dying screams were heard and Tawell was followed to the station. Railway staff at Slough were able to telegraph their Paddington colleagues:

> A murder has just been committed at Salt Hill and the suspected murderer was seen to take a first-class ticket for London by the train which left Slough at 7h. 42m. p.m. He is in the garb of a Kwaker with a brown great coat on, which reaches nearly down to his feet; he is in the last compartment of the second first-class carriage.

The reason for the odd spelling of 'Quaker' is because on these early machines only twenty letters of the alphabet could be sent – there was no C, J, Q, U, X or Z (other misspellings that would have resulted from the limitations of the technology have been tidied up in our text). Within minutes the reply came back:

> The up-train has arrived; and a person answering, in every respect, the description given by telegraph came out of the compartment mentioned. I pointed the man out to Sergeant Williams. The man got into a New-road omnibus, and Sergeant Williams into the same.
>
> (*Illustrated London News*, 11 January 1845)

In due course, Mr Tawell was given his appointment with the hangman. But a combination of human error and low cunning meant the police failed to capitalise on another telegraphed alert along the same stretch of telegraph wires:

> One notable and well-prepared forger on the run is said to have joined a lady in a compartment in Paddington; as the train sped westward, he asked her to cut all his hair off and then to look the other way while he changed his clothes. Despite

the alarm having been sent ahead by the electric telegraph, the police failed to recognise him at Reading.

(Sowan, p. 26)

Unfortunately, the universal installation of the telegraph across the railway network proceeded rather more slowly than might have been hoped, partly due to the fact that so many of the early railway staff were illiterate. The GWR's system actually fell into disuse for a time, until it was installed on all major lines in the 1850s. The system proved to be revolutionary, and not just in arresting murderers and aiding the operation of the railway. It also meant that information could be relayed the length of the country instantaneously, which was important for the content of newspapers, among other things. This is discussed in more detail elsewhere in the book.

Fraud

The building of railways required vast sums of capital. For those so inclined, the scope for fraud was equally boundless. For fraudulent activity on a truly grand scale, we need look no further than the man once known as 'The Railway King'. George Hudson was born in 1800, the fifth son of a farmer who died when George was just nine. By the age of fifteen he was apprenticed to a draper in York, and went on to work his way up in the business (a process aided by marrying the daughter of one of the partners). At the age of twenty-seven he inherited a fortune of £30,000 from a great uncle. This immediately propelled him into the ranks of the local great and good and in 1833 he was appointed treasurer of a company promoting a railway between York and Leeds. A meeting with George Stephenson the following year enthused Hudson with the idea of a network of railways across the nation, and started him on a career of building, or acquiring, as many railways as one man could.

Prior to 1849, railway companies needed no independent audit, allowing Hudson to use each new injection of investors' money to pay the unrealistically high dividends he had promised to his existing shareholders. His accounting procedures were notoriously vague and he used to pack shareholder meetings with his supporters, to ensure any dissent was shouted down. Having said this, the shareholders themselves – in the grip of the railway mania of the period – did not appear to be too scrupulous about their investments, provided the dividends kept coming. In one case, Hudson was even able to raise an investment of £2.5 million to fund railway construction, without telling the investors where the railway was going to or coming from.

In 1844 he carried out his greatest amalgamation, with the establishment of the Midland Railway. By this time, he had acquired his nickname and was already the most powerful figure in the British railway world. He was lionised by the great and the good, from Prince Albert down; a public testimonial for him raised £30,000 in three months, and another £25,000 was subscribed for a statue in his honour. He was said to have been largely responsible for emasculating most of the more radical proposals in Gladstone's 1844 railway Bill, by which Parliament had hoped to control some of the excesses of the early railways.

Hudson's ambitions as a railwayman were matched by his civic and private aspirations. He became Mayor of York in 1837 and by 1845 got himself elected MP for Sunderland and Deputy Lord Lieutenant of Durham. He bought the Duke of Devonshire's 12,000-acre estate at Londesborough and by 1848 controlled 1,450 of the nation's 5,007 miles of railway, in a network stretching from Berwick to London and Yarmouth to Bristol.

These toadying extracts from an *Illustrated London News* article about him illustrate the deference he received from all and sundry, as long as he was still making money for everybody:

His career in railway enterprise has been, it is well known, attended with unprecedented success, attributable, in no trivial degree to his ability, judgement and integrity.

Mr Hudson enjoys unbounded popularity in his own district, and people of all ranks would be glad to confide any sum of money to his discretion and speculative enterprise. His sudden rise has not blunted his naturally kind disposition.

We have known Mr Hudson for many years and whether in private life ... or in his more arduous engagements in the railway world – we have ever found that his politics (to us) were objectionable, yet his course was always straightforward and highly honourable.

(*Illustrated London News*, 6 September 1846)

But it was as the railway mania died down and the nation went into recession that the cracks began to show in his multi-million-pound empire. He fell seriously ill while struggling to juggle his finances so as to balance the books, and more and more of his former fawning devotees turned into his bitterest critics. His dubious business practices began to come into the public arena and the *Illustrated London News* (who, as we saw, had ingratiated themselves with him as much as anybody) highlighted the hypocrisy of the Establishment that had previously beaten a worshipful path to his door: 'Before he was detected in his malpractices he was the host and guest of peers of the realm, who would have disdained to speak to him when he kept a mercer's shop at York.' (*Illustrated London News*, 22 November 1856)

Society turned against him; he was stripped of his honours and prestige. Hudson Street in York had its name changed to Railway Street and Lord Macauley spoke for the nation in calling him 'a bloated, vulgar, insolent, purse-proud, greedy, drunken blackguard'. Investors lost a total of nearly £80 million in his downfall. To his credit, Hudson owned up to his misdeeds and sold off his possessions to pay back at least some of his creditors before fleeing overseas to live in poverty for the next twenty years.

For all that he was just as Macauley described him (to which others added 'obnoxious', 'personally charmless' and other unflattering epithets), Hudson's commitment to a unified national railway network was undoubtedly the way for the railways to go, and his vision and determination made an important and positive contribution to the development of the national network.

Less well known than Hudson but still fraudulent on a grand scale was the rise and fall of Leopold Redpath. He was an office worker with the Great Northern Railway, based at King's Cross, whose job was to issue (and account for) shares in the company. His salary did not exceed £250 a year, but this was difficult to square with the fact that he lived at Chester Terrace in Regent's Park (at a rental of £200 a year), owned another property in the same exclusive terrace outright, along with a £30,000 mansion at Weybridge, ran three carriages, had an extensive art collection and was a generous philanthropist. The railway company rather implausibly assumed either that he had an uncanny gift for playing the stock market, or that he was a man of substantial independent means, whose work for the railway was merely a hobby.

The truth was very different. Redpath was issuing false share documents to imaginary people, which he then resold to real investors, pocketing the proceeds. His ill-gotten gains were then invested in real railway stock, whose value he enhanced with a simple stroke of the pen (so that, for example, £250 of stock became £1,250). It took the railway company at least eight years to spot that it was paying out £15,000–20,000 more per year in dividends than their books could account for, by which time Redpath had defrauded them of some £250,000 (or £25 million in modern values). Their lax bookkeeping even gave Redpath's accounts a clean bill of health, despite them showing a deficit of at least £180,000 (or possibly even up to three times that amount). Redpath fled to Paris, but was detained and brought back to London, where he became one of the last people to be sentenced to transportation to Australia for life for his crimes. The loss of the money that Redpath defrauded led to a delay in the construction of the Metropolitan underground railway.

The case of Cornelius Stovin smacks not so much of criminality as incompetence, and also raises some questions about the competence of his employer, the London & South Western Railway. He was a Cambridge graduate from a wealthy background, whose first business as a brass-founder failed. He then displayed his business acumen by setting up a Liverpool-based coaching company in the same year that the railway between Liverpool and Birmingham opened. Predictably, it too failed and in 1839, just three days before he was declared bankrupt, he was appointed traffic manager of the Railway. His account-keeping proved to be chaotic and he was told to reduce the losses. Instead, in March 1852 he disappeared rather suddenly to the United States. The Railway made every effort to get him back, even offering to repay his return fare, but he proved strangely reluctant to return. In time his family left Britain to join him and they all decamped for Canada, where he got a new job – as a railway manager.

Small wonder, perhaps, that some railways had a contingency item in their accounts for 'Forged Stock Transfer Reserve', against the possibility of fraudulent staff. The LMS kept it until 1947.

But fraud was not the exclusive province of the management and staff of the railways. The law relating to liability for passengers and their luggage was at first unclear until resolved by legislation in 1845. Strangely enough, this clarification of the railways' responsibilities led to a surprising number of passengers on the Liverpool & Manchester claiming for large sums of money that had been salted away in luggage which had unaccountably gone astray. Smelling a very big rat, the L&M declined to pay out and instead offered future customers the option of taking out insurance against the loss of any small fortunes contained in their luggage.

Theft and Robbery

Theft has been a problem associated with the railways (as with every form of transport) since the earliest days. The first mail was carried by rail in 1838 and it did not take long after that for the first mail robbery to occur. The Eastern Counties Railway reported losing no less than seventy-six items of luggage in a single day in 1848 (whether by criminal activity or staff error is not clear) and, by the following year, thefts from just the six largest railway companies were costing over £100,000 annually.

The form of crime most associated with railways in the public imagination is robbery from a moving train, the modern equivalent of holding up of a stagecoach. One of the first ever narrative moving pictures to be shown in cinemas was *The Great Train Robbery* of 1903. This was inspired by the real-life exploits of one Robert LeRoy Parker, better known to cinemagoers as Butch Cassidy.

In Britain, everybody knows about the Great Train Robbery of 1963, in which Ronnie Biggs gained a form of celebrity for his minor part in the theft of £2.6 million from a railway mail coach. But its predecessor, the Great Gold Robbery, took place on 15 May 1855. Three London firms loaded 91 kilograms of gold (worth almost £1 million in modern values) onto a train bound for Folkestone, where it was to be shipped across the Channel to Boulogne. Intricate and apparently foolproof security measures were put in place. The boxes containing the gold were weighed at Boulogne; one was found to be under the expected weight, the other two slightly over. Nonetheless they were accepted and put on a train for Paris.

On arrival, it was found that the gold had been replaced by lead shot, and the search was on to establish exactly where the substitution had taken place. The French blamed the British railway company; the British said it had happened in France. Four police forces in the two countries plus a private investigator employed by the South Eastern Railway and a substantial reward yielded nothing but false trails.

In August 1855 a career criminal named Edward Agar was arrested for passing a dud cheque. Facing transportation for life, Agar decided to turn Queen's evidence, revealing his part in the Gold Robbery and incriminating two railway employees, William Pierce and William Tester, and railway guard James Burgess. The conspirators had waited until being tipped off that there was a good haul of gold to be had, then travelled on the train on which it was being transported, carrying carpet bags full of lead shot. The guard on the train was Burgess, who let them into the guard's van. The journey to Folkestone gave them time to unlock the boxes with duplicate keys they had obtained and force the other security measures, replacing the gold with the lead shot. While the boxes of 'gold' were being offloaded at Folkestone, three of the conspirators travelled on to Dover with their carpet bags full of the real thing.

The three others were eventually arrested and tried in January 1857, with Agar and his common law wife Fanny Kay as the chief prosecution witnesses. Two of the accused got fourteen years' penal transportation, and Pierce got two years in prison for his lesser part in the robbery.

The most famous attack on an actual train was of course the aforementioned Great Train Robbery of August 1963, in which a gang of fifteen tampered with the signals at Mentmore (Buckinghamshire) to stop the Glasgow–London overnight mail train. They coshed the driver and made off with the £2.6 million (£43 million at 2012 values) in used notes the train was carrying. The raid was poorly executed and eleven of the gang received long terms of imprisonment (between twenty and thirty years). But only 13 per cent of the stolen money was ever recovered and some of the gang (including a mysterious 'Ulsterman', thought to have been a key figure in planning the crime) were never captured. The disappearance of the money seems particularly surprising, since most of it was in £1 and £5 notes and it weighed in at some 2.5 tons.

Like its twentieth-century counterpart, the 1855 robbery caught the public imagination. It spawned a Victorian mystery novel called *Kept* and (later) a film, *The Great Train Robbery*. In both of these fictionalised versions, the criminal mastermind behind it evades capture.

But some, far from believing that the railways provided new opportunities for crime, saw them as a solution to the problem. The Liverpool & Manchester Railway prospectus, written in 1824, claimed:

> There is still another ground of objection to the present system of carriage by canals, namely, the pilferage, an evil for which there is seldom adequate redress, and for which the privacy of so circuitous and dilatory passage affords so many facilities. Whereas a conveyance by Railway, effected in a few hours, and where every delay must be accounted for, may be expected to possess much of the publicity and consequent safety of the King's highways.

This added security was not realised in practice, if the despairing words of David Stevens, the Goods Manager of the LNWR in 1853, are anything to go by:

> Thieves are pilfering the goods from our wagons here to an impudent extent. We are at our wits' end to find out these blackguards. Not a night passes without wine hampers, silk parcels, drapers' boxes or provisions being robbed; and if the articles are not valuable enough they leave them about the station.
>
> (Quoted in Whitbread, p. 62)

Some of the proceeds of crime went beyond the 'not valuable enough' category. Among the items reported stolen over the years were people's dirty laundry, a traveller's samples of false teeth, a box of turnips, baby alligators, doorknobs and rotting cheese. Railway property was itself a tempting target for some. Today we are all familiar with the theft of copper cable and the disruption it causes to the railway, but over the years other targets have included tarpaulins (valued by farmers as covers for haystacks – the Eastern Region alone lost 10,000 of them in 1951), the pictures of holiday resorts that used to adorn carriages and even the horsehair stuffing for seats (for which there is apparently a ready market among upholsterers).

Railway Stations

While the railways may not have invented a new class of crime, they provided a promising new venue for it to take place. While not strictly illegal, some child beggars in railway stations could batten onto travellers with such determination that they could only be removed with a clout – or a penny. Over and above them, if contemporary reports were to be believed, the Victorian railway station teemed with criminal scoundrels, waiting to relieve the traveller of their valuables – or their virtue:

> It is no wonder that a station has always been a Mecca of thieves. What could provide better cover, with its multitudinous throng? The problem of the thief is not so much what to steal, but which of the many articles will prove the most lucrative 'lift' … Railway stations must be unique in one respect. Besides providing a rich, albeit risky, hunting ground for the luggage thieves, they also supply, for only a modest charge, the ideally convenient hiding place for the plunder: the station cloakroom.
>
> (Whitbread, p. 175)

Towards the bottom of the criminal pecking order came 'the station lounger', a social problem described in an Edwardian study of youth crime:

There is a floating population of station denizens who are not there to travel. Dossers, derelicts, drifters, drug addicts, the homeless and the friendless find in the station, open twenty-four hours a day, warmth, shelter and light...

The typical lad of this class can be seen any day outside most of our big railway stations ... trying to get a 'carry' from some bag-laden passenger; now and then a traveller for the day brings joy to his heart, but most of the day he is filling up his time in spending pennyworths at the coffee shop on the corner, gambling with the rest of the boys and dodging the police.

(T. Norman Chamberlain, quoted in Whitehouse, pages 151–162)

They do not appear to have been spectacularly successful in dodging the police, for they were frequently fined for sleeping out, gaming, jostling and trespass. Many of them, unable to pay their fines, ended up in gaol.

Henry Mayhew, chronicler of London's low-life in the fourth volume of his *London Labour and the London Poor*, devotes an entire section to railway pickpockets. He provides a detailed description of their appearance. They 'are generally smartly dressed as they linger there – some of them better than others. Some of the females are dressed like shopkeepers' wives, others like milliners, varying from nineteen to forty years of age'. (Mayhew, p. 200)

As for their behaviour, 'they are generally seen moving restlessly about from one place to another, as if they did not intend to go by any particular railway train. There is an unrest about the most of them which to a discerning eye would attract attention.'

The level of detail in his description of their techniques almost amounts to a training manual for the would-be pickpocket. This is a small part of it:

They sometimes go into first- and second-class waiting rooms and sit by the side of any lady they suppose to be possessed of a sum of money, and try to pick her pocket by inserting their hand, or by cutting it with a knife or other sharp instrument. They generally insert the whole hand, as the ladies' pockets are frequently deep in the dress...

They occasionally travel with the trains to the Crystal Palace and other places in the neighbourhood of London, and endeavour to plunder the passengers on the way. Frequently they take longer excursions – especially during the summer – journeying from town to town, and going to races and markets, agricultural shows or any places where is a large concourse of people.

(Ibid., pages 201–202)

A particular target for pickpockets were would-be spectators at bare-knuckle boxing matches. Their combined railway and fight ticket could be worth £2 or more, and the victim was hardly likely to report to the police the theft of a ticket to an illegal event. The theft of luggage could be no small matter. In the mid-1870s a minor epidemic of jewellery robberies took place in London stations. Among others, Lady Dudley lost £25,000 worth at Paddington station and Countess Grey £2,000 worth at Waterloo. An 'educated young lady', working the Great Eastern stations in 1890, took hundreds of pounds worth of property before being caught and sentenced to what some thought was an overly generous nine months' imprisonment. They may have been right, for she was caught doing the same thing on the very day of her release.

Social commentators also catalogue a whole host of other criminal activity being conducted at the station: prostitutes plying their trade, pimps on the lookout for innocent youngsters to corrupt; paedophiles, drug pushers and homosexuals in pursuit of their then-illegal liaisons. Not even railway hotels were safe. Chesney reports a specialised form of villainy in them, called 'snoozers'. These were people who took a room at a railway hotel and befriended the other guests, to see who might be worth robbing. Once everybody was asleep, they would break into the victims' rooms and relieve them of their valuables, leaving the hotel early the following morning on the pretext of catching an early train, hopefully before the loss of the valuables was even discovered.

It is worth being shot at to see how much one is loved.

(Queen Victoria, 1882)

Turning to a more specialised area of criminality, railway stations were a good place if your objective was to assassinate a member of the royal family. In March 1882, a deranged citizen named Roderick McLean made one of his eight unsuccessful assassination attempts upon the queen, as she was passing through Windsor's Central station. She had apparently given a 'curt' reply to some poetry he had sent her. The attempt was later immortalised by another 'poet', William McGonagall. No doubt inspired by all of this, in 1900 an attempt was made on the lives of the Prince and Princess of Wales, as they were waiting in the Gare du Nord in Brussels.

Concessionary Fares?

An interesting example of concessionary fares was the arrangement the Liverpool & Manchester Railway had with the local constabulary. Under this, the police were allowed free travel on the trains 'if pursuing a criminal'. However, the police superintendent had to authorise the journey in writing (which may have created some interesting difficulties in cases of hot pursuit). More curious still, if the officer made an arrest, he would be charged full fare, whereas if the villain got away, the journey was free.

Terrorism

The railways, being heavily used and highly visible parts of the urban fabric, were a natural target for terrorist outrages. The 1880s saw a series of bomb attacks by Irish Fenians, the forerunners of the IRA. In 1880, a charge of dynamite was placed under the tracks between Bushey and Watford to catch the Irish Mail. Fortunately, the charge failed to go off. On 30 October 1883 two bombs were detonated, one near Praed Street station, Paddington, and the other on a District line train between Westminster and Charing Cross. Nobody was killed or badly injured, but the culprits were never caught. The following February four stations were attacked – Victoria, Charing Cross, Ludgate Hill and Paddington. Only the one at Victoria exploded, again without fatalities and without the perpetrators being caught. A tunnel between Gower Street and King's Cross on the Metropolitan line was bombed in January 1885, and this time one James Cunningham was convicted of the crime, receiving a life sentence with hard labour. Further bombs were planned, but either informants enabled police to arrest the bomber or they blew themselves up before planting the device.

Fare Dodgers

Last, and quite possibly least, how did the railway companies deal with those who committed the minor crime of buying a ticket to travel part-way, then staying on for the complete journey? Joseph Peace of the Stockton & Darlington was asked that question by a parliamentary committee in 1839. He told them: 'On one or two occasions … we have got them into a separate coach, drawing the bolt between the coach and the engine; and as they all agreed they were going half way, we left them to walk home, and that has cured it.' (Parliamentary papers, 1839, x. 332)

This chapter may seem like an alarming catalogue of criminality, but it has been able to draw upon the infinite fertility of the criminal mind over almost two centuries. It would be difficult to argue that the railways gave rise to the disturbing consequences for the safety of people and property that some of the early opponents of the railways feared. On the other hand, they did not prove to be the security breakthrough that the Liverpool & Manchester Railway prospectus claimed, in fighting the theft en route that plagued the canals. As for railway stations, while they provided something of a focal point for Victorian criminality, who today would regard them as hotbeds of crime, to be entered with trepidation?

CHAPTER 5

The Railways and Regulation

The folly of 700 people going 15 miles an hour, in six carriages on a narrow
road, exceeds belief.

>(Lord Chancellor Henry Brougham, 16 September 1830, on the death of
>William Huskisson at the opening of the Liverpool & Manchester Railway)

When I see so many young engineers and such a variety of notions I am convinced
that some system should be laid down to prevent wild and visionary schemes
being tried, at the great danger of injury or loss of life to the public.

>(George Stephenson, addressing a Parliamentary Select Committee in 1839)

The railways were born into a world of extreme laissez-faire. Free competition
and an absolute minimum of regulation to interfere with the 'natural laws' of
supply and demand were seen (at least by most of those in authority) as creating
the best of all possible worlds. But the railways created a need for people's
travelling habits to be managed to a degree that could not have been imagined
(or possibly even tolerated) beforehand. They posed a number of unprecedented
problems.

Some related to safety. The railways were many times faster than any known
form of transport and the vehicles were massive, a combination which meant they
could do extreme damage to anything that got in their way. The early trains were
extremely poor at stopping and, being on tracks, they had nowhere else to go if
they encountered someone else using the same section of track – swerving was
not an option. Also (as early operators were to find out) the railways could not
be operated in the same way as other modes of transport – they were 'a natural

monopoly', as Parliament conceded, and ways had to be found of reconciling this monopoly with the prevailing values of Victorian England.

It fairly soon became clear that laissez-faire had its problems as well as its advantages, and that there were other possible models for the development of the rail network. The French, for example, sought a partnership between government and the rail companies, with the government planning the network and being represented on different railway boards, where they could impose conditions on rates, safety or other matters. In Britain, a Royal Commission took stock of progress so far on the network in 1866/67 and revisited the possibility of greater national control. Their conclusions were predictable:

> The Royal Commissioners on Railways have at length made their report. The document sums up in great detail the results arrived at from the mass of evidence adduced before the Commission, and gives judgement against the proposition that the railway system should be taken under the control of the state. The general conclusion of the Commissioners is, in short, that no comprehensive plan shall be undertaken and that the dealing with the railway system shall be confined to modification in private bill legislation, and in the management by the companies. The report says:[a]

> We are of the opinion that it is inexpedient at present to subvert the policy which has hitherto been adopted of leaving the construction and management of railways to the free enterprise of the people, under such conditions as Parliament may think fit to impose for the general welfare of the public...

> We recommend that Parliament should relieve itself from all interference with the incorporation and the financial affairs of railway companies, leaving such matters to be dealt with under the Joint-Stock Companies Act, and should limit its own action to regulating the construction of the line...

> We do not consider that it would be expedient, even if it were practicable, to adopt any legislation which would abolish the freedom the railway companies enjoy of charging what sum they deem expedient within their maximum rates...

> We are unable to see any method of ensuring punctuality in passenger trains by means of legislative enactments, except that proposed by the Committee of the House of Commons in 1858 – viz., that punctuality should be guaranteed, and that passengers injured by delay should be enabled to recover summarily a fixed sum; but we have already referred to the objections to this proposal.

Parliament has relied for the safe working of railways upon the efficiency of the common law and of Lord Campbell's Act, which gives persons injured and near relatives of persons killed a right to compensation. We consider that this course has been more conducive to the protection of the public than if the Board of Trade had been empowered to interfere in the detailed arrangements for working the traffic.

(*Illustrated London News*, 18 May 1867)

Despite these views, the railways were regulated more than any other area of Victorian activity (with the possible exception of mining), and helped to establish a precedent for a culture of government control that survives across a far wider range of activity to this day.

Regulation Before the Railways

Before the railways, there was precious little regulation on the nation's transport networks (such as they were). There had been no national network of roads since Roman times and the parish-based system of maintaining such roads as existed was hopelessly inadequate. An Act of 1555 required parishes to appoint two unpaid surveyors to oversee repairs to the parish's roads and for each able-bodied parishioner to contribute two days' unpaid labour for road mending. The system was 'universally hated, widely ignored and almost impossible to enforce'. (Hylton, 2009, p. 10)

The parishes could not borrow money to fund major works and in any event had little incentive to do so, since the main beneficiary of improved roads was through, rather than local, traffic. So the standard of the road network, in terms of its safety and navigability, was worryingly variable, to put it mildly. The eighteenth-century writer Arthur Young, travelling on a stretch of highway that formed part of the Great North Road (the future A1), feared compound bone fractures as he bounced over broken stones, before nearly being buried alive in muddy sand. In Berkshire, the Marlow Road was favoured by the Marquis of Salisbury and many other westbound health tourists over the main Bath Road because it was slightly less bumpy and therefore easier on their gout. It even became known as the Gout Track.

The coming of the turnpikes from the second half of the eighteenth century at least created a financial incentive for the trusts who built them to maintain them but, after their initial sanction by Parliament, which set limits on the tariffs to be charged, there was no set standard for their maintenance and no idea of creating a coherent national network. Part of Arthur Young's nightmare journey, described in the previous paragraph, was over a turnpike. Nor was there any rule about how to use the road. Even travelling on the left-hand side was not enshrined in law until the Highways Act of 1835, after that principle had already been adopted by the Liverpool & Manchester Railway in 1830. The same convention was adopted by most (but not all) of the railways that followed.

The canals had to be rather more heavily engineered than the roads, but even they were not regulated after the initial parliamentary approval of the route. Again, there was no idea of a coherent national network, and Parliament did not even set a standard for the dimensions of canals and their locks, making the potential for different sized boats navigating from one part of the canal network to another a very hit-and-miss affair. So, for example, the types of barges that traded along the Bridgewater Canal could enter the adjoining Rochdale Canal but not the narrower Ashton Canal.

The earliest Railway Acts sought to follow the same free and easy approach to their operation as they had taken with the turnpikes and canals. The Stockton & Darlington Railway Act was based upon an 1811 one for the Berwick & Kelso Railway. It did not specifically allow for the carriage of passengers, since it assumed that the railway company would build the track, but that others would provide and run vehicles along it, on the same 'open to all' principle as the turnpikes. This quite quickly proved to be unworkable, though it did not finally disappear from railway legislation until 1859. It was unclear as to the form of motive power to be used, referring at one point to 'men, horses or otherwise' (elsewhere in the Act, reference was at least made to 'loco-motive or moveable steam engines', though a number of the legislators did not have the faintest idea what a 'loco-motive' was). The Act also made vague references to the railway providing 'proper books of account', without in any way clarifying what these meant (something that was not cleared up until the Regulation of Railways Act 1868).

Health and Safety Building the Railways

But there were health and safety nightmares lurking even before the first railways opened for business. Construction of the canals and the early railways was left in the hands of an army of contractors and subcontractors, ranging from individual labourers, taking the first steps towards becoming employers, to some of the wealthiest businessmen in the land. In the latter category was Sir Samuel Morton Peto (1809–89), who in 1850 employed some 14,000 workers and who was able to underwrite the Great Exhibition of 1851 to the tune of £50,000. These contractors were left to their own devices in carrying out their work by the railway promoters and, provided it was completed on time and within budget, not too many questions were generally asked about the methods they employed.

This is not to say that no railway promoter took any interest in their contractors' health and safety, though not perhaps in the terms we would use the words. In the case of the Stockton & Darlington, the sternly Quaker promoter Edward Pease checked out all the would-be contractors beforehand to ensure that none of them was 'a friend of publicans'. In one case where the verdict was in doubt, it was written into his contract that 'the first time he is seen intoxicated, he will be dismissed and the sum due to him as wages shall be forfeited'.

As for the people the contractors employed, the itinerant armies of navvies included refugees from the Irish potato famine, displaced and desperate agricultural workers and, in some cases, outcasts from the law. There were thought to be 200,000 of them working on new lines in 1845. As we have seen, they lived in the most squalid and primitive conditions, terrified local communities with their wild and lawless behaviour and operated in an unregulated and dangerous work environment. In the eyes of many, navvies were seen as less than human and accident reports would speak of the deaths of 'three men and a navvy'. Only after 1854, when gangs of navvies went out to Crimea to build a railway to supply the suffering British troops at Sevastopol, was their reputation to some degree salvaged. The following reflects the pre-Crimean view of the navvy:

> When the rail first began to spread its iron road through England, the labourer attracted no attention from politician or philosopher, from statistician or from statesman; he had joined no important body, he had not made himself an object of dread.
>
> With all the strong propensities of an untaught, undisciplined nature; unable to read and unwilling to be taught; impetuous, impulsive and brute-like; regarded as the pariahs of private life, herding together like the beasts of the field, owning no moral law and feeling no social tie ... They lived for the present; they cared not for the past; they were indifferent to the future...
>
> A perfect dread was on the minds of the people of the town near which the railway labourer was expected.
>
> Living like brutes, they were depraved, degraded and reckless. Drunkenness and dissoluteness of morals prevailed. There were many women but few wives; loathsome forms of disease were universal.
>
> ...Crimes of the most atrocious character were common, and robbery without any attempt at concealment was an everyday occurrence.
>
> (From *A History of the English Railway*, 1851, quoted in Morgan, p. 215)

Meanwhile, health and safety was ignored, as contractors cut corners to speed up work or reduce their costs·

> Vertical banks of rock and earth were undermined to bring them down, the navvies' chances of survival depending upon their ability to spot them collapsing and their speed in running when they did so. Safety fuses were discarded upon the grounds that they caused delay. Cheap iron 'stemmers' were used, instead of the safer copper ones, to ram home explosive charges. The iron ones could make sparks and set the charges off prematurely. In one particularly horrifying accident, a navvy called William Jackson had a stemmer shot through his head like a rocket-propelled javelin, killing him instantly.

(Hylton, 2007, p. 134)

Unsurprisingly, the casualty rate of the navvies working on the Woodhead tunnel contract (thirty-two killed and 540 injured, 140 of them seriously) was reckoned to be worse than that of the soldiers fighting with Wellington in the Peninsular War and the Battle of Waterloo (itself hardly a recipe for a long and healthy life). The Royal Berkshire Hospital in Reading was nearing completion in 1839, just as the construction of the Great Western Railway was passing through the town. The hospital's first patient was fifteen-year-old George Earley, a railway labourer who was run over by a railway wagon, causing his arm to be amputated. In the hospital's first year, sixty-one of the eighty-six patients treated for accidents were railway employees. Add to this the eight people killed and seventeen injured in the Christmas Eve 1841 train crash in nearby Sonning cutting, and it is small wonder that the railway directors were persuaded to pay 100 guineas and a further annual subscription of 10 guineas towards the hospital's running costs. Even this modest contribution seems relatively generous when compared with some others. As a new railway neared Northampton, the local infirmary treated 124 rail-related injuries, at a cost of £590. The contribution the contractors made to that bill came to just £15 1s 0d.

Rarely did the railway companies or the contractors compensate workers for injury or death. All the victims had to fall back on in many cases was the navvies' own contributory sickness club. Samuel Peto was unusual among contractors in encouraging his employees to get medical insurance. In France, a law had been enacted to make contractors compensate any employees who were killed or injured at work, even if it appeared that the fault lay with the individual. This had had the effect of greatly reducing the accident rate. The Select Committee on Railway Labourers was called upon in 1846 to enact something similar in Britain, but they declined to do so. Parliament did, however, legislate that year to compensate passengers injured or killed in rail accidents. Between 1848 and 1857 the South Eastern Railway paid out a total of £61,897 in such payments, but no company ever had to devote more than 1 per cent of its total expenditure to compensation.

As for railway staff, they often fared little better than those employed by the contractors. The North Eastern Railway was considered one of the more enlightened employers of the day but, even in 1870, the family of an employee killed in a work-related accident could expect no more than a nominal £10 gratuity, and an offer by the company to employ any children of the deceased. Railway companies managed to conceal their figures for accidents to staff until 1871, when it was revealed that one in 167 railway workers was killed or injured at work each year – a worse casualty rate than even the mining industry. The year 1875 saw 767 railway workers killed and 2,815 injured at work.

That said, there were also pockets of good practice. The Great Western retained a company surgeon and ran a small hospital at its Swindon works; the London & South Western set up a home for the orphaned children of its railway employees and several railways established savings banks and friendly societies for their employees. There was also a Railway Benevolent Institution, set up in 1858 to support all railway workers in need and their families. By 1921 the Institution had paid out grants totalling £1,600,000. However, the funds for this came from subscriptions from railway officers and servants, and from donations from the public, rather than the railway companies themselves.

The Railways and Monopoly

Parliament recognised relatively early on that this new phenomenon at least needed special control, even if not directly run by the state. A parliamentary Select Committee in 1839, investigating complaints about monopolistic practices by the London & Birmingham Railway, conceded two principles that normally tended to be anathema to the Victorians – not just the granting of a monopoly, but also one that had to be subject to detailed government regulation:

> The safety of the public also requires that on every railway there should be one system of management ... On this account it is necessary that the company should possess complete control ... although they should thereby acquire an entire monopoly.

> (Bagwell and Lyth, p. 58)

The general interests of the community must sometimes be at variance with the interests of the railway proprietors ... and it becomes more important that they should be so far controlled as to secure the public as far as possible from any abuse which might arise from this irresponsible authority.

(Evans, p. 288)

So it was that the railways were brought under the control of a railways inspectorate of the Board of Trade. The original 1840 Regulation Act gave them very limited powers; notice had to be given to them before anybody opened a railway, the Board of Trade could appoint inspectors to vet the new railway and the railway had to file returns of traffic, the charges they made and personal accident injuries. But the inspectors had no powers initially to stop a railway opening, even if it were found to be dangerous – though this did not stop the inspectors holding a number of inquiries without the necessary authority. Not until the 1842 Act did they have proper powers of inspection and accident investigation, and the ability to postpone opening if the railway were dangerous.

The logical people to staff the inspectorate were civil engineers, but most of those with the relevant experience were already heavily engaged in railway building and there were doubts whether they would be: (a) available and (b) sufficiently independent of the railway promoters. So then, and for a long time afterwards, inspectors were drawn from the ranks of the Corps of Royal Engineers.

Health and Safety in Operating the Railways

Nobody anticipated the new challenges the railways would create, in terms of the volume and speed of traffic they would generate and the need for it to be organised in a different way. As we saw, when the promoters of the Stockton & Darlington Railway opened for business, it was initially assumed that they could be run in the same free and easy way as a turnpike. Thus, anybody who turned up with a wagon with wheels of the right gauge was entitled to use it; there was no control over the design or standard of maintenance for these wagons. Trains could be drawn by horses, steam locomotives, stationary engines (or, on the downhill sections, by gravity); there were no timetables, no signalling and just a single track with passing places, giving rise to endless arguments about who had priority (though the promoters did at least specify that minerals wagons got priority over passengers, and passenger carriages were known to have been bodily lifted off the tracks to resolve heated disputes). It was left to the Liverpool &

Manchester Railway, the world's first railway as we would understand the term, to start working out the rules for operating one.

As for the Stockton & Darlington, it took them until 1833 to accept the error of their ways and take over as sole provider of transport services along the line, after which it became possible to introduce a timetabled, steam-hauled passenger service. It took until 1854 before they stopped entirely trying to mix steam and horsepower on the same line.

The early public were equally clueless about how to behave in the vicinity of railways. They would climb on top of coaches to travel, stagecoach-style, oblivious of the danger of being knocked off at the first bridge or overhanging tree. Some early railway carriages (presumably on lines without low bridges) actually had open, rooftop seats. Because these were cheaper, passengers used to cram onto them and ran the risk of being pushed off (the railway's response was to fit nets below the carriage door levels, to try and catch the fallers). If a passenger's hat blew off in mid-journey, they would very likely leap from the train to retrieve it, fondly imagining: (a) that they would survive the fall and (b) that, having picked up their hat, they would be able to catch up and rejoin the train. When their train stopped at an intermediate station, they would get out and wander about on the opposite track, possibly invisible to oncoming trains due to the steam from their own locomotive. There were also a number of early cases of death due to people falling asleep (with or without the aid of alcohol) while lying across the line. One was so drunk that he slept through having his hat run over by a locomotive, while he was still wearing it.

Some of the employees of the railway were as guilty as the passengers. During the first year of the Liverpool & Manchester's operation, accidents to employees included them jumping off before the train had stopped and falling under a carriage; falling out of the brake van while drunk and going under its wheels; leaving a plank lying across the track, to sit on while they were having lunch, with the result that the fireman of the locomotive that hit it was thrown fatally from the footplate; crushing their head between two sets of buffers while attempting an uncoupling.

Long working hours (twelve- to sixteen-hour days) meant that fatigue added to the danger. One guard fell asleep as his train passed through the tunnel at Liverpool. There was fortunately no accident, but that did not save him from being taken to court and given two months' hard labour by the magistrates. Danger lurked in the most unexpected places. In Reading, the water pipes used to fill the locomotives were heated by gas, to stop them freezing. In November 1851 the pilot light went out and a railway employee went looking for the problem with a naked candle. The resultant gas explosion injured a man and tore up part of the platform.

The railways initially developed in a very fragmented manner, and one of the themes of their evolution in the nineteenth century was that of amalgamation. Something like 1,000 railway companies had disappeared by 1914, though there were still 247 survivors in 1875 and 120 by the time of the 1921 Railways Act (though the market was by then dominated by fourteen major players). One of the consequences of all this amalgamation was to do with safety, in that it brought together fleets of wagons with different couplings, braking and other incompatible features. These pushed up operating costs and slowed the assembly and running of goods trains. More to the point from a health and safety perspective, they helped to make the shunter's job, coupling the wagons, the most hazardous on the railway. Their union, the Amalgamated Society of Railway Servants, brought pressure to bear on both rail companies and Parliament to regulate their working.

A Royal Commission on Railway Accidents was convened in 1877. When they asked George Finlay, the general manager of the London & North Western Railway, what the primary cause of railway accidents was, he told them it was 'the neglect of servants'. The truth was that the biggest causes were defective brakes, faulty engine boilers, inadequate signalling and the difficulty of persuading shareholders to spend profits on safety measures. Some railway companies freely confessed to their extreme reluctance to spend money on safety. In 1876 J. Staats Forbes, chairman of the London, Chatham & Dover Railway, frankly admitted that, despite the railway's vast increase in custom and profitability over the past five years, they had spent next to nothing on improved safety. He said that:

> He had had these things urged on him for some time, but he had been as reluctant as any man could be to involve the shareholders in a single shilling of outlay which could be avoided and he had required, not mere theory, but the strongest evidence that these things were required before he would allow them to be done.
> (Dendy Marshall/Kidner, p. 345)

Two years later, his railway suffered its worst ever accident – five passengers were killed and many wounded, in an accident that would not have been possible had the then widespread safety measures been in place on his railway.

Even Brunel – and the early Great Western generally – had a remarkably casual attitude towards safety. When a train was delayed, they did not send someone walking back along the line to look for it – they would send a locomotive along the same line, but going in the opposite direction to the missing train. Brunel himself seemed to think that he had carte blanche to travel where he liked, at whatever speed he liked, on 'his' railway. He once had a narrow escape at 50 mph, and was asked what he would have done had he seen the train coming towards him. His chilling reply was that: 'I would have put on all the steam I could command with a view to driving off the opposite engine with the superior velocity of my own.'

It took the appointment of Daniel Gooch as locomotive superintendent to start creating some track discipline on the Great Western. Even so, part of the train could still become disconnected from the rest without being noticed by either the driver or the policemen who served as human signals along the track. The disconnected part would then come to a halt, waiting for the next service to crash into it. Brunel's solution to this (from 1847) was to have an iron seat fixed onto the back of the engine's tender, from which a lookout could look back along the train for uncouplings, fires or other problems. The exposure to the elements of these seats and their general discomfort earned them the nickname 'iron coffins'.

Despite all this resistance, enforced safety measures were one of the factors that contributed to the railways' spiralling operating costs. In the 1860s, these operating costs consumed around 48 per cent of the railways' total receipts. By the start of the twentieth century, this had risen to 63 per cent.

Signalling and the general management of train movements left much to be desired on the early railways. Timetabling – saying that train X had the exclusive right to use a length of track between two times – was one of the earliest means of traffic control, of keeping trains apart. However, this first meant that all concerned had to memorise the schedule. Nor, without any means of communication, was there any way of knowing whether the previous train had cleared the next length of track. It was also extremely inflexible, with no way of rescheduling trains possible, at least until the use of the electric telegraph became widespread. For these reasons it was also extremely inefficient. Timetabling certainly would not have helped in the case of the Southern Railway's disaster at Staplehurst in June 1865, in which Charles Dickens was a passenger (fortunately unscathed). A ganger had temporarily removed some lengths of track on a bridge undergoing repairs when, to his surprise, the boat train appeared earlier than expected. Its running varied from day to day, according to the tide, and the ganger had got the day wrong. His error cost ten people their lives.

The scope for human error with timetabling or time interval methods of keeping trains apart is illustrated by the fact that the Great Western would pay a bonus of a week's wages to any policeman (signalman) who went a year without making a mistake (the time interval system of traffic management had to be reintroduced during the First World War, when bad weather knocked out the mechanical signalling system).

Nor did the first mechanical signals always inspire confidence. Some of the earliest versions displayed a painted metal plate. This plate was either directly facing the oncoming driver, or turned parallel to the tracks so as to be virtually invisible to him. Asking a driver to respond to a signal he cannot see for part of the time does not sound like the most foolproof of systems, but that is precisely what the Great Western asked their drivers to do in this instruction from 1840: 'A signal ball will be seen at the entrance to Reading Station when the Line is right for the Train to go in. If the Ball is not visible the Train must not pass it.' (Quoted in MacDermot, p. 310)

The semaphore signals that were for many years the industry standard started to be introduced in 1841, though other types were not entirely phased out until the 1890s. But even semaphore signals could be prone to error. One of the London & North Eastern Railway's signals at Abbots Ripton froze in the 'safe' position during a blizzard in January 1876. The crash which followed resulted in the deaths of fourteen people. Others could stick halfway in normal use, giving an ambiguous signal. A curious accident involving a semaphore signal occurred on the Southern Railway in May 1904. A signal linesman stepped on a cable while carrying out repairs, causing another signal to go to 'clear'. The driver of a milk train took this as a signal to proceed and collided with a passenger train, killing a passenger.

There were at first no signal boxes taking an overview of points' settings. The first signal box is thought to have been a curious structure known as 'the Lighthouse' (which it resembled) that opened on the London & Croydon Railway in 1839. This used a system of coloured discs (and, at night, coloured lights) to tell oncoming trains whether the points were set for Croydon or Greenwich.

Elsewhere on the network there could be individual point operators with their individual point levers. A pointsman outside somewhere like Reading station would be expected to know whether each oncoming train was a non-stop express service, or whether the points had to be changed to let it into the station (Reading and some other Great Western stations at first had a curious and dangerous one-sided station arrangement, with both Up and Down platforms to the same side of the tracks). One pointsman made a mistake, and sent an express service careering at high speed into Reading station. It is a testament to the stability of the broad gauge rolling stock that the train stayed on the tracks, albeit shooting the luggage off the carriage roofs onto the platform. As for the pointsman, he was found still upright and clutching his point lever, but in a dead faint! It may be safely assumed that he missed out on any bonus that year.

Not even a serious accident, like the one at Shrivenham in 1848 that left six dead and thirteen seriously injured, could prompt the Great Western to review its operating practices. In this case, two porters had pushed a couple of wagons onto the main line to free up a wagon turntable, and a train had crashed into them. The Great Western's main response to it seems to have been simply to urge their staff to greater vigilance.

Edward Bury, the locomotive superintendent for the London & Birmingham, had an unusual approach to gaining the undivided attention of the men on the footplate at key danger points on the network. A trackside device would trigger a lever on the locomotive that sounded a steam whistle and shone a bright red light on the engine straight into the face of the driver. But there are some accidents for which no health and safety policy can legislate. Heacham in Norfolk was badly affected by the floods of 1953, during the course of which a stationary locomotive, caught in the floods, was struck by a moving wooden bungalow, which had floated off its foundations.

Railway Regulation

Moving from health and safety itself to more general government intervention in the running of the railways, there was certainly no shortage of legislative activity:

> Robert Stephenson calculated in 1856 that 186 separate pieces of legislation pertained to the London and North West Railway alone, yet the practical effect of railway legislation had been to allow 'competition to be obtained, wherever it has been sought'.

> (Evans, p. 288)

There were differing views as to how far state control of the railways should go. Gladstone held what was perhaps an extreme position at the time, believing that the railways, like their contemporary, the newly formed Post Office, should be a state enterprise (an idea that the industry lobbyists addressing the 1844 Railways Bill managed to knock on the head). Others, like Robert Stephenson and contractor Thomas Brassey, envisaged a mixed economy of state control and private investment, whereby a rational network could be built but shareholders would still get their dividends. But many others adhered to the traditional Victorian view that free competition remained the cure for all ills. If one accepted the principle that a railway had to be a 'natural monopoly', this compensatory free competition could take the form of allowing the construction of many competing (for which, read 'duplicating') lines, serving broadly the same set of customers. Having allowed this unprofitable duplication, the government then imposed all sorts of public service obligations on them all, which prejudiced the already dubious profitability of some of them.

Some schemes were financially crippled before they began operating, or even building, the line by the sheer wasteful cost of navigating their Bill through Parliament. The Great Western promoters spent £75,000 (at 1835 values) proving the obvious, that a railway from Bristol to London would be a public benefit. They then had to compensate the owners of the land for having compulsorily to sell their land to the railway company (with the result that the landowners were paid twice for their troubles) and the railway cost twice its original estimate. Parliamentary approval, land acquisition and compensation cost the Eastern Counties Railway £370,000, while the cost of obtaining consent for the Trent Valley line – £630,000 – was more than the railway cost to build.

Small wonder that some landowners saw the coming of the railways as a licence to print money, and their 'principled opposition' turned out to be nothing more than a way of maximising income. Disraeli satirises this in his novel *Sybil* (1845):

'I fear [the railroad] has a dangerous tendency to equality' said his Lordship, shaking his head: 'I suppose Lord Marney gives them all the opposition in his power?'

'There is nobody so violent against the railroads as George,' said Lady Marney, 'I cannot tell you what he does not do. He organised the whole of our division against our Marham line.'

'I rather counted on him,' said Lord de Mowbray, 'to assist me in resisting this joint branch line here; but I was surprised to learn that he had consented.'

'Not until the compensation was settled,' innocently remarked Lady Marney: 'George never opposes them after that. He gave up all the opposition to the Marham line when they agreed to his terms.'

(Quoted in Hylton (2007), pages 192–93)

Robert Stephenson, when president of the Institution of Civil Engineers in 1856, complained that 'the ingenuity of man could scarcely devise a more costly system of obtaining a railway Act', while Samuel Smiles, secretary to the South Eastern Railway, condemned Parliament's handling of the 1840s railway mania, calling it:

A tissue of legislative bungling involving enormous loss to the Nation. The want of foresight displayed by both Houses in obstructing the railway system so long as it was based on sound commercial principles was equalled only by the fatal facility with which they granted projects based on the wildest speculation.

           (Quoted in Vaughan, p. 10)

But it was not just safety considerations that attracted calls for greater regulation, as this editorial from 1844 explains:

When the various leading Railway Companies were first formed, the public hailed their formation, because they were led to believe, that the principal object which their originators had in view, was the accommodation and benefit of the community. The proprietors disclaimed all intention of seeking to obtain anything more than the ordinary rate of interest for the capital invested in these undertakings. And they assured the public, times without number that they would, by a reduction of fares, give them the benefit of whatever success should attend their enterprise.

In this, the public have been grossly deceived. The Railway Proprietors, instead of reducing their fares, have kept them up at the rates which had been fixed on, before it could be ascertained what would be the result of the new experiment. The leading lines have proved more successful than the most sanguine had ventured to anticipate. But the benefit is exclusively enjoyed by the shareholders. The public have derived no advantage from the success of these undertakings. Instead of lowering the fares, as the country had been led to expect, the Railway Directors have proposed dividing the unexpectedly large revenue derived from their respective line among the shareholders...

The public are grossly and grievously wronged in this matter. And they have a right to look to the Legislature for redress. The Railway Companies having broken faith with the public, it is the duty of Parliament to interfere, and see that the public be righted. Passengers ought to be travelling in the leading lines at from 50 to 75 per cent cheaper than they are at present.

           (*Illustrated London News*, 24 February 1844)

Over the years, successive governments imposed a string of obligations on the railways and their fare structure. The 1844 Act imposed a duty on them to carry third-class passengers for a penny a mile in trains that met minimum standards of accommodation and speed. They were also required to transport the armed forces around the country at the (not overly generous) rates prescribed by the government. Parliament set the maximum rates for the railways' charges, and the Liverpool & Manchester was required by its Act of Parliament to reduce its charges if its profits exceeded 10 per cent. An Act of 1854 required them to build any facilities a trader might request while, from 1873, all the railway's charges had to be on public display at every station.

The railways also had to become a common carrier. This put them under a duty to transport, at rates fixed by government, any goods a customer might require of them, from anywhere to anywhere (unless the items were too big to carry or might otherwise damage the railway). Almost everything was moved by rail. House moves, unless very short distance, tended to be containerised and taken by wagon to the nearest railway station, for onward transmission. Entire farms were moved this way, and when the circus came to town, the parade of their menagerie from the station to the big top was part of the spectacle.

From 1870, at the height of the Franco-Prussian conflict, the government even gave itself powers to take over the railways entirely in the event of war. None of these obligations applied to the road-using competition. To cap it all, from 1842 all railway tickets were taxed and the railways became the biggest contributor to the rates of every parish they passed through, typically contributing 80 per cent of a parish's rateable income. Part of their contribution would be spent on the upkeep of the roads that their rival carriers used without charge (the road users' contribution through the Road Fund licence did not come in until 1910). Only in 1929 were the railways relieved of 75 per cent of their rate payments, but a cynical government immediately took all those savings and converted them into subsidies for the railways carrying iron, steel, coal and agricultural produce, leaving the railway companies no better off.

Much of this legislation was based upon fears of a railway monopoly, and the abuses that might follow, but by the interwar period the growth of the road haulage industry meant that any talk of monopoly was outdated. The railways were still campaigning for a level playing field when the Second World War broke out.

CHAPTER 6

The Railways and Leisure

We must have railways for the millions!

(Thomas Cook)

A Short History of Holidays

As the first railways were coming into being, the idea of holidays as we know them – travelling to the seaside or other resorts for a week or more – was unknown to large parts of the population. This is not to say that they had no leisure, but rather that their pattern of recreation was dictated by the rhythms of the agricultural or the Church year, and that it took place largely within the communities in which they lived. Holidays were sometimes marked by traditional plays, feasts and sporting fixtures (such as cricket and the often violent and unruly predecessors to football). This rural pattern of leisure formed an uneasy relationship with the more urban, industrialised society that Britain was becoming, where life was tied more closely to the relentless demands of the factory system. Industrialists likened this to trying to harness deer to the plough, and bemoaned the observance of 'Saint Monday', where employees took Mondays off to recover from the weekend's excesses.

Up until 1834, the Bank of England observed no fewer than thirty-three saints' days and other religious festivals as holidays. In that year, the number was cut to just four – May Day (1 May), All Saints Day (1 November), Good Friday and Christmas Day. While these gave bank employees holidays, the rest of the population had to wait until the Bank Holidays Act of 1871 extended the privilege to them. This gave the nation four new bank holidays (Easter Monday, Whit Monday, the first Monday in August and Boxing Day – Good Friday and

Christmas Day were not included, since they had been recognised as days of rest since time immemorial). This Act resulted from a campaign by Liberal Member of Parliament Sir John Lubbock, and the holidays were also initially known as 'Saint Lubbock's Days'. They were not universally welcomed by the poorest in society, since these were not statutorily paid holidays and much of the workforce could ill afford the loss of a day's income (let alone any longer period without pay).

Since 1971 bank holidays have been announced each year by royal proclamation and can be varied, either to mark special events or to control the activities of the banks (for example, to prevent a run on the pound).

Some parts of England and Scotland – in particular the industrial North and Midlands – had long-established arrangements for taking a week or more as unpaid holiday. Wakes weeks have origins going back to the seventh century, to a time when the Anglo-Saxons were being converted to Christianity. They started out as a celebration relating to the saint's day of the patron saint to whom the local church was dedicated, and evolved into a week's unpaid holiday, during which all the local mills and factories closed for maintenance. Each town in Lancashire would take off a different week between June and September.

Whole communities could virtually become ghost towns during wakes week once the railways came. Oldham got its rail link to Blackpool in 1846 and, at its height in 1860, over 23,000 of its citizens made their way to Blackpool during their week. Local schools would even close, to enable pupils to go on holiday with their parents. Mill workers would pay for their holiday by enrolling in a wakes saving or Going Off Club, right up until the Second World War. These could be big business; the Holiday Savings Club in Oldham collected a total of £228,000 in 1906. Wakes weeks have gradually died out with the decline of traditional industries, and as the national curriculum and the standardised timing of school examinations have prevented schools from fitting in with them.

However, for large parts of the working population no such arrangements as wakes weeks existed in Victorian times. Most clerical workers had some sort of entitlement to holidays with pay by the end of the nineteenth century, but it took much longer to extend them to the industrial working class. In 1911 the TUC adopted holidays with pay as policy and in 1912 Labour Member of Parliament George Lansbury began a campaign to legislate for statutory holidays with pay for all full-time workers. They were a long time coming, initially via negotiations between employers and unions on an industry by industry basis. The print workers were among the first to win them, in 1918. By 1925 around 1,500,000 workers had them, but the number had only risen to around 3,000,000 by 1938 (leaving some 15,500,000 workers without paid holidays). It was in this year that the Holidays With Pay Act extended the right (or, to be strictly correct, recommended that the right be extended) to some 11,000,000 full-time workers.

However, there were still obstacles. The following summer – 1939 – was somewhat more preoccupied with events on the Continent than with holidays, so the law could not be fully implemented and its effects measured until after the war. Second, a holiday away from home was still unaffordable for many of the 19,500,000 workers earning less than £250 a year. A *News Chronicle* survey in 1939 found that only a third of those earning less than £4 a week could afford to travel on holiday. A further problem came from within existing seaside resorts, many of whose residents opposed the democratisation of holidays. Used to a more genteel middle-class clientele, they feared that an influx of the proletariat would lead to 'vulgar behaviour and anti-citizenship'. As for the holiday industries themselves, they painted a spectre of overcrowded resorts, inadequate facilities, increased prices and staff shortages.

The answer to many of these objections was to be found in the holiday camp and, from the 1930s onwards, the likes of Billy Butlin and Captain Harry Warner provided holidays which were affordable ('a week's holiday for a week's pay' was a slogan they both used); mass-produced (at their height, Butlins alone took over a million guests in a season); and relatively self-contained, so as not to frighten the middle-class residents of seaside resorts.

Mass holiday-making meant mass transport and, in the days before mass car ownership, this meant railways. When Butlin reopened his Filey camp after its wartime requisition by the armed forces, it had its own railway station, and he had a business relationship with the LNER to provide rail access to his camps generally. His camps were built close to railway lines and some had their own branch lines or dedicated stations constructed. It may have been this that led the rival LMS Railway to collaborate with Thomas Cook in building their own holiday camp at Prestatyn.

Some Case Studies

Simmons (1986) identifies four categories of resort: first, those that catered for the mass market, such as Brighton, Blackpool, Hastings and Southend; second, those that wished to remain elite and in some cases resisted the coming of the railway in doing so – places like Bournemouth, Eastbourne, Torquay and Worthing; third, ports that evolved into resorts – like Lowestoft, Weymouth and Yarmouth; and finally smaller resorts.

It had long been thought that sea-bathing had health-giving properties – they called it 'physic in the sea'. Scarborough had introduced it by 1730 and Brighton, Worthing and Margate had followed suit by the 1750s. What started out as a health cure blossomed into a social event, nowhere more so than in the case of Brighton, which enjoyed the patronage of the future Prince Regent from 1783 onwards. Scarborough, meanwhile, had to make do with the patronage of the local Yorkshire gentry.

Some venues received large volumes of visitors before the railways, particularly after the introduction of steamships from 1815. Margate received some 90,000 visitors from London in 1830, while the numbers going to Gravesend were over 120,000. The coming of the railways made it possible for an even wider group of people to go to the seaside – particularly to resorts not conveniently placed to get large numbers of seaborne visitors. Different seaside resorts attracted different clienteles. Blackpool became a Mecca for the Lancashire working classes, while Southport appealed to the slightly better-off and Morecambe served the West Riding textile towns (it was known as 'Bradford-by-the-Sea').

There was huge competition for the prestige of building a railway line from London to Brighton, with six competing schemes coming before Parliament in 1834 and 1835, costing the competitors nearly £200,000 simply to submit them. The successful scheme opened in 1841, at a time when Brighton was in something of a recession. Royal patronage was coming to an end (Queen Victoria could not stand the town and regarded its inhabitants as 'very indiscreet and troublesome'); it was thought to be getting overdeveloped and the sanitary arrangements were not ideal – until 1839, its raw sewage was discharged directly onto the beach. Such tourist traffic as there was arrived by road, since there was no seaborne trade to speak of and attempts to run a steam carriage from London had failed.

But the railways soon changed the town's fortunes. Whereas a stagecoach might bring in up to fourteen tourists, an ordinary rail service could supply at least ten times that number and an excursion train could supply tourists by the thousand. Many of the excursions ran on a Sunday, which incurred the wrath of the Sabbatarians. They complained of the idleness and drunkenness the visitors brought to the town, and considered their complaints vindicated by God when two London excursion trains crashed in nearby Clayton Tunnel one Sunday in 1861.

The railway also made Brighton a commuter town serving London. As early as 1845, a first-class season ticket could be had for £50 a year – the railway deliberately targeted first-class custom. Furthermore, it became an important part of the town's industrial employment from 1852, when the railway moved its locomotive works to Brighton. By 1881 it employed around 600 people.

Most towns disliked the idea of being served by a monopolistic railway – as we have seen, the Victorians were great believers in competition as the way to improve service. Brighton was an exception, and the Corporation forged an alliance with the London, Brighton & South Coast Railway to oppose plans for a competitor line from London. There was of course a price for the railway company to pay for municipal support, in terms of reduced freight rates to London and cheap local passenger services.

Heading north, from the 1780s and for the next sixty years Blackpool was a small bathing place serving a local Lancashire clientele. When the Preston–Wyre railway opened in 1840, it brought steam trains within 4 miles of Blackpool and visitor numbers started to grow. They grew further from 1846, when a branch line brought trains into the town itself, and tensions started to grow between what might be called the seclusionists, who wanted to limit Blackpool to the genteel visitor, and those hankering after a more boisterous mass market. The seclusionists provided a gated community at Clarement Park to keep out the riff-raff but, from the 1860s onwards, the mass market began to take over the rest of the town, with its first pier opening in 1863. By the 1890s, Blackpool was getting 2 million visitors a year, almost all of them brought in by rail.

A number of resorts feared that the coming of the railway would lower the tone of their town. Bournemouth had its battle between the seclusionists and the mass marketers. Having originally marketed itself on its seclusion, it was quite late (1870) in getting its rail service. The local MP expressed his constituents' concerns about 'the suicidal policy of allowing one of the most beautiful portions of Bournemouth to be cut up by a railway'. So when it eventually came, it was kept at a distance (today, the expansion of the town has brought the station well within the urban envelope). Cromer was even later (1877) getting its railway and Weston-super-Mare's first branch line (in 1841) was horse-drawn.

The attitude of local landowners could be important in settling the town's relationship to the railways. The Duke of Devonshire saw the benefits to Eastbourne, both as a seaside resort and a superior commuting suburb for workers in the City. A branch of the Hastings–Brighton line opened there in 1849, initially serving a small new town the duke had a hand in developing. Even more entrepreneurial was the Earl of Scarborough, who had interests in Skegness. When the railway provided Skegness with a station that was larger than the local population of 349 could justify, the earl stepped in with a development plan for a leisure resort. He funded a number of the amenities himself and brought in others to develop a pier and baths. By 1913, what had been a tiny village was drawing in over 750,000 visitors a year from the East Midlands and Yorkshire.

Throughout the south-west of England, all along the coasts of Cornwall, Devon, Dorset and Somerset, the growth of small settlements into holiday resorts was driven to no small degree by the marketing efforts of the Great Western Railway. Torquay was in 1800 a tiny village of some 800 people. The railway reached it in 1848 and by 1901 it was a town of some 35,000, augmented in the summer by another 20,000 tourists in a good week. By contrast, Ilfracombe, which had been a much larger place than Torquay at the start of the railway age, was much less well connected to the rail network and had only grown to 8,557 by the turn of the century.

In some resorts, the railway did much more than just deliver the tourists. Cleethorpes was a long-established bathing place and in 1863 got an extension to the Manchester, Sheffield & Lincolnshire Railway. A pier followed in 1872 and the line was doubled and the station rebuilt by 1880. The railway then purchased the pier and added other attractions, such as a promenade and gardens, and a brisk business in day excursions grew up.

A particularly strong relationship developed between the railway and the town of Whitehead in what is now Northern Ireland, where the Belfast & Northern Counties Railway undertook many of the functions of a local authority. They built a landing stage and a ½-mile-long promenade (made of old railway sleepers, and lit by railway-style oil lamps) and even imported sand for a beach, which they kept in place by groynes (again built of surplus sleepers).

By the 1920s holiday traffic was a major part of the railways' business. The Great Western retained fleets of superannuated coaches to cope with the peaks in demand and the Saturday changeover was run like a military operation. Trains consisting entirely of restaurant cars headed west on Fridays, ready to feed the returning holidaymakers, and every available tender locomotive was pressed into service. Many holidaymakers sent their baggage in advance, and special trains were laid on for the purpose. Eight 200-ton trains an hour would leave Paddington on Saturday mornings, and they were in danger of encountering congestion problems as they reached the West Country branch lines. If there were any failures of the rolling stock, queues of trains would soon build up.

Railways and Excursions

Genteel parties will find the trip an agreeable and healthful mode of spending part of the day.

(Early excursion advertising by the Garnkirk & Glasgow Railway)

All that was horrible: long and unearthly hours, packed carriages, queer company, continual shunting aside and waiting for regular trains to go by, and worst of all the contempt of decent travellers.

(An alternative view of excursions, quoted in Faith, p. 273)

In addition to holidays away from home, the railways also gave us the day trip – the excursion. One of the founding fathers of the railway excursion was an enthusiastic opponent of the demon drink. The inspiration for it came to him as he was making his way – on foot – to a temperance meeting:

From my residence at Market Harborough I walked to Leicester (15 miles) to attend that meeting. About midway between Harborough and Leicester – my mind's eye has often reverted to the spot – a thought flashed through my brain, what a glorious thing it would be if the newly developed powers of railway and locomotion could be made subservient to the promotion of temperance! That thought grew upon me as I travelled over the last 6 or 8 miles … I broached the idea of engaging a special train to carry the friends of temperance from Leicester to Loughborough and back to attend a quarterly delegate meeting appointed to be held there in the two or three weeks following. The Chairman approved, the meeting roared with excitement and early next day I proposed my grand scheme to John Fox Bell, the resident secretary of the Midlands Counties Railway Company.

(Thomas Cook, writing in *Leisure Hour*, 1860)

Thus was the travel empire of Thomas Cook born. It was in July 1841 that over 500 supporters of teetotalism each paid a shilling (5p in modern money – children went half price) to make the 12-mile trip from Leicester to Loughborough. Music accompanied them en route and another band met them at Loughborough station. Crowds turned out to cheer the trippers as they made their way to a private park, thrown open to them for the day, and where tea, ham sandwiches, cricket and other sports were included in the price of the excursion.

This is sometimes claimed as the first railway excursion, but there are other, earlier potential claimants to the title. One early one went into Leicester itself on 24 August 1840:

It had four engines to drag it forward and to the beholder appeared like a moving street, the houses of which were filled with human beings … the number of carriages was sixty-seven and the number of passengers nearly 3,000, most of whom were well and respectably attired.

(Quoted in Robbins, p. 42)

Earlier still was a trip to Liverpool by 120 members of Manchester's Bennett Street Sunday School in June 1831. All sorts of bodies organised excursions, from social reformers like Thomas Cook's temperance friends, through promotions by the railways themselves, works outings, Sunday School treats, Trade Union 'galas', Friendly Society festivals and even treats for workhouse children organised by Boards of Guardians. There can have been few individuals who could not have afforded, or been eligible for, a trip. At first, do-gooders welcomed these holiday excursions, as a more wholesome substitute for the drunkenness and disorder that accompanied urban holiday celebrations. But it gradually became clear that, all too often, the excursion simply transported the drunkenness and disorder from the town or city to the seaside, or wherever the excursion was bound.

The excursions were cheap, the rolling stock used for them often substandard and the safety standards lamentably absent. Hall describes one Glasgow excursion train of 1850 as comprising eighteen covered coaches, along with three open cattle trucks and three open sheep trucks – the latter provided for the benefit of passengers 'who refused to get off the roofs of the covered carriages'.

Unlike Thomas Cook's temperance train, the destination of the excursion was not necessarily always an improving one. Another early but striking example was one organised by the Bodmin & Wadebridge Railway in Cornwall on 14 June 1836. The 'attraction' was reported to be a public hanging in Bodmin. There is some question as to whether a public execution actually took place in Bodmin on that date but, even so, there were other examples of equally gruesome attractions being used to promote rail travel. In 1849, both Norwich and Liverpool had their audiences attending public hangings considerably increased by rail-borne excursionists. In Norwich's case they travelled from as far afield as London (and, it is said, added considerably to the public disorder often associated with such occasions). In Liverpool, John Gleeson, 'a murderer of some note', drew a crowd of 100,000 for his execution outside Kirkdale Jail. Chesney describes the carnival atmosphere:

Like any other open-air festivity, executions were marked by high spirits and hearty appetites. Sellers of fried fish, hot pies, fruit and ginger beer commonly drove a humming trade, as did hawkers of mournful ballads and fake condemned-cell confessions – known in the business as 'lamentations'.

(Chesney, p. 356)

The execution of the railway murderer Franz Müller (see the chapter on crime) drew a very healthy (if badly behaved) audience of around 50,000. This grisly line of business for the railways was closed by the ending of public executions in 1867.

Railways could also swell their income with the help of excursion trains to other disreputable or even illegal events. A number of sporting activities, such as horse racing, hunting, pugilism and, to some extent, cricket, attracted a following which was curiously composed of the cream of society and its dregs.

Prizefighting in early Victorian times was bare-knuckle and brutal, where the participants could die from the injuries they suffered and the crowds often got involved in disorderly conduct of their own. If the authorities heard of such fights taking place, the police or the Army could be despatched to break them up. For this reason, promoters would often hold the matches near to the county boundaries so that, if disturbed, they could relocate across the boundary and complete the event before the neighbouring authorities got wind of it. So the railway brought crowds to Sawbridgeworth, near the Hertfordshire/Essex border, for a bout, and the Caunt/Bendigo fight of 1845 was staged at Newport Pagnell (in Bucks, but convenient for Bedfordshire and Northants). When Kent police stopped a trainload of fight fans near their destination at Tonbridge, they simply diverted to Etchingham (Sussex), where a police-free alternative venue was found.

The railway could even have a more direct involvement in the proceedings. Thus it was that, on 12 July 1842, a trainload of 'swells, nobs and fancy men', along with 'the sweepings of St Giles and Whitechapel', travelled from Paddington to Twyford (which was on the Great Western Railway and close to the Berkshire/Oxfordshire border). There, in the station yard (and so presumably with the connivance of the railway company), a prizefight was to be held, with a purse of £50 for the last man standing. The event lasted over two hours, and the loser, known as Tom the Greek, later died from his injuries.

One of the most famous of the bare-knuckle fights took place at Farnborough (on the Hampshire/Surrey border and served by two railway lines) on 17 April 1860, after a long cat and mouse game between promoters and the authorities. To fool the authorities, the railway companies sold spectators three-guinea tickets stamped 'to nowhere' and Metropolitan policemen stood at intervals along the route out of Waterloo, to make sure that at least the event did not take place on their patch. A crowd of some 30,000 assembled to see Britain's champion Tom Sayers take on the American John Heenan (intriguingly billed as 'half horse, half alligator and a bit of snapping turtle') in the first world championship fight, for a purse of £400. The match had reached its forty-second round when the police arrived to break it up. By this time, Heenan was badly damaged and Sayers was 'almost unrecognisable as a human being'. The fight was declared a draw and the crowd closed ranks around the fighters, preventing police access to them. Prizefighting had a good many rich and influential supporters, and among those forced to beat a hasty retreat that day were the Prince of Wales, Prime Minister Palmerston and the novelists Charles Dickens and W. M. Thackeray.

Part of the authorities' opposition to prizefights came from the disorderly behaviour of the crowds associated with them, and an ugly riot at Paddington in 1863 increased pressure for the 'sport' to be banned. The Marquis of Queensbury rules, which cleaned up prizefighting and by which modern boxing is governed, were endorsed by Parliament in 1865. The importance of the railways to prizefighting was shown by the fact that Parliament deemed it necessary to pass the Regulation of Railways Act 1868, which made it illegal for the railways to run prizefight specials. It also provided for half of the fines (of up to £500) imposed on the railways for breaches of the regulation to be paid to informers reporting forthcoming events, and this gradually helped to kill off the bare-knuckle version of the sport. Wadhurst (on the East Sussex/Kent border and on a railway line since 1851) now claims to have been the venue for the last bare-knuckle fight (8 December 1863), in which Britain's Tom King beat John Heenan in thirty-six rounds.

But the railways were by no means limited to purely disreputable sporting events. They were central to the development of many of the nation's current favourite leisure activities. Horse racing was one of the first sports to be transformed by the railways from a casual pastime for the rich to a nationally organised mass leisure activity. It had started even before the first railways; in 1825, the attraction of the Darlington Races had would-be passengers clinging to the side of any coach or wagon heading in the right direction. The racecourse at Newton got its own dedicated branch line within two years of the Liverpool & Manchester Railway opening, and the arrival of the Great Northern Railway transformed Doncaster's St Leger meeting into a major entertainment for working people. (This included railway employees, and Doncaster railway works used to close for the St Leger week in September, so as to avoid mass absenteeism among its workers.) In 1839, when the Great Western ran its first excursion to the Ascot races, the train became overcrowded. Displaced passengers protested by climbing on the roofs of the carriages and it took half an hour to talk them down. Epsom and Chester were served by rail by 1840 and Goodwood at least had a rail link as near as Chichester. As Wilson points out: 'There was an enormous growth in the popularity of the turf – with sixty-two new racing events added to the calendar in the 1850s, ninety-nine in the 1860s, fifty-four in the 1870s. The growth of railways, combined with the growth of free time, made this possible.' (Wilson, p. 409)

The democratisation of the sport was not universally welcomed; those who had enjoyed it as an elite activity felt that the intrusion of the great unwashed (which the railways had abetted, but did not start) had robbed it of much of its attraction, and devices like the enclosure were invented, to keep the common herd at arm's length. But this did not prevent racecourse owners being among the main supporters of new lines that would serve their needs. Sandown Park was sold to potential investors in the 1860s, partly because of its proximity to Esher station, as was Kempton Park in the 1870s. Epsom also got its own branch lines and the promoters of Newbury racecourse in 1905 managed to get their own dedicated station. By contrast, the lack of a nearby rail link was one of the reasons given for the failure of the racecourses at Monmouth, Weymouth and Stockbridge. Even Cheltenham, a course not blessed with particularly good rail access, today runs 'luxury steam rail packages' to their National Hunt Festival meeting for their elite guests.

Special race day excursions were common from the earliest days of the railways to the Second World War and beyond, and carried vast numbers of racegoers (and not a few confidence tricksters). The railways would offer reduced fares and kept carriages in reserve for them. Dr Beeching later claimed that British Railways kept some 2,000 carriages for excursion traffic generally and that these were used, on average, just ten times a year. These would not be of the highest quality and, in the 1840s, lords going to the Derby meeting could be seen clambering into the open trucks normally associated with third-class travel. In fact, the general standard of excursion services – their nickname of 'wagon trains' may give a clue – was such that the Board of Trade felt obliged to intervene, specifying minimum numbers of guards, an end to the dangerous practice of pushing overloaded trains from behind and adequate levels of braking (one excursion that crashed in 1860 had only one brake wagon per eight vehicles, which the Board deemed 'quite insufficient').

The railways were important to horse racing not just for bringing in the crowds, but also for moving the horses. In pre-railway days it could take weeks to transport a racehorse from one part of the country to another. With rail, horses could now be moved 200 miles from training ground to racecourse in a day and national competition became a realistic possibility. The *Newcastle Courant* reported, as 'a remarkable proof of the wonders of steam travelling', that Lord Palmerston's mare Iliona was able to run at Newcastle on a Wednesday and at Winchester (almost 400 miles away) on Friday.

A fixed, national annual calendar of events began to develop from around 1835, though this still tended to reflect the annual migrations of the upper classes (Newmarket in April, Epsom in June, Goodwood in July and Doncaster in September). But the prize money for racing remained very small, in relation to the cost of running a racehorse – the top seven courses in England could only manage £15,000 in prize money between them in 1859. The railways were criticised in some quarters for investing so little in a sport from which they made a great deal of money.

Many other sports were invented or made subject to a standard set of national rules during the mid-Victorian period – golf, football, rugby union, athletics and tennis, among others – and the railways made competition at a national level possible. Cricket developed its county-based structure for national competition and this was well established by the time the first touring Australian XI made its appearance on our shores in 1878.

Speedy rail travel was important at a time when many of the participants were still amateurs, and unable to take a lot of time off work to play. One example often quoted is of Queens Park, then a Scottish amateur football team, being able in 1879 to leave Glasgow late on Friday night, arrive in Manchester at 4 a.m. on Saturday, play a game that afternoon and travel back to Glasgow overnight on Saturday. It also meant that large numbers of spectators could follow their sporting heroes to their matches. By the 1880s, Spurs could get 10,000 fans arriving at White Hart Lane for a match, and the station had to be fitted with extra-wide doors to ease the overcrowding. Manchester United's new ground at Trafford Park, opened in 1908, promised the local railway company an extra 220,000 passengers a year.

Ambitious football clubs began relocating so as to be close to a station. In London, Chelsea chose Stamford Bridge, close to what is now Fulham Broadway station, in 1905 and the needs of the football fans were designed into the station's 1910 rebuild. Charlton's ground, the Valley, was next to a station and Queens Park Rangers got the site for their stadium near Park Royal station off the Great Western Railway. Arsenal relocated to Highbury, near the underground station at Gillespie Road, in 1913 (a station later renamed 'Arsenal'). In Birmingham,

Aston Villa was close to Witton on the Birmingham–Walsall line. But can any of them match Manchester United for their railway connections? They were actually formed in a railway works, starting life as Newton Heath FC, and were made up of workers in the carriage and wagon department of the Lancashire & Yorkshire Railway in Manchester.

The FA Cup posed particular transport problems for supporters. The Final was traditionally held in London, but from the foundation of the professional Football League in 1888, the contest was dominated by northern clubs (the original League contained no club from south of Birmingham and only two southern clubs reached the Final between 1883 and 1914). This meant moving very large numbers of northern fans into and out of London (the 1901 final attracted a crowd of 110,000). One of the reasons for relocating it to Wembley from 1923 was that it had good rail links, not just from London but also from the north. For many years, until growing car ownership and football vandalism did for it from the 1960s onwards, the railway football excursion was an important part of both railway traffic and football life.

London's two great cricket grounds, Lords and the Oval, both pre-dated the railway age. Lords was for a long time a barrier to the extension of the Underground, though it was eventually served by St John's Wood on the Metropolitan line, and the Oval even had an Underground station named after it. In Manchester, the Old Trafford station that later also served Manchester United also catered for the cricket fans going to the Old Trafford ground. As for golf, the great centres of Gleneagles (Caledonian Railway, 1924) and Turnberry (Glasgow & South Western Railway, 1903) started life as railway promotions.

Once every four years the nation becomes fans of (and overnight experts in) winter sports, as it indulges in wall-to-wall television coverage of the Winter Olympics. Such success as we enjoy in such sports as curling, skating and the like could originally be laid at the door of the railways. In the days before we had artificial rinks, these sports could only be played when the frosts were hard enough to provide ice thick enough to support people. Participants had then to be brought together quickly, before it thawed, making it very much a local sport. But this started to change from the 1890s, when railways like the Great North of Scotland started (at very short notice) laying on winter sports specials. These brought enthusiasts from far and wide, turning them from local to national (Scottish nationalists would no doubt say international) sports, and driving up standards in the process. In similar fashion, skiing enthusiasts could be transported at short notice to the unpredictable snows of Aviemore.

Another Highland activity that benefited greatly from the railways was game shooting. The railways opened up vast areas of hitherto inaccessible moorland and gave them a much wider potential market for the game they shot. Special trains were laid on in the run-up to the glorious 12 August and the value of a particular shoot was closely linked to its accessibility by rail.

The Great Exhibition

But the single event of Victorian times that generated the most excursion traffic must be the Great Exhibition of 1851. It drew more than 6 million visitors over a six-month period, of which an estimated 5 million came by rail. A whole generation, most of whom had never before seen the nation's capital, came to London for it. The 400-mile round trip from Leeds or York could be made for just 5s (25p) and the London & North Western Railway alone brought in about 775,000 visitors. Thomas Cook organised some 150,000 excursions, with combined rail and admission tickets. The original admission fee (£3 for gentlemen and £2 for ladies) was soon relaxed, enabling ordinary people to see the Exhibition for just 1s. Many of those who could not afford even that had their visits subsidised by benevolent landowners or industrial employers (especially those who were proud exhibitors at the event). But the experience was not always a pleasant one, especially for those travelling in the cheapest carriages. Thomas Hardy describes the arrival of one such party in London (a fictional account, but no doubt based on observation):

The seats for the humbler class of travellers in these early experiments in steam-locomotion, were open trucks, without any protection whatever from the wind and rain; and damp weather having set in with the afternoon, the unfortunate occupants of these vehicles were, on the train drawing up at the London terminus, found to be in a pitiable condition from their long journey; blue-faced, stiff-necked, sneezing, rail-beaten, chilled to the marrow, many of the men being hatless; in fact they resembled people who had been out all night in an open boat on a rough sea, rather than inland excursionists for pleasure. The women had in some degree protected themselves by turning up the skirts of their gowns over their heads, but as by this arrangement they were additionally exposed about the hips, they were all more or less in a sorry plight.

(Thomas Hardy, from his short story 'The Fiddler of the Reels', quoted in Simmons, ed. 1991, p. 95)

Somewhere to Stay

The railways gave rise to a quantum leap in the number of people travelling, which could overwhelm a hotel industry based on the numbers travelling by coach. News of a distressing example of the suffering this caused came in from Birmingham: 'Last week so great was the difficulty of securing accommodation that the Countess of Chesterfield was obliged to sleep at the Acorn, in Temple Street.' (Robbins, p. 34)

London went from being the far-off capital of the Empire to a daily excursion trip away: 'Thirty years ago, not one countryman in one hundred had seen the metropolis. Now there is scarcely one in the same number who has not spent the day there.' (*The Times*, 12 April 1850)

Just as the stagecoach era gave rise to a nationwide network of coaching inns, so the railways gave rise to railway hotels. There can be few towns of any size on the railway that do not have (or at least did not at one time have) its station hotel. These are likely to have been geared more to the business traveller than the holidaymaker, for only the most affluent of vacationers could have afforded to stay at some of them. Arguably the greatest of them was the Gothic fantasy of the Midland Grand Hotel, at the Midland Railway's St Pancras terminal, designed by the eminent Victorian architect George Gilbert Scott. It opened in 1873, closed as a hotel in 1935 and was thereafter used as offices. Following a threat to demolish it in 1967, it was made a Grade 1 listed building and reopened as a hotel in 2011. While it may be the grandest station hotel, it is not the earliest surviving example. One possible candidate for that title is the Crewe Arms Hotel, built opposite the railway station in 1838.

For those who did not want the expense of a hotel or the regimentation of a holiday camp, the railway companies for many years offered the inexpensive self-catering option of camping coaches. The railways had a problem of what to do with superannuated railway carriages – the wooden-bodied ones had little or no scrap value. A number of them were converted (sometimes in a fairly rudimentary way) into residential holiday accommodation and placed in sidings at rural stations. Cynics have suggested that the railway companies chose the most out-of-the-way locations for them, less for the rural idyll than to maximise fare income (since it was a condition of hire that you travelled to them by rail). The first of these was introduced by the LNER in 1933, with other companies following close behind. By the end of the decade there were some 400 sites, offering six to ten people a week's holiday for between £3 and £5. During the Second World War many were used to house railway workers, or pressed into government service, but they were reintroduced in the 1940s and 1950s. They gradually went out of favour in the 1960s as other types of holiday became more fashionable, and there were fewer staffed rural stations at which to locate them. The last one made available to the general public by the railway companies was by the LMS in 1971. There are still some operating today, associated with heritage railways and other private operators.

Railways and the Weekend

The idea of the weekend short break pre-dated the railways, but it was at that time very much one for the more wealthy portions of society. The railways helped to popularise it. An early example came in 1842, when the London & South Western started offering cheap tickets from London to Southampton or Gosport, travelling down on Friday evening and returning on Monday morning. While the idea started out in London, it soon took hold in Manchester as the practice of closing warehouses, public offices and banks on Saturday afternoons became more widespread. In this case the excursions were to places such as Blackpool and Fleetwood. As we saw, the railways were already involved in the promotion of a range of seaside resorts as leisure destinations – places like Southport, Llandudno, Eastbourne, Ramsgate and Yarmouth – and weekend vacationers were a useful addition to the traffic. By the 1870s 'the weekend' was very much part of the English language and, for those who could afford it, part of the English way of life.

Railways and Seaside Postcards

The railways were partly responsible for the practice of sending holiday postcards – not the comic cartoon ones, but the scenic views of seasides and other tourist attractions. Scarborough lays claim to being the first to be immortalised in this way. Many of these were produced by the railway companies as publicity for their excursions, and from 1894 it became possible to send them by post. These became hugely popular in the earliest years of the twentieth century – in 1913–14 some 927 million were sent, but the practice began to decline after the First World War, when the naughty variety became even more popular.

The Railways and Culture

The railways also did culture. What was then open ground between the Albert Hall and South Kensington (later to become the site of the Victoria and Albert

Museum) was the setting for many an exhibition. Some of these drew visitors in their millions. The District line provided a subway link from its South Kensington tube station, under the busy Exhibition Road, which visitors to an event would pay a penny to use. The District even offered artisans a combined Underground and exhibition ticket for a shilling.

As for the theatre, the railways are said to have made three major contributions. First, they provided new themes, settings and plot lines for the playwright. One of the earliest must have been *The Lucky Hit* (1836), based on the first round of railway mania that was then in full swing. Many a Victorian pantomime or farce would feature fanciful railways that carried the actors off to the moon, or China. Between 1908 and 1914 over fifteen plays with railway themes were licensed by the Lord Chamberlain. But the most successful seems to have been Arnold Ridley's 1925 hit *The Ghost Train* (later filmed three times).

The railways' second contribution was the late-night service, put on to allow theatre-goers from outside London to enjoy a late-night supper after the performance before travelling home. Some of these went as far out as Aylesbury and Brighton. Finally, they made lives a lot easier for travelling theatre companies, providing them with faster, cheaper transport for their actors and special low wagons for transporting large props and pieces of scenery.

1. This early cartoon predicts the effects of the railways on their competition. (Courtesy of Manchester Libraries, Information and Archives, Manchester City Council)

2. Art critic John Ruskin, one of the early Railways' bitterest opponents. (LoC)

3. British engineering not only built our railway network – it supplied the world's railways. Here, Beyer Peacock locomotives wait at the Manchester Ship Canal to be exported to Turkey in 1949. (Courtesy of Manchester Libraries, Information and Archives, Manchester City Council)

4. The railways and class. As might be expected, locomotive number 55 *Queen* bears the royal coat of arms and was frequently called upon to pull the royal train for Queen Victoria. (GWS)

QUEEN ADELAIDE.

QUEEN ADELAIDE'S RAILWAY SALOON.

5. The railways and class. Queen Adelaide, widow to King William IV, was an early and enthusiastic royal railway traveller. This is her railway saloon dating from 1842, now in the National Railway Museum.

6. The railways have transported the royal family – dead or alive – since the start of Queen Victoria's reign. Here, George VI's funeral cortège passes through Paddington on 15 February 1952. (GWS)

7 and 8. The railways and class – early rail travel for the lower orders. Didcot Railway Centre's replicas of 1840s Great Western carriages (a) for second-class passengers (with a roof, but no glass windows) and (b) third-class (open wagons with wooden benches for seats). (Author's collection)

9. The railways and safety. This head-on crash at Norton Fitzwarren, near Taunton, in November 1890 was caused by a signalling error. It left ten dead and eleven seriously injured. (GWS)

10. The railways and literacy. Travelling post offices played an important part in the nation's mail service for many years. This shows part of the Great Western service in around 1890. (GWS)

11. The railways provided the sellers of books and magazines with a captive audience. (GWS)

12. As common carriers, the railways were required by law to deliver most cargoes, large or small. This huge girder was part of a bridge-widening scheme between Maidenhead and Reading in 1892. (GWS)

13. As well as delivering very large objects, the railways spent much time and effort (not always profitably) moving small items of freight around in a piecemeal manner. (GWS)

14. Far from making the horse extinct, the railways themselves kept a small army of horses and carts to deliver goods to and from the railhead and its final destination. (GWS)

15. A taste of luxury that is no more – the railway restaurant car. (GWS)

16. The railways and leisure. They aimed to cater for the holiday needs of all income groups. (GWS)

17. The railways and leisure. Dressed for seaside fun, Victorian-style, these revellers make their way from railway station to beach. (GWS)

18. The railways and war. British navvies build the Grand Crimean Central Railway, relieving the suffering of the allied forces at the siege of Sevastopol and enhancing their reputation in the process.

Opposite top: 19. The railways and war. British rolling stock and railwaymen served on many fronts during the First World War. This primitive ferry is carrying a Dean goods engine across the Bosphorus straits in Turkey. (GWS)

Opposite bottom: 20. The railways in the First World War. This train, operated by the War Department's Railway Operating Division, appears to be delivering sleepers for railway construction 'somewhere near the Western Front' in France or Belgium. (GWS)

21. The railways at war. They were a prime target for the Luftwaffe in the Second World War. Bristol was one of our most bombed cities, and this picture shows some of the damage, possibly from the raid on 3 January 1941, when Temple Meads station was hit. (GWS)

22. The railways and architecture. The north portal of Clayton Tunnel, near Brighton, one of the railways' more unusual contributions to the nation's architecture. (David Porter Collection)

23. Integrated transport – the railway provides buses to ferry its customers to Newbury racecourse, despite the course having its own dedicated railway station. (GWS)

24. Integrated transport – Railway Air Services: a big idea that did not come to fruition. (GWS)

25. Integrated transport – railway-sponsored bus services fed passengers into the station, and from the station to their final destinations. (GWS)

26. More integrated door-to-door transport, with this steam-hauled road freighter acting as an agent of the railway company in the 1920s. (GWS)

27. The steam railcar – precursor to the modern diesel multiple unit – was one of the ways the railways tried to find a cost-effective method of serving lightly trafficked and suburban lines. (GWS)

28. Charles Dickens chronicled the chaos of early railway construction, and was traumatised by the Staplehurst railway crash, in which he was involved. (LoC)

29. Dove Cottage, Wordsworth's most famous family home in Grasmere, though he had moved on by the time the railways threatened his beloved Lakeland. (LoC)

30. St. Pancras Station, known as the Cathedral of the Railways. It had the largest single-span roof in the world when the Midland Railway opened it as their London terminus in 1868. (LoC)

CHAPTER 7

The Railways at War

The army which is concentrated at one point is difficult to supply and can never be billeted; it cannot march, it cannot operate, it cannot at all exist for any length of time; it can only fight.

(Helmut von Moltke the elder, Chief of German General Staff (1869))

The railways have become an instrument of war without which the great modern armies are not able to be assembled or moved forward. Today you no longer ask how many battalions your enemy has but how many railway lines.

(Count Alfred von Schlieffen, Chief of German General Staff until 1906 and author of their strategic plan for the First World War)

There comes a time when locomotives are more important than guns.

(Erich Ludendorff, commander of the German army, 1918)

The First World War had begun – imposed on the statesmen of Europe by railway timetables. It was an unexpected climax to the railway age ... Railway trains go faster than men walking. This is the strategical reason why the defence was stronger than the attack throughout the First World War. Defence was mechanised; attack was not.

(A. J. P. Taylor, *The First World War* (1963))

Transport and War Before the Railways

The importance of good transport to military operations has long been understood by governments. Some of Britain's first government-sponsored road-building since

Roman times took place in the Highlands of Scotland, where the Jacobite uprisings of 1715, 1719 and 1745 prompted them to build highways that facilitated the movement in of troops to crush further dissent.

As a maritime nation, much of our trade was conducted by coastal shipping, and one consequence of the Napoleonic wars was that French privateers declared open season on British ships. Parliament looked for more secure ways to keep the nation supplied with its essentials. Could coal be brought from Newcastle to London in sufficient quantities by inland waterway or road, they wondered? A canal was proposed across Somerset and Devon, to enable shipping to get from Bristol to the South Coast without having to make the dangerous passage around Lands End, and another linking the naval base at Portsmouth to London. One of the purposes of the Caledonian Canal was to provide a more secure route between the east and west coasts of Scotland while the Royal Military Canal (discussed later) was built entirely for military reasons. As early as 1798, the Grand Junction Canal was reserved for the transfer of troops on exercise between Blisworth and Liverpool, with civilian canal users being made to wait their turn.

War in the Railway Age

The railways would have a dramatic effect on the conduct of war. Before them, it was difficult to maintain a large army in one place for any length of time, since they had to rely largely upon any supplies they could appropriate from the immediate area. An army of 60,000, with 40,000 horses, needed 450 tons of food a day, so local supplies would rapidly become exhausted and no means existed for importing them in sufficient volumes. The problem became worse as armies modernised and demanded an ever-growing mountain of munitions and the other instruments of war. The railways made it feasible to conduct war on a much larger scale than hitherto.

The railways made warfare both more and less mobile; more mobile, in that large bodies of troops and their equipment could be moved rapidly over long distances. But, as the Western Front in the First World War was to demonstrate, the railways could also help produce stalemate by making it much easier to defend a position than it was to advance. The defending side had an established rail network behind it to keep it supplied with munitions and reinforcements, while the advancing side was doing so on foot across land generally without railway support and often churned up to impassability by shelling.

Napoleon's nemesis at Waterloo – the Duke of Wellington – was by 1830 the prime minister who presided over the opening of the Liverpool & Manchester Railway. It was therefore natural that the military implications of this new mode of transport should be explored. The first British use of the railway to move troops was at the actual opening ceremony of the Liverpool & Manchester Railway. The troops in this case were being brought in purely for ceremonial purposes, though the hostile reception the Duke of Wellington received in Manchester suggests they might have been needed for other purposes, had not the duke left Manchester rather hurriedly. Shortly thereafter, the railway was used to convey a regiment of troops from Manchester to the Liverpool docks, en route to Ireland to quell rebellion there. A journey that would have entailed a two-day march was completed in two hours.

The Better Regulation of Railways Act of 1842 established the principle of the railways carrying troops at a rate to be negotiated between the railway and the government. (In addition to carrying the soldiers, the railways were also expected to carry 'women belonging to the regiment', at a rate of up to ten women per hundred soldiers.) The first use of this power was made the same year, but once again for the suppression of civil unrest rather than any threat from a foreign power. Around 2,000 troops were transported into the Manchester area to help put down the so-called Plug Plot Riots among textile workers. Within two years, the Future Railways Act took away any question of the railways negotiating charges for troop movements by setting a maximum rate, and the Regulation of Forces Act 1871 gave governments the power to take over the railways entirely, on a temporary basis, in the event of war.

Continental Europe lacked the watery barricade of an island nation, and began using the railways as an instrument of war rather sooner. The first large-scale troop movement was in 1846, when 12,000 Prussian troops were sent to Krakow, in what is now Poland, to quell a rebellion there. The French moved some 640,000 troops and their horses into Italy in 1859 during the Franco-Austrian War, but were rather less good at the logistics of keeping such a large army fed. One downside of the military importance of railways in Continental Europe was that governments sometimes found themselves having to build expensive lines that had a military purpose, but little or no peacetime rationale.

The Crimean War was the first non-domestic conflict involving Great Britain in which railways played a significant part. The British Army had had its own transport corps until 1833, when it was disbanded on cost grounds. Come the Crimean War, individual regiments were left to organise their own transport.

It was predictably a shambles, with the Crimean roads impassable and supply chains non-existent. Troops were starved of food and munitions and the wounded could not be evacuated. When word of this reached England, railway interests offered to build a railway between the port of Balaclava and the front line, at Sevastopol.

Two of Britain's leading railway contractors – Samuel Peto and Thomas Brassey – oversaw the works and the 8-mile Grand Crimean Central Railway was built in just seven weeks, opening in March 1855. The Army, initially sceptical (they had wanted a road), were delighted. Field Marshal Burgoyne said, 'It is impossible to overrate the services rendered by the railway, or its effect in shortening the time of the siege and alleviating the fatigues and suffering of the troops.' One side effect of this project was to rehabilitate the reputation of the people who built it – the navvies – in the eyes of the nation. A group which hitherto had been viewed with fear and hatred by the general public suddenly became heroes.

But it was soon seen that the military potential went far beyond just moving troops about; armoured trains and mobile guns were just two of the further possibilities, envisaged as early as the 1860s:

> Supposing that a railway were made in a line parallel to the coast, with a parapet embankment, no troops could get inland without crossing it; and supposing that the opposing troops, riflemen and artillerymen were carried on moving forts along the line, the invaders could be destroyed at will, unless we suppose vessels to lie close to the shore to support them … A moving fort on a railway, as compared with a stationary fort, has the same advantage that a vessel has on water, and the invading enemy, to be on a par with the invaded, must bring batteries of railway artillery with him…
>
> The most economical method of using artillery is to mount it on rail platforms instead of on fixed forts or batteries, because by this process one gun becomes the equivalent of many. The obvious advantage is that an ordinary enemy can actually be pursued by the fort, instead of being permitted to move around it at a distance. The invading army would experience a difficulty of the same kind after landing as before landing – land ships, instead of water ships, carrying the heaviest projectiles at the longest ranges.
>
> (Adams, pages 332–53)

Adams (and others) also suggested a series of circular railways at different radii around London, linking the various radial routes coming out of the city and forming a series of defensive lines against a possible invader. Using a corridor of communication as a barrier to an invading force was by no means a new idea. During the Napoleonic wars, the government spent £200,000 on the Royal Military Canal, running 28 miles between Hythe and Rye in Kent and Sussex, and combining a defensive obstacle with a means of moving troops about more swiftly on what might become the front line in the event of an invasion. The canal network served a similar defensive barrier role against possible German invasion in the Second World War.

Military considerations also entered into the planning of the railways:

> When Parliament was considering lines in Dorset and Devon, the Great Western saw them as their – and broad gauge's – natural territory, since Parliament had specifically excluded railways in these counties from the provisions of the Gauge Act. However, Parliament preferred standard gauge for them, not least on the grounds that it could link seamlessly with the lines between Dover and Portsmouth. This would be important in supporting military operations along the coast in the event of an attempted invasion.
>
> Brunel attempted to counter these arguments by claiming that the greater carrying capacity of the broad gauge meant that they could move 15,000 troops in a shorter time than standard gauge would take to move 10,000. Military requirements also dictated the route of some railways. In vulnerable coastal areas, they specified that the main line should follow a more defensible line some miles from the coast, with ports being served by branch lines. This influenced Brunel's designs for the Devon & Dorset Railway which, contrary to good railway practice, left even major stops like Bridport stranded on a branch line, 4 miles from the main route.
>
> (Hylton (2007), p. 190)

The Agadir diplomatic crisis of July 1911 led to the role of railways in wartime coming under renewed scrutiny. The Under-Secretary of War met with senior railway figures to consider the feeding of London in the event of war. Some potential clashes became evident, like the conveyance of food from Liverpool to London interfering with the delivery of naval coal from south Wales to the north-east Scottish coast (the Admiralty had hired around 4,000 wagons for this purpose and, at the height of the war, were moving some 56,000 tons of coal a week from south Wales to Scotland). Another major additional load at the outbreak of war was the delivery of the British Expeditionary Force to their ports of embarkation for France. Over a three-week period in August 1914, 711 trains rolled into Southampton Docks alone, disgorging 5,006 officers, 125,171 men, 38,805 horses, 277 motor cars and diverse other equipment.

The day after the First World War broke out, the government took control of the nation's railways under the 1871 powers. They retained that control – under a body known as the Railways Executive Committee (REC) – until four years after the end of hostilities. The railway companies were to be compensated on the basis of their net receipts for 1913, the last full year before hostilities (some adjustments were made for the fact that some railways would bear more of the brunt of additional military traffic than others – the LSWR, for example, had to cope with the immense amount of military movement around Salisbury Plain). Overall, this fixed-price deal was a good move on the part of the government, as it meant they could commission as many additional services as they wanted, at no cost to themselves, as well as setting their own service priorities.

They certainly took advantage of this; in the case of the Great Western, the first two weeks of hostilities alone saw 632 troop trains run, along with forty-one Admiralty coal trains and 149 petrol and oil trains. In 1915, the railways as a whole carried 13.9 per cent more traffic than in the most prosperous pre-war years, and this excluded government traffic, whose volume was not even recorded. Ambulance trains formed a significant part of that wartime traffic. In total, 1,234,248 wounded troops came back through Southampton alone, and were carried off by 7,822 trains to 196 receiving stations. In just the one week ending 9 July 1916, 151 trains brought home 30,006 wounded through Southampton, following the carnage at the opening of the Battle of the Somme. In total, some 9 million soldiers travelled through Folkestone and 7 million through Southampton during the course of the war.

All this had to be done in the face of greatly reduced staffing, despite many key railway jobs being classified as Reserved Occupations, exempt from conscription. By the end of the war the total number of volunteers from all railway companies was 184,475 – about 49 per cent of the railway staff of military age at 1914. Over 21,500 of them would be killed. Recruiting offices were told to ensure that railwayman volunteers had the permission of their railway company to sign up, and the GWR was one company that threatened financial penalties against employees who volunteered for military service without their permission. But even this only reduced, rather than prevented, the loss of staff. Numbers of these staff went to operate the railways in France that served the Western Front. Some of the volunteers' places were filled – at least for the duration of hostilities – by others, including more than 55,000 women. Women were allowed to fill almost any railwayman role, except on the footplate.

Overseas battlefront railways also benefited from a considerable amount of British rolling stock and infrastructure (including over 1,000 locomotives, 20,000 wagons and in some cases track, uprooted from British railway lines). At the sharp end of the Western Front, lightweight, prefabricated narrow gauge railways, like a giant version of Hornby model railway lines, were developed to get men and munitions to the very front line, often within range of the enemy's guns, and to evacuate the wounded.

Coal – in particular Welsh steam coal – was a major concern for the Admiralty, most of their fleet being coal-fired. Before the war they would have relied on a fleet of colliers to deliver it to their headquarters at Scapa Flow in the Orkneys, but the submarine menace ruled this out and the railways had to bear the brunt of delivering the huge amounts required. As in the Napoleonic wars, coastal shipping generally ceased to be a safe way of moving goods around Britain and, in the absence of a well-developed road haulage network, the responsibility for this too fell largely on the railways.

Fear of German sabotage of the domestic rail network was widespread and sentries were initially stationed at strategic points. But, after fourteen of them had been run over by trains and two others mistakenly shot by their comrades, it was decided that the saboteurs would probably do less harm and most sentries were withdrawn.

The Western Front placed a huge demand on the rail network. The Great Western alone had 277 ammunition factories in its network and just one of these, at Hayes, could fill 3,800 wagons a month. But the biggest concentrations of dangerous cargos came from the industrial areas served by the LNWR. In the course of the war, they had to deliver over 10 million tons of TNT, nearly 11 million hand grenades and several million tons of poison gas. An even more perilous cargo came in the form of nitroglycerin, which had to be moved (very gingerly) around the network in specially sealed, temperature-controlled wagons. All of the railways' assets were put at the disposal of the war effort. Some 126 railway-owned steamers were requisitioned by the government, to be used as everything from hospital ships to seaplane carriers. In both World Wars, the railway companies' locomotive workshops were pressed into use, making a variety of military hardware, large and small, ranging from armoured trains to ambulance stretchers. Even some of the companies' railway hotels found a military purpose.

Air raids had only a limited impact on Britain in the First World War, and blackout arrangements were correspondingly primitive. The railways' advice to passengers to keep the carriage blinds closed at night was a request, rather than an instruction, and consequently often ignored. Trains, and the stations they stopped in, therefore made tempting targets for bombers, and Liverpool Street and St Pancras were among the stations suffering major bomb damage.

As the war progressed, things grew steadily more difficult for the civilian traveller. By 1917 the number of services was being cut, cheap fares were scrapped and there was a 50 per cent increase in fares generally from January of that year (hitherto, they had been frozen at 1914 levels, despite the wartime inflation in prices generally). Pre-war levels of maintenance also deteriorated. This led to at least one major accident, at Weedon in Oxfordshire in August 1915, when ten passengers on the Irish Mail were killed in a derailment.

Conditions for the staff also deteriorated, with an increasing workload and a diminishing wage packet and, on 26–27 September 1919, a national rail strike began. Having seen what started as a strike in Russia in 1917 end in revolution, Prime Minister Lloyd George was desperate to see that the British strike did not escalate. However, it was the railways themselves that suffered from the industrial action. During the eight days the strike lasted, a fledgling road haulage industry, reinforced by large numbers of newly released army surplus lorries, began to demonstrate the role it could – and in future would – play in keeping the country moving.

If the First World War started with railway timetables, it ended in a railway carriage, in the forest at Compiègne outside Paris, where the Germans were made to sign the Armistice in November 1918 (and where Hitler would exact his revenge in 1940).

In both World Wars, the burden of supplying the nation's needs, both war-related and civilian, fell heavily onto the railways. In the Second World War in particular, petrol shortages meant that much of the road haulage sector's cargo had to be transferred to rail.

The development of aerial warfare by the Second World War created new pressures – both offensive and defensive – on the railways. The building of concrete runways on bomber airfields required the delivery of almost 750,000 tons of London's bomb damage rubble as foundations, courtesy of the railways. Each thousand-bomber raid took eight trains worth of bombs and twenty-eight fuel trains (carrying over 2,500,000 gallons of aviation spirit). Once again, the railways' engineering works were pressed into war service with, for example, the Crewe and Horwich works producing over 500 tanks by 1942, and Swindon turning out 171,000 components for Hurricanes at very short notice while the

Battle of Britain was at its height. Other products ranged from munitions by the million, to landing craft and midget submarine superstructures.

But the major difference from the First World War was the scale of the disruption caused by German bombing of the rail network. The railways were a prime target, but they became skilled at repairing the most major damage at almost unbelievable speed. Repairs to the track were generally reckoned to be completed within twelve hours and even more major works might take little longer:

At one town bombs hit a station building, severed four through lines and damaged a train. Almost before the noise of the explosions and falling masonry had ceased, working was resumed. 'Shuttle' services of buses were arranged within fifteen minutes; newspapers, mails, milk, fish and other perishable traffics were diverted, and engineers were hard at work clearing the debris to restore the tracks. The damaged train was removed in a few hours, and within twenty-four hours a load of steel plates for shipment was delivered without delaying a ship, passenger train services being resumed within forty-eight hours after the raid.

(From the government's *Facts about British Railways in Wartime*)

Large quantities of spare parts were set aside for repairs; the LMS alone had enough tracks, sleepers and points in safe storage around its network to replace 22 miles of track. Bombproof duplicate railway control rooms were set up around the country and signal boxes were also made less vulnerable to air raids.

The railways suffered some 10,000 raids, with a loss of 14,000 carriages and 24,000 goods wagons. The most bombed station was Poplar, near the East London docks, which was hit by 1,200 high-explosive bombs, 50,000 incendiary devices and fifty-two rockets. The very first V2 rocket to land in Britain hit the railway line in London's Bethnal Green. But it was not only direct hits that disrupted services. An unexploded bomb anywhere within 400 yards of a railway line could bring services to a halt, for fear of the vibration detonating it.

One allied response to bombing was the blackout, which affected the railways just as much as everyone else. Blacked-out trains made for a gloomy journey for passengers and unlit stations made it next to impossible to tell whether you had reached your destination. Having the station names painted out added to the confusion. Wartime censorship could prevent you being told why your train was late, or what the destination of the train now standing in the station was. With 15-watt blue bulbs in the compartments, you could barely even make out your fellow travellers. A. A. Milne's sad little poem neatly sums up the miseries of wartime rail travel:

We were alone, I hailed the fellow blindly,
'Excuse me, sir, I live at Wavertree.
Is it the next but one?' She answered kindly,
'It was the last but three.'

Passengers even disembarked when the train was not even in a station, some of them falling to their doom off bridges or down embankments. Platforms became dangerous places to be, with invisible luggage to trip over and platform edges to fall off. Workers in the railway yards had to make do with the absolute minimum of lighting (which they referred to as the 'gloomy glim'). Even the footplates of the locomotives had to be covered in with anti-glare sheets, to stop the glow from fireboxes being seen by enemy bombers. This also made it stiflingly hot for the crew and difficult to see the track ahead.

Civilian travel took the lowest priority in wartime. The posters during the Second World War asked 'Is your journey really necessary?' and, even if necessary, it certainly was not pleasurable. Trains were slow, uncertain (with frequent delays or cancellations) and overcrowded. Restaurant cars were withdrawn entirely from May 1942 and train toilets often lacked essentials like soap and towels. First-class travel was abolished on suburban services, as were bargain and leisure-related tickets, and, from 1942, sleeper cars were only available for people travelling on government or military business. Despite all this, passenger traffic increased substantially over peacetime levels.

The railways played an important part in some of the major campaigns of the war. First was the evacuation of vast numbers of civilians from our major cities at the outbreak of war (having first had a practice evacuation at the time of the Munich Crisis). By the end of 1939, over 1.4 million people had been removed from London, along with over 700,000 from our provincial cities. The first 158,000 members of the British Expeditionary Force also had to be delivered to their ports of embarkation for France during this period, later to be followed by mass troop movements to Norway, the Middle and Far East and North Africa. Large numbers of food trains were run at this time, moving food away from the London docks to safer storage around the country. Treasures from our museums, art galleries and places of worship were also evacuated, along with large quantities of government records.

When a third of a million British and French troops were evacuated from the beaches of Dunkirk in 1940, the railways ferried them back from the South Coast ports to their barracks, hospitals or homes. As D-Day approached in 1944, some

7,000 additional train services a week were being run to get men and materials into the right place. By the end of the Second World War the railways had run 451,765 special trains for the armed forces.

Huge depots were established to keep the forces supplied after D-Day. The four weeks after the landing were said to have been the busiest in the entire history of the railways. Before the war, Micheldever had the dubious distinction of being regarded as the most remote station in Hampshire. In 1939 it became a fuel depot and during the course of the war it acquired 14 miles of new sidings with room for over 2,500 wagons, along with a 2,000-foot-long shed. This was crammed with everything an invading army could need and was nicknamed 'Woolworths' for the variety of goods available from it. They prided themselves in their rapid turnaround of orders, and aimed to have items ordered late one afternoon in the hands of their customers in Normandy the following day.

As in the First World War, maintenance standards slipped, with locomotives frequently covering 100,000 miles between general overhauls. At the same time the locomotives were being asked to draw ever-heavier loads. Peacetime passenger trains of eleven carriages were increased to sixteen or seventeen and freight trains of between 1,500 and 1,700 tons were being run. One consequence of this was that the railways would be in a very dilapidated condition when peace finally came. The ruinous cost of recompensing the owners of the railways for the running down of their assets was one of the factors that would influence the decision to nationalise them in 1948 (a Conservative government would probably have had little choice but to do the same thing).

The railways had started the war with a staff of around 600,000. By the end of it about 110,000 of these were serving in the armed forces or civil defence. In addition, some 170,000 of the remaining staff had to be trained for air raid precautions (ARP) duties. In some cases, staff shortages became so severe that some former employees who had joined the forces had to be recalled from their overseas postings to keep domestic services running.

Today, military aviation and road transport carry many of the burdens previously borne by the railways. But should we ever again face the threat of enemy blockade and fuel shortages, the railways would need to fill the enormous gaps that would be left by the lack of capacity among those alternative modes of transport.

CHAPTER 8

The Railways and Literacy

The train was a natural place to sit (or stand), and read, and it remains so: a railway carriage probably plays host each day to more people reading than the average small town library.

(Harrington)

The early railway years saw some significant advances in the nation's literacy. One estimate has 75 per cent of the population of 1840 able to do some reading and 60 per cent some writing. Male literacy, by another estimate, rose from 67 to 80 per cent between 1841 and 1870, with the rate for women going from 51 to 73 per cent. Any figure is likely to be subjective, depending upon how high the bar is set; by no means all of those classed as literate would have been familiar with the complete works of Shakespeare, but how many of them could do much more than scratch their names in a marriage register?

Whatever advances took place over these years can be attributed to many factors. The rise of industrial capitalism, with its work ethic and its emphasis on self-improvement, is one, as is the transformation of the state's view of education, from laissez-faire, through support of voluntary providers, to the Education Act of 1870, providing compulsory education for all children between the ages of five and thirteen. In among these causes, the railways have made some contributions – both major and minor – to the spread of literacy in nineteenth-century Britain. At a local level, and courtesy of the Great Western Railway, Swindon had a library almost a decade before the authorities in much larger places such as Manchester followed suit. Other changes had an impact on a much wider level.

Reading on the Move

The choices for readers in pre-railway days were fairly limited. A newspaper cost 7*d* (most of which was government stamp duty) and a three-volume novel was £1 11*s* 6*d*. It was not until 1850 that local authorities were given powers to spend public money on the buildings and fittings of a public lending library (though, curiously, not on books – these had to be contributed by public donation). So, before that, even if someone had the ability to read, the raw materials for doing so were not easy to come by for those on modest to middling incomes. Charles Dickens' *Pickwick Papers*, first published as a serial between 1836 and 1837, was one of the first works to begin widening the market for fiction.

The enforced inactivity of a train journey created a huge captive market for readers (60 million passenger journeys a year by 1850) and retailers spotted the opportunity. On the London Underground an advertising contractor named J. Willing bought the exclusive rights to sell books and post advertisements throughout the network in 1863. The original contract cost him £1,150 for three years and must have been a money-spinner since, when he later sought a seven-year extension, the price had rocketed up to £34,000. But prior to this, in 1841 a shop for the sale of newspapers had been let at Fenchurch Street station to a Horace Marshall, and another at Euston went to a Mr Gibbs. When the railway company discovered that Mr Gibbs' £60 a year rental was bringing him in an annual income of £1,200, his contract was swiftly terminated, making way for what was to become a household name in the promotion of literature.

It all started in 1792 as a small newsagent, which opened for business in Little Grosvenor Street, London. By 1828 the business was being managed by the founder's son, one William Henry Smith, and had taken his name. His son, also William Henry, would follow him into the business in 1846. Two years later, they succeeded Mr Gibbs, opening their first railway bookstall at Euston, and their business expanded with the railway network. This time, the contract included a share in the profits for the London & North Western Railway and an agreement for Smith to extend his operation into all the LNWR stations. Alongside newspapers, they also sold cheap editions of other publications, known as 'yellowbacks' and aimed specifically at rail travellers. By 1851/2, Smith had contracts with eleven railway companies. Many leading writers of the day found their way onto the station platforms, sometimes, like Dickens, publishing their novels in instalments.

Another application of steam – the steam printing press – made it possible for many more copies of books to be published. When Dr Livingstone wrote up his *Missionary Travels and Researches in South Africa* in 1857, a first edition of 70,000 could be run off. Before the steam press, 10,000 sales would have been a huge bestseller.

Before W. H. Smith, the sale of newspapers and other reading matter on stations was a job sometimes given to railwaymen invalided out of other railway occupations, and many of these independent retailers (knowing what would sell) specialised in material that dealt with forbidden topics such as sex, religion and politics in a salacious way. There were a good few Victorian precursors to *Fifty Shades of Grey*. Smith (who came to be known by *Punch* as 'Old Morality' and by others as the 'North West Missionary') was having none of this, and did much to clean up the standard of literature available to travellers. Poetry, history and books on self-improvement took the place of the unsuitable material. He was actively supported in this by the LNWR, who insisted that he sold nothing indecent, nothing advertising patent medicines and no trade union material. *The Times* noted his efforts with approval, reporting: 'A wholesome change in railway bookstalls ... at the North Western terminus we diligently searched for that which required but little looking for in other places, but we poked in vain for the trash.' (Quoted in *History Today*, Volume 48, 1998)

Publishers were also quick to see the market. Routledge's Railway Library was launched in 1848 and Murray's Railway Reading offered cheap and healthy literature. Longmans produced a Travellers' Library of improving literature, including practical scientific works for 'the mechanics, engine drivers and others employed upon the line'. Not only did the subject matter of railway reading expand, the format also underwent a transformation. The smaller format, often paperback, book, easier to fit into pocket or handbag, was designed with the railway traveller in mind. Books with shorter paragraphs and more legible typefaces, books with disjointed paragraphs that could be dipped into at random and even puzzle books appeared. There were also accessories – a book cushion, on which your book could sit comfortably in your lap, and a battery-powered railway reading lamp for dimly lit carriages.

The railways thus did much to encourage reading, but, for the literary elite, 'railway literature' would remain a term of abuse. Even so, by the end of the Victorian era, H. G. Wells could still see the railway train as:

a perfect symbol of our times, an image of a Democratic century: uncomfortably full in the third class – a few passengers standing – and everybody reading the current number either of the Daily Mail, Pearsons Weekly, Answers, Tit-Bits or whatever Greatest Novel of the Century happened to be going.

(H. G. Wells, *Anticipations*, quoted in Harrington)

The younger W. H. Smith would later withdraw from the business to pursue a career as a politician, becoming a Member of Parliament and eventually First Lord of the Admiralty. This latter appointment also earned him the lasting (if unwelcome) fame of being satirised by Gilbert and Sullivan. In their operetta *HMS Pinafore* the song 'When I was a lad', with the famous line 'now I am the ruler of the Queen's Navy', was about him, mocking his lack of qualification for the job.

In 1905 the railway companies tried to impose a further steep rental increase on W. H. Smith. Smith responded by opening 150 shops in the high streets leading to the nation's main stations. This was to work to their advantage sixty years later, by immunising them from the worst effects of Doctor Beeching's cuts.

The Railways and National Newspapers

Before the railways, there was no such thing as a real national newspaper. By the time the London papers got out into the remoter parts of the provinces, their news was getting out of date, and they generally carried little of specific interest to the provinces. By the same token, provincial newspapers like the *Manchester Guardian* (founded 1821) carried only 'late echoes of the London press'. Circulations were also limited, both by the absence of universal literacy and by the ruinous level of stamp duty imposed on newspapers by governments that were none too keen to have the lower orders reading news, lest they came upon something subversive. Stamp duty was gradually reduced, but only finally abolished in 1855 – though even then the paper on which all written media depended still had to wait a further six years for its excise duty to be abolished. The *Manchester Guardian*, a quarter of a century after its foundation, still only had a circulation of 9,000. (But, by the same token, London newspapers were by that time selling only 1,500 copies in Manchester.)

W. H. Smith also took advantage of the rail network to become the country's leading distributor of newspapers. In 1838 they contracted with the Grand Junction Railway to carry papers from Birmingham to Manchester and Liverpool and soon had a fleet of express trains delivering newspapers. In December 1849, in a special promotion, the London *Times* was made available to dealers on the Paris Bourse by 1.30 p.m., 6½ hours after leaving London, and national papers regularly left the London termini on express trains by 6 a.m., bound for the far corners of the British Isles. By 1850 Smith had wholesale newspaper warehouses in Dublin, Birmingham, Manchester and Liverpool and a London newspaper could be bought in Bristol by 11 a.m. For many years, the 2.32 a.m. newspaper train between Marylebone and Sheffield was the fastest train in Britain.

The Railways and the Electric Telegraph

The railways were instrumental in giving Britain the mid-nineteenth century equivalent of e-mail. By the 1850s a network of telegraph cables was in place, making it possible to transmit news from one end of the country to the other (from capital to provinces, or vice versa) almost instantaneously, putting newspapers produced in both areas on a relatively equal footing. Although the electric telegraph was not invented by, or specifically for, the railways, they were one of its most important users and the railway network proved to be the ideal channel for its overhead lines.

Telegraphy had been in use at least since the eighteenth century, primarily for military use, but this had relied on a chain of stations within line of sight of each other, sending messages by means such as flags or semaphore. In ideal conditions they could send complex messages relatively quickly over long distances, but in bad weather or at night they were virtually useless.

The railways were an ideal market for high-speed communications. With their trains operating at much higher speeds than any other form of transport, they needed to know where each one was at any given moment. Various advances relating to electricity culminated in 1837 in two Englishmen, Charles Wheatstone (an academic) and William Cooke (an entrepreneur and businessman), coming up with a system of telegraphy that could work day or night, in all weathers, and beyond the line of sight.

In that same year, Cooke proposed installing a sixty-code telegraph system on the Liverpool & Manchester Railway, but this proved to be more complex than the railway needed. At the Liverpool end of the line, trains needed to be cable-hauled on the incline out of Lime Street, and their main requirement was for something to tell the winchman when to start (and stop) winching. Cooke proposed a simplified system, but the railway opted instead for a pneumatic version, using whistles as the signals. An almost identical situation developed that same year at the Euston end of the London & Birmingham Railway, where outward journeys were cable-hauled as far as Camden town. Again, the railway settled for the pneumatic option.

Wheatstone and Cooke's first commercial success was on the Great Western in 1838 where, at a cost of £3,270, they installed a 13-mile stretch of telegraph between Paddington and West Drayton, which was extended as far as Slough in 1843. In the chapter on crime, the arrest and conviction of a notorious murderer by means of that railway's telegraph is described, and this did much to raise public interest in the invention. Another, happier application of it related to the birth of Queen Victoria's second son, Alfred, news of which (courtesy of the telegraph) was able to appear in *The Times* within forty minutes of the announcement from the palace. The invention of the telegraph was certainly one whose time had come: in America, Samuel Morse was busy independently inventing his own system (along with the code that bears his name) and inventors in other countries were coming up with similar devices that (for one reason or another) failed to succeed commercially.

From the 1840s the telegraph network spread steadily. The UK had 10,000 miles of telegraph line and 1,300 telegraph stations by 1868, but the network's biggest expansion came in the next four years, by which time the network had grown to 87,000 miles of line and 5,179 stations. This spread was closely related to the railways. Eight of London's first seventeen telegraph offices were based at rail termini, and in country areas the local telegraph office was almost always at the railway station. By this time, there were telegraph lines all around the world, with the transatlantic one being completed in 1866 and that to Australia in 1872. Just as the telegraph was establishing its universality, Alexander Graham Bell in 1876 rendered it obsolete by inventing the telephone. However, railways in Britain were still using some 15,000 sets at the end of the nineteenth century and some were not taken out of service until the 1930s.

As far as the railways were concerned, the telegraph more than paid for itself:

> The cost of maintaining and working a single pilot engine (all of which have been superseded by the telegraph) amounted to a greater sum than is now required to defray the expense of the entire staff of telegraph staff and the mechanics and labourers employed in cleaning and repairing the instruments and maintaining the integrity of the lone wires.
>
> (C. V. Walker, Telegraph Superintendent of the South Eastern Railway, 1850)

As for the telegraph companies, the railways were a vital part of their early development. The preferred option for telegraph wires was to hang them on poles, but this meant the use of a continuous strip of land between point A and point B. The telegraph companies did not own – or want to own – long strips of land.

Instead they negotiated wayleaves with the landowners, to allow them to erect the poles and to enter their land to maintain them. The railway lines offered long uninterrupted strips of land in a single ownership (for ease of negotiation) and much of the early telegraph network therefore followed the railways. By 1848, about half the rail network of the day had telegraph wires along it.

Literacy and Operating the Railways

The complexity of a railway's operations made it essential to maintain detailed and accurate records and, for this reason, demanded high (for the day) standards of literacy from its staff. Simmons says that a variety of staff would need literacy skills – obviously those doing clerical jobs, handling money or operating the telegraph. He also mentions those checking tickets, though some early railways used to show the destination on the ticket by means of a symbol, for the benefit of illiterate ticket collectors.

From the very earliest days, applicants for clerical jobs with the Great Western had to apply for the post in their own handwriting – but was literacy needed to be an engine driver? Opinion was divided. Charles Hutton Gregory of the London & Croydon Railway said in 1840 that his drivers 'must be able to read and write and, if possible, understand the rudimental principles of mechanics' and the Board of Trade concurred the following year, telling Parliament: 'There can be no doubt that an engine driver should be able to read his instructions.'

Not everyone agreed. Edward Bury, who became superintendent of locomotives for the London & Birmingham in 1839, was asked how his drivers got 'sufficient practical knowledge' of their craft, and replied: 'We do not want them to have much; I would rather the men should not touch the engine themselves.' (Simmons (1991), p. 187)

Brunel was even more definite on the matter in his evidence to a parliamentary committee in 1841:

I would not give sixpence in hiring an engine man because of his knowing how to read and write. I believe that of the two the non-reading man is the best, and for this reason. I defy Sir Frederick Smith, or any person who has general information, and is in the habit of reading, to drive an engine ... It is impossible in a man that indulges in reading should make a good engine driver; it requires a species of machine, an intelligent man, an honest man, a sober man, a steady man; but I would much rather not have a thinking man. I never dare drive an engine, although I always go upon the engine; because if I go on a bit of the line without anything to attract my attention, I begin thinking about something else.

(Simmons (1991), p. 187)

Brunel's colleague, Daniel Gooch, disagreed with this view.

So it was that some railways had illiterate drivers (as we know from the fact that they signed accident reports with a mark, rather than a signature) while others did not. One 1856 accident report speaks of the driver involved being unable to read the book of regulations, some of which were quite long and complex, requiring a well-developed vocabulary. Take this one, issued by the LNWR in 1846, which requires the skill of a parliamentary draftsman to disentangle:

> The fan or arm of the auxiliary signal at Cheddington, Leighton, Roade, Blisworth and Weedon are repainting to a yellow colour which will be more discernable than green, the ground colour is obliged to be nearly red, the signal will, however, continue to be shown for the assistance of the drivers, although it is not intended they should stop thereat but come on heretofore as far as the stationary post, when the policeman will tell them why the train has been stopped.

Some illiterates still had to issue written orders. On the Great Western, as late as the 1890s, the regulations had to be read out to the staff at least once a week, and an illiterate foreman at Reading was provided with a clerk to write his letters for him. Only by 1904 were all Great Western staff required to supply a signature. Other railways required literacy much earlier. The Southampton & Dorchester made it a requirement from 1847 and the London, Brighton & South Coast were issuing written questionnaires to all staff by 1856. All would-be staff of the London & South Western Railway had to be able to write 'with reasonable facility' and were examined on it as part of recruitment. Some rail companies did more to further the cause of literacy. The Grand Junction provided a reading room for its men at its new Crewe works from 1843 and the Great Western funded a circulating library for its Paddington staff from 1852. The LNWR ran weekly evening schools for adults from 1847.

The Railways and the Post

The growth in literacy went hand in hand with that of letter writing, and the railways played their part in accommodating that growth. The first real national postal service could be said to have been established in 1657, when an Act of Parliament created the position of Postmaster General, in charge of a government monopoly of mail-carrying. At first they were carried by ordinary stagecoaches, with journeys from London to York taking four days 'if God permits'. Journey times were somewhat reduced by the building of turnpike roads in the eighteenth century and the introduction of mail coaches (from 1784). By 1837 twenty-seven mail coaches were leaving London nightly, but they were still limited to the speed and distance the horses could gallop between changes. The service to Bristol still took 12¼ hours, which the railway reduced to 4 hours 10 minutes.

The Stockton & Darlington got around the government monopoly of mail-carrying by tying string around bundles of letters and calling them parcels, but the Liverpool & Manchester were one of the first lines where the GPO first started making official use of the railways, adapting carriages to carry mail. An Act of 1838 gave the GPO wide-ranging powers, to put mails on any train, to demand special trains if needed and to stop railway companies changing the times of trains without notice. The railways could be required to provide carriages in which to sort the mail, and wagons on which to transport mail coaches or carts. That same year, the Grand Junction Railway became the first to provide a carriage (a converted horsebox) for mobile mail sorting. The introduction of Rowland Hill's penny post in 1840 gave a great boost to the volume of letter writing (123 per cent in the first year, 441 per cent by 1854), strengthening the case for rail to be used to carry that additional volume. Lineside apparatus for picking up and dropping off the mail on the move soon followed (though Brunel resisted it for a time, regarding it as dangerous). The subsequent growth of the travelling post office network may be judged from the fact that the service, for which the Government paid £1,743 in 1838, was by 1896 costing them £1,000,000.

CHAPTER 9

The Railways and Time

Everything is near, everything is immediate – time, distance, and delay are abolished.

These cottagers told the time by the smoke of the trains which passed in the valley. They got up by the milk train between four and five; they had breakfast by the paper train at half past seven; the London express at half past twelve was their dinner bell. If they had a clock, they did not use it or even wind it up.

God's Time to Railway Time

In this chapter we look at two separate but related issues – the adoption of a standard national basis for timekeeping and using it to produce timetables. Both are vital to the conduct of our modern lives and both were, to a considerable degree, the result of the railways. Prior to the coming of the railways there was no nationally agreed basis for setting time. It was done at a local level, based on the rising and setting of the sun (also known as God's time). One problem with this was that the sun was not a particularly accurate timekeeper, being subject to the Earth's erratic orbit around it and seasonal variations, not to mention being invisible when cloudy. On which subject, the original Liverpool Road station in Manchester had a sundial mounted on its wall as a timekeeper. Given that city's reputation for rainfall, it is hard to think of any railway location (except perhaps the platform of an underground railway) where a sundial would be of less use. But more serious was the fact that the sun rose and set at different times, depending upon how far east or west you were – almost half an hour earlier in Yarmouth than in Penzance.

Stagecoach operators were relaxed about timings. These differences in time had been noticed since the start of mail coach services in 1784, but the coaches' progress was sufficiently slow for it not to be a problem for them. The longest east–west stagecoach journey was between London and Plymouth, between which there was a twenty-minute time difference, but since the journey took twenty-two hours by mail coach the gap was not too noticeable. Some coach drivers even carried watches that could be calibrated to gain or lose time by up to a quarter of an hour a day, depending on the direction in which the coach was heading. However, with more rapid means of communication, problems did begin to arise. With the arrival of the electric telegraph, for example, you even had the anomaly that a telegraph message between London and Dublin could arrive before it was sent (according to local time).

At the very beginning, the directors of the Liverpool & Manchester Railway were content to time their train departures to the nearest half hour. But discrepancies began to matter on the railways, particularly as the network grew and making connections between services became more of an issue. Accurate timetabling was also a help in avoiding collisions and near-misses. It was not such a big problem for Liverpool–Manchester services, where the local time differential between the two ends of the line was only about three minutes, but Great Western services covered longer east–west distances and the gap grew wider, so that Bristol time ran some eleven minutes behind London time. Someone using local time for their arrival at Bristol station ran a real risk of missing a train running on London time. At first the Great Western tried making their passengers at least aware of local differentials. Their 1841 timetable told its passengers that 'London time is about four minutes earlier than Reading time, seven and a half minutes before Cirencester and fourteen minutes before Bridgewater.' (Hylton (2007), p. 104)

To add to the confusion, different companies, sometimes sharing the same stations, applied different policies. At Rugby, the London & North Western used local time, while the branch from the same station to Leeds on the Midland line worked on London time. The Chester & Holyhead Railway set its clocks by the Craig-y-Don gun, fired daily some 16½ minutes late by London time, even though the railway's principal duty was to carry the Irish Mail train, which ran to Greenwich Mean Time. Just to confuse matters further, a specially regulated watch was sent daily with the service from Euston to Holyhead, to time the departure of the mail steamer. Despite the ability of the telegraph to send instant time signals, this practice was not discontinued until 1939.

Passengers complained and sometimes even tried to sue the railways as a result of being stranded. From 1845, a campaign began to build for standardisation. The Liverpool & Manchester, the London & South Western and the Great Western were three of the first railways (all running east–west services) to support the use of Greenwich Mean Time as a basis for timekeeping. The Great Western had standardised on it from November 1840 and the Liverpool & Manchester even petitioned Parliament to adopt it nationwide for all purposes in 1845, albeit without success.

An early victory came in 1847, when the Corporation of Manchester agreed, at the request of the Lancashire & Yorkshire Railway, to reset all its official clocks to railway time. In the same year, the Railways Clearing House, set up to improve coordination between the multitude of different railway companies, recommended that all its members go over to Greenwich Mean Time 'as soon as the General Post Office permitted it', and many railways made the switch more or less straight away.

Some pockets of resistance remained for a while. In Exeter and Bristol public clocks had two minute hands, showing both GMT and local time, due to the opposition of the Dean of Exeter to the new arrangement. The same was true of the public clocks at Great Tom and Christ Church, Oxford, and there was also opposition in towns like Bath, Devonport and Plymouth. Traditionalists generally lamented the change. These included Charles Dickens, who says of the new order in *Dombey and Son* 'there was even railway time observed in clocks, as if the sun itself had given in'.

An important further step forward came in October 1852, when the Astronomer Royal started transmitting GMT signals from the new electromagnetic clock at Greenwich to the railway network.

The last bastion of the old system fell in 1852, when the Dean of Exeter succumbed to the standard (the day after Exeter started receiving GMT signals from Greenwich). By 1855, 98 per cent of towns and cities had access to GMT. But it was only in 1880, with the passing of the Statutes (Definition of Time) Act, that GMT became the nation's official time. Four years later it became the world's standard basis for timekeeping, as twenty-five nations signed up to Greenwich Mean Time at the Prime Meridian Conference in Washington.

So the railway became an important local reference point for the time, and stations would have their clocks checked once a week to make sure they were keeping good time. Moreover, 'under the station clock' became a common meeting place for travellers and those awaiting them.

Timetabling

The word 'timetable' derives from 'tide table', something used by sailors since the sixteenth century. Before the railways, timetabling was as vague as timekeeping. Some coach operators would even allow anyone booking all four inside seats on the coach to specify when they would like to leave. In any event, such were the uncertainties of stagecoach travel (affected by road conditions, frequent stops to change horses, highwaymen and the weather, among other things) that any mention of timings tended to be accompanied by worrying caveats like 'barring accidents' or 'God willing'. The mail coaches had something called time bills, but these were simply for internal use, for the Post Office to check the punctuality of its mail service, rather than for the benefit of passengers.

In the very earliest days, it seemed that the railways would take an equally vague view of timetabling, as Henry Booth, secretary to the Liverpool & Manchester Railway, explained to a parliamentary Select Committee in 1841:

Booth: 'We have twenty stopping places ... but if we are to be limited to a timetable, we must be stopping at every one of the twenty stations...'
Committee: 'Do you keep a record of actual departure times from the intermediate stations?'
Booth: 'No, it is hardly desirable with the number of stations on the line. Our man merely has to open and shut the gate; the train stops, takes up the passengers, and goes on.'

Charles Saunders, Booth's opposite number on the Great Western, was even more candid to the same Select Committee:

At the opening in 1838 we found the engines were so inefficient that timetable working was hopeless; one or two engines might keep time, the other eight or ten were always out of time. So we suspended timetables till the locomotive power became sufficient.

The Liverpool & Manchester were at least persuaded initially to publish a 'scheme of departures' from its two terminals, though they were markedly coy about when the train might get to its destination. They later specified that their first-class trains would arrive at the other end after an hour and a half, and second class after two hours, but even then they would not speculate as to when services might reach the intermediate stations. Passengers from there had to guess. More conventional timetables would follow, as the operating arrangements bedded in and the locomotives became more powerful and more reliable. The London & Birmingham had the first timetable as we would know it in 1838. Meanwhile, 'Railway King' George Hudson had his own unique take on timetabling. When confronted with statistics showing how many of his trains were late, he responded with figures for the number that were early, showing that, in net terms, his railway ran roughly on time. The South Yorkshire Railway's 'timetable' of 1851 went a stage further, and refused to give times of arrival or departure, adding unnecessarily that 'no guarantee of punctuality' could be given.

Bradshaw

One important impetus towards standardisation came in 1838, when George Bradshaw, a Quaker map-maker from Manchester, diversified into railway timetables. The earliest surviving (1839) *Bradshaw* (or, to give its original full name, *Bradshaw's Railway Timetables and Assistant to Travelling*) consisted of just eight pages of railway times and cab fares, and five pages of maps and plans. By the end of the century it was approaching 1,000 pages in length and 'Bradshaw' had become the generic term for a railway timetable. From 1847 it even ran to a Continental edition. Throughout the nineteenth century, its price never varied from its original 6*d*, and even in 1937 the price for what was by then a mammoth tome had only risen to 2*s* 6*d*.

But even Bradshaw suffered from the vagaries of local time before Greenwich Mean Time became broadly accepted in most areas (by around 1852). As Henry Booth reported in 1847, a 250-mile journey going west–east might take 7½ hours, whereas the identical journey, run at the same speed east–west, would reach its destination in 6½ hours local time.

Bradshaw was authoritative and a national institution. It was said that the two books you would find in every Victorian home were the Bible and *Bradshaw*. But it was also impenetrable to all but the most dedicated code-breaker, and was lampooned by Charles Dickens, *Punch* and any music-hall comedian looking for a sure-fire laugh. It was printed in a tiny typeface on poor-quality paper and populated by a host of obscure symbols and abbreviations. Author Anthony

Trollope despaired of having the strength and mental ability to make sense of it and *Punch* called for reading *Bradshaw* to be made part of the school curriculum.

It almost was. Archbishop William Temple, the headmaster of Repton School, did not set errant pupils lines, but instead gave them the more challenging task of finding the best way from Great Yarmouth to Exeter without passing through London, with the help of *Bradshaw*. *Punch* also said of it in 1865 (presumably tongue in cheek) that 'seldom had the gigantic intellect of man been employed on a work of greater utility', and in their 'Tourists' Alphabet', 'B is the Bradshaw that leads you to swear'. An article in 1885 alleges that a witness once told the court that he had on one occasion spent twenty consecutive minutes studying the pages of *Bradshaw*, whereupon the judge advised that the evidence of such a man could not be relied upon, and suggested that his sanity needed investigating.

In 1876, the music hall duo Albert and Leigh had a hit with their number 'Bradshaw's Guide', which tells how love blossomed on a train as a helpful swain assisted a bewildered damsel in making sense of her *Bradshaw* (not helped by the fact that she could not remember the name of the town to which she was trying to travel). *Bradshaw* also made its appearances in fiction. Jules Verne had Phileas Fogg relying on *Bradshaw* for part of his journey around the world in eighty days, and whenever Sherlock Holmes leapt from his chair crying, 'The game's afoot!' it was a reasonable bet that he had his *Bradshaw* near at hand. But even the gigantic intellect of Sherlock Holmes struggled with deciphering *Bradshaw*. As he said of it: 'The vocabulary of Bradshaw is nervous and tense, but limited. The selection of words would hardly lend itself to the sending of a general message.'

John Pendleton was less polite in his comments on the impenetrability of *Bradshaw*: 'With your head in a fog and your eyes aching, on the encouraging words in italics "see above" or "vice versa" you feel inclined to fling "Bradshaw" out of the window.' (Pendleton volume 2, pages 153–4)

From 1838 until 1961, George Bradshaw produced what tried to be a comprehensive schedule, except that he encountered initial non-cooperation from some railway operators. They refused to provide him with the information he needed, on the grounds that it 'might make punctuality a sort of obligation and that failure to keep the time announced would bring penalties'.

But, for all the early railways' vagueness about arrival (and sometimes departure) times, this local newspaper tried to encourage its readers to be punctual travellers, and perhaps overestimated the punctuality of the railway company in doing so:

The method [punctuality], so strictly adhered to at every station on the line is perhaps one of the most admirable lineaments of railway travelling; and it is highly important that the public should bear in mind the absolute necessity of passengers procuring their tickets at least five minutes before the departure of each train.

(Reading Mercury, 4 April 1840)

Punctuality was also enforced upon one group who were more accustomed to having others wait on their pleasure. The London & Birmingham Railway in 1839 advised that, 'Gentlemen's carriages and horses must be at the station at least a quarter of an hour before the time of departure.' This was to enable the private carriages of the rich to be loaded onto the flat wagons that would enable them to travel without having to mix with the common herd.

The Railways and Speed

Related to ideas of time and timetables was the concept of speed. By the 1840s the fastest express trains were capable of 60–70 miles an hour. Compared with the stagecoaches, which were previously the fastest things on wheels, the transformation this involved would be the equivalent for us of modern family saloon cars suddenly being capable of 400 mph. Even the minimum average speed for the slowest parliamentary trains prescribed by Gladstone's 1844 Act was 12 mph. If it sounds slow today, it needs to be borne in mind that this minimum speed was faster than the maximum average speed that was available to the most affluent traveller by horse-drawn coach at the time. But it was perhaps the Rainhill trials of 1829 that gave the first intimation of the transformation in man's understanding of speed that the railways were to bring:

The most sanguine advocates of travelling engines had not anticipated a speed of more than 10–12 miles an hour. It was altogether a new spectacle, to behold a carriage crowded with company, attached to a self-moving machine and whirled along at the speed of 30 miles an hour.

(Booth, p. 74)

But even in 1830 some, like Henry Booth, the secretary to the Liverpool & Manchester Railway, had the vision to see the wider transformation in ideas of time and space that would be wrought by the railways:

But perhaps the most striking result produced by the completion of this Railway, is the sudden and marvellous change which has been affected in our ideas of time and space. Notions which we have received from our ancestors, and verified by our own experience, are overthrown in a day, and a new standard erected, by which to form our ideas for the future. Speed – despatch – distance are still relative terms, but their meeting has been totally changed within a few months; what was quick is now slow; what was distant is now near ... Our notions of expedition, though at first having reference to locomotion, will influence, more or less, the whole tenor of business and life ... A saving of time is a saving of money. For the purposes of locomotion, about half the number of carriages will suffice, if you go twice the speed.

(Booth, Pages 89–90)

CHAPTER 10

The Railways and Women

Women as Travellers – and the 'Ladies-Only' Compartment

> She was the kind of woman who, on a long journey, always goes into the compartment labelled 'ladies only'.
>
> (Herbert Williams MP recalls a conversation overheard between two women in March 1950. What kind of woman did they have in mind?)

What, if anything, did the railways do for women? Before the railways, the perils associated with public transport for women were largely limited to the middle classes. The really rich would travel in their own private coaches and the likes of public stagecoaches were beyond the means of most working-class women. Few women travellers would embark on a journey without a husband or some other male chaperone to accompany them. It was thought at first that the railways, by making travel both more affordable and quicker, would reduce the dangers of travelling and bring about 'the emancipation of the fair sex, and particularly the middle and higher classes, from the prohibition of travelling at all'. (*Quarterly Review*, June 1844)

From the early days of the railways, ladies-only waiting rooms started being introduced in some stations, some of them staffed with female attendants. It was around this time that some railway companies also started introducing ladies-only accommodation on trains. The Grand Junction Railway appears to have been the first to do so, followed by what the *Railway Chronicle* called 'the Brighton Company'. The *Chronicle* ran an article (22 November 1845) asking whether 'shutting them (women) up' was really the answer and questioning whether women were in any more danger than they would have been, say, walking on Hampstead Heath. If the railways really were that dangerous, they suggested that the only advice to women would be not to travel at all.

Nonetheless, pressure for the universal provision of ladies-only compartments grew in the 1860s, no doubt fuelled by lurid and sensational accounts in the popular press of the hazards facing female travellers. They reported cases of rudeness, bad language and, worse, assaults. The *Penny Illustrated* carried an account (26 September 1868) of two women who were followed from compartment to compartment by a man who acted in 'an insulting and obtrusive manner', and a letter in the *Standard* (13 September 1864) told of a female servant who was assaulted by two men. They pushed her to the ground and grabbed her knee, before leaving the carriage, laughing. According to the *Railway Chronicle*, some of these miscreants would even go so far as to dress in women's clothing, to help them pursue their vices. Novelist Anthony Trollope has his character Mrs Stanbury saying: 'There's no place a young woman is insulted in so bad as those railway carriages, and I won't have her come by herself.' (from *He Knew He Was Right* (1868))

Many railways resisted the demand for the universal provision of ladies-only compartments, on the grounds that it made it more difficult to assemble some trains. In contrast, the Metropolitan Railway announced the introduction of ladies-only compartments to all their services from October 1874, to much praise from the public and press. However, it turned out that the ladies-only facility was only available in first and second class – this may have been a reflection of the cost of providing it, or perhaps a view that third-class female travellers were not ladies, but just women.

If proof of this last point were needed, it came in a sensational court case involving a Colonel Valentine Baker in 1875. Baker was a well-connected and highly regarded cavalry officer, whose circle of friends included no less than the Prince of Wales. He was charged with 'attempting to ravish' a young lady he met in the first-class compartment of a London & South Western Railway carriage. Possibly in an attempt to bolster his bona fides as a gentleman, he refused to allow his counsel to cross-examine the young lady, and relied on his assertion that it had been no more than a friendly kiss that had been misunderstood. However, the young lady's evidence showed that it had been considerably more than a kiss that had led to her hanging out of the open door of a moving train, screaming for help. The episode cost Baker a fine, a year's imprisonment and the end of his British Army career. The upper reaches of society were shocked, not least by the fact that it had taken place in a first-class compartment. Had he tried the same thing in a third-class compartment, they argued, he would have got away with it. The case contributed to a fear among men of travelling 'singly with a stranger of the weaker sex, under the belief that it is only common prudence to avoid in this manner all risk of being accused, for purposes of extortion, or insult, or assault'. (Report to Parliament, quoted in Faith, p. 248)

The Metropolitan's ladies-only experiment was discontinued after just a few months, after it was found that they were very little used. Similar conclusions were reached in relation to many other similar experiments carried out by different companies and the Board of Trade confirmed them in their findings (in 1887). The *Newcastle Weekly Courant* was clearly of the view that the press (apart from themselves, naturally) was partly to blame for female concerns: 'There are women who, believing that all they read in the newspapers is as true as gospel, think they are in mortal terror when they find themselves alone with a man in the carriage.' (*Newcastle Weekly Courant*, 10 October 1884)

In the reporter's view, men were more likely to search the train for a spare seat, rather than sit with an 'unattended female', for there was a fear that a man in this compromising position could be blackmailed with bogus claims of sexual assault: 'Apparently, most men thought that it is best to leave female travellers alone, as they are generally well able to take care of themselves.' (Ibid.)

It was a view shared by the *Railway Times*, who referred to: 'That portion of humanity which sterner beings sometimes characterise as the weaker sex, but who in these days of women's rights spurn the soft impeachment and claim to be superior beings'. (*Railway Times*, 3 March 1888)

There was a further danger for an innocent male who found himself alone in a compartment with a lady. The activities of this particular fraudster were even immortalised in a music-hall song, about 'a charming young widow I met on a train'. Dressed in deepest mourning and carrying a (dummy) baby, she would feign a paroxysm of grief over her recent bereavement and, as the gallant gentleman sought to console her, her light fingers would relieve him of his watch, purse and other valuables. It was also not unknown for prostitutes to use ladies-only compartments as their business premises.

Sensational reports of assaults continued to appear into the 1880s. In 1888, a Miss Scragg was attacked on the London & North Western Railway, and an attack on a woman in a ladies-only compartment of the same railway led to the victim falling from the moving train while trying to escape her assailant. But by now, more responsible sections of the press had to concede that the number of attacks was minimal, relative to the numbers of women travelling, and began to cast doubt on whether even women wanted to be separated. The Manchester South Junction & Altrincham Railway had long provided segregated compartments but, as the *Manchester Guardian* reported: 'Many ladies objected to riding in them as they felt it actually increased their exposure to predators, especially on long journeys or if they were the only occupant.' (*Manchester Guardian*, 11 November 1905)

'Women themselves do not ask for isolation, nor do they desire it.' (*Railway Times*, March 1888)

Enforcement of the ladies-only rule could also be problematic. While some railways had their own by-laws to make male trespass into ladies-only compartments an offence, no such universal power existed until there was a change in the national rules in 1906, and a railway official could be reduced to appealing to the better nature of the trespasser in an effort to get them out. The new rule provided for fines of 40s for a first offence and up to £5 for repeat offenders, but the first people prosecuted under the new powers got away with a derisory fine of one shilling, plus costs.

What is perhaps little known now (and was virtually unknown then) was that since 1912 the Metropolitan and some other lines had issued an instruction to guards that – on request – they were to reserve a compartment as ladies-only: provided (a) there was a spare compartment to reserve and (b) that it was outside peak travelling hours. The service was little used, not least since the railway did not tell the travelling public about it. Moreover, a guide to good practice for all British railways had since 1884 called upon guards to assist ladies travelling alone, and where possible find them a compartment with other ladies (though not necessarily one reserved exclusively for them).

One thing that was certain was that the railways increased the range of employment opportunities accessible to women. In 1881 the census showed that nationwide, there were some 7,000 women working as clerks. By 1911 the number had risen to 146,000 and by 1931 women made up 42 per cent of the clerical workforce. They could travel on the workmen's trains on an equal footing with male workers, and those peak-hour commuter services were sufficiently well patronised for the molestation of isolated women not to be a problem.

There was a revival of interest in segregated accommodation after the First World War, by when a greatly increased number of women were working (and commuting), or travelling on rail for shopping or leisure trips. A later survey by the London & North Eastern Railway found that public opinion was fairly evenly divided on the matter though, strangely, twice as many men as women supported the ladies-only idea. The following newspaper correspondence may help to explain why:

> I observe that women hate each other so intensely that they will not willingly travel in the same railway carriage with each other ... I find one corner in every smoking carriage occupied by a woman. She faces the engine and she is invariably a non-smoker.
>
> As soon as the male pipes and what-nots are burning well she opens the window and we are all subjected to fierce draughts to which she, swathed in fur, is insensible...
>
> I have ostentatiously turned up my collar and reached my hat from the rack, I have made pointed remarks as to my bald head, and I have wrapped my paper around my legs, but all to no purpose.
>
> I am no hater of women. I shall always have as many wives as the law allows. But I behold that womankind, like fresh air, should be kept strictly in its place. In this instance, outside the window of a smoking carriage.
>
> (*Daily Telegraph*, 13 December 1935)

The *Manchester Guardian* reported (on 9 December 1931) that the Metropolitan Railway was introducing ladies-only smoking compartments in some of its night trains and for once it appears that these proved highly popular. A letter to the *Telegraph* in November 1963 took the argument about segregation to its logical (if ludicrous) conclusion and called for the introduction of men-only compartments, where males could 'retreat from the huge bags, umbrellas and empty chatter of female travellers'.

Ladies-only space continued to be provided on the post-war, nationalised British Rail. In 1957, a guard named Purdy was put in hospital by three youths after trying to enforce it. The arrangement only came to an end in 1977, with the Sex Discrimination Act. British Rail received conflicting advice as to whether ladies-only compartments were, or were not, illegal under the Act. However, they were not keen to invite a test case in the courts, and the provision was allowed to lapse.

But no account of ladies-only travel would be complete without a reference to 'Angela'. She was, according to railway folklore, a doctor's daughter in Wendover who regularly commuted to London by train in the 1950s. The ladies-only compartment was situated next to the guard's accommodation (to make it easier to police) and she would often strike up an acquaintance with whichever guard happened to be on duty. It seems: (a) that she must have had the compartment to herself quite a lot and (b) that some of the guards rather exceeded their job description in assisting their passengers, for she is alleged to have given birth to five children of different railway employees.

Today, ladies-only accommodation is still available on many nations' railways, including Japan, Egypt, India, Iran, Taiwan, Brazil, Mexico, Indonesia, the Philippines, Malaysia and Dubai. Japan has had such provision since 1912, and some new provision was made after the Second World War on the Keihin–Tohoku line, at a time when the railway was so crowded that it was almost physically impossible for women and children to force their way on board.

But mostly the ladies-only space is provided to counteract the problem of groping which, if the statistics are to be believed, has become a Japanese national sport. In a survey, two-thirds of women passengers reported having been assaulted in this way, and the police recorded a threefold increase in the number of reported incidents in the eight years up to 2004. Apparently, the high level of overcrowding throughout the network makes it difficult to identify and apprehend the guilty parties. The Osaka Municipal Subway, which is said to have the worst incidence of the problem, runs at 160 per cent of its official capacity. In addition to being less crowded than the rest of the trains, the ladies-only compartments are said to be 'less smelly'.

India has introduced entire women-only trains, patrolled by police, which appear to have been a great success. They offer women protection from both would-be molesters and bag snatchers. They are less popular with dutiful husbands who try and accompany their womenfolk on their journey, only to find they have to make separate travel arrangements. Taiwan goes a stage further and also designates ladies-only sections of the platform for waiting at night, and the segregated Israeli accommodation is provided to comply with religious requirements that the womenfolk of one sect have to travel separately.

Women Railway Employees

Women have long been employed by the nation's railways, though the range and number of tasks entrusted to them varied mostly between war and peace. Just before the First World War about 13,000 of the national railway workforce (about 2 per cent of the total) were women. Their roles were predominantly traditional female ones, including large numbers of waiting room attendants and catering staff; they worked in railway hotels and laundries, and as cleaners and managers of railwaymen's lodging houses. In the railway workshops, they performed roles that included machinists and seamstresses.

Just a few managed to cross the boundary into areas of male employment. The first women station-mistresses were seen as early as 1832, and in the 1851 census a couple of female labourers are recorded among the navvies; there was the odd bridge-keeper and signalwoman and, from the late nineteenth century, women clerks were being employed in ever-increasing numbers. These latter upset their male counterparts, since they were paid about half the going male rate for the job, making the men fearful for their futures. The railway companies assuaged these fears by getting the women to concentrate on the new technologies – telephones, telegraphs and typing – denying them the usual channels to promotion and (in line with a number of other employers of the day) dismissing them when they married. These artificial limits to their advancement were in turn used as an excuse not to develop the potential of female staff or to give them equal pay.

A lot of this changed (temporarily at least) during the First World War. The railways were a reserved occupation, which could exempt railway staff from conscription once it was introduced in 1916 (until then, Britain's Army was a purely volunteer organisation). But this did not stop railway staff volunteering in their thousands (184,000 in total, including a good number who were needed to run the many railways supporting the battlefronts in Europe and elsewhere). By April 1915 the railways were forced to reassess the limits on female employment on the railways. Within eighteen months, some 34,000 women had been engaged, many of them stepping into occupations that were hitherto the exclusive preserve of men – cleaners of locomotives and carriages, porters, drivers of electric trucks and horse vans, operators of points, cranes and lifts. As the manpower shortage grew worse, they even diversified into areas such as signalling, shunting and train guards – much to the concern of many male railwaymen. The National Union of Railwaymen did not lift their ban on female membership until July 1915, once it had negotiated the conditions of their employment. The railway companies agreed to the automatic reinstatement of enlisted male railwaymen after the war and, so as not to depress wage rates, the unions insisted on female staff receiving no less than the male rate for the job. However, this did not mean equal pay, because only male employees received the wartime cost-of-living bonus, which meant that male railwaymen could still be paid virtually twice as much as females doing the same job. This was the cause of much resentment and at least two episodes of industrial action by female staff.

By September 1918, over 50,000 women were filling the vacancies left by male railway workers. Come the Armistice and the men's return, those women were laid off, despite the fact that wartime fatalities meant that the railways were left with some 20,000 vacancies. Some of the women were allowed to be redeployed into work such as carriage cleaning and clerking, where the substitution issue did not apply to the same extent.

Inequalities persisted throughout the interwar years. Manual staff eventually saw the end of the marriage bar (for railway clerks the ban was not lifted until well after the Second World War), but they were in almost every case excluded from male pay scales. They made some progress in entering male areas of work, such as crossing keepers, but on lower rates of pay. By 1939, 26,000 women worked on the nation's railways, 11,500 of them as clerks.

The year 1939 brought about a repeat of the changes seen in the Great War, except that women now took on a much wider range of what were previously male roles. They became signalwomen, maintained the track, operated heavy machinery and did other demanding manual tasks in the workshops. Once again, some male railway workers were angered, as management ignored height restrictions and established priorities for promotion, to allow women to become train guards. Men also found themselves, as they saw it, relegated to operating older, dirtier steam-hauled services, to allow women to work on the cleaner (and more prestigious) electric trains. By June 1944 over 114,000 women were working on the railways, 74,000 of them in jobs normally reserved for men in peacetime. In addition to the physical demands of these jobs, railway workers of both sexes had to contend with the attentions of the Luftwaffe, with almost 400 railway workers being killed and 2,500 injured.

The restoration of peace brought with it another clear-out of female employees from jobs traditionally reserved for men. This was relaxed to some degree in the late 1950s, during a peacetime period of labour shortage, to allow women in signal boxes and track maintenance. But when Dr Beeching raised the possibility of female guards in 1960, protests from male workers led to the idea being dropped. Equal pay for women doing equal work finally came in 1958, some seventeen years before it was enshrined in national legislation. However, the sexes were still segregated, with women in most cases barred from promotional ladders. It was the Sex Discrimination Act of 1975 that finally gave women equal access to traditionally male areas of employment, on equal terms to men. Only then did women finally get the opportunity, always open to their brothers, to be engine drivers.

CHAPTER 11

The Railways and Vandalism

The unfettered reign of private enterprise, which, under the dictatorship of the engineer, has of late so much prevailed in this country, has been no doubt a grand source of works of commercial utility, but it has doomed us to much bitter humiliation in matters of art and taste.

(Engineer William Pole (1814–1900), quoted in Simmons (1991), p. 159)

Railroads … are to me the loathsomest form of devilry now extant, animated and deliberate earthquakes, destructions of all wise social habit or possible natural beauty, carriages of damned souls on the ridges of their own graves.

(John Ruskin, letter to *The Times*, 3 March 1887)

Change Before the Railways

This chapter is not so much about what the railways did for us, as what they took (or in some cases tried to take) from us, even if I do try to end on an optimistic note. The impact of the railways on the environment of Britain was both precedented and unprecedented. It was precedented in that there had been other major changes to the landscape within living memory of the first railways. Between 1750 and 1830 England had seen over 4,000 Enclosure Acts passed – affecting roughly 21 per cent of the land area of Britain. Around 6,800,000 acres had been enclosed, turning them from medieval areas of communal mixed agriculture to pasture. Then there had been the civil engineering work associated with the building of the canals, some of it impressive enough in its day, and the turnpikes, which could be driven across country with little regard for the landscape. But the railways were also unprecedented, because nothing before them compared to the scale and extent of the change they wrought.

In the early days in particular, public appreciation of our national heritage was not as well developed as it is today, and some railway builders thought – perhaps with some justification – that their railway had the right to go pretty well wherever and however it wished, knocking down whatever stood in its way. John Moxon, chairman of the London & Croydon Railway, said as much to a Parliamentary Committee in 1839. 'What?' said horrified committee chairman Lord Granville Somerset, 'Would you knock down Westminster Abbey and Blenheim Palace?' Moxon considered the question and conceded that he might at least spare the Abbey – probably.

Long before the railways, there had been a tradition of removing anything ancient that obstructed the free flow of traffic or otherwise impeded modern life. To take just a few examples: the High Cross at Bristol was erected at the centre of the town in 1373, on the site of an earlier Anglo-Saxon cross. For centuries it was the focal point of civic life until, in 1733, it was condemned as 'a ruinous and superstitious relic which is at present a public nuisance'. It was dismantled and eventually re-erected at Stourhead gardens. In London, the city walls and their associated gates, dating back largely to Roman times, were retained for many years as a symbol of the city's prestige, despite having become something of a pinch point in its traffic movements. In 1760 all but one of the gates – Newgate – were demolished to ease the flow of traffic. In similar vein, the gates were removed at Leicester (1776) and Canterbury (1781–91).

Ancient bridges tended to be another inconvenience, and those at Chester and Bedford, not to mention the original London Bridge, were all victims of progress. The construction of St Katherine's Dock, London, in 1825 involved the demolition of St Katherine's Hospital, including its fifteenth-century chapel, not to mention 1,250 houses.

Not that everything that was lost was necessarily an architectural gem. Reading's medieval crossing of the Thames, removed in 1869, was an unsightly mishmash, built half in stone, half in wood (being the shared and disputed responsibility of two often warring local authorities). But long before the coming of the railways history is littered with examples of what we would now regard as our heritage being destroyed, for military or political reasons (such as the slighting (demolition) of castles occupied by the losing side in civil disputes, or the asset stripping following the Dissolution of the Monasteries) or simply because they got in the way of progress.

The railways continued this tradition of clearance with a vengeance. An early piece of vandalism occurred at Edinburgh, in the shadow of the castle. The Trinity Hospital and church (founded in 1460) stood there and in 1848 the North British Railway Company made a bid for the site, to form part of Waverley station. Among others, the Society of Antiquaries of Scotland objected and, to address their concerns, the railway gave Edinburgh Town Council £22,000 to dismantle the church carefully and re-erect it elsewhere. The rebuild never happened, apart from one transept and the choir, which were belatedly reconstructed in the 1870s (by which time, much of the original stonework had been 'lost'). This is not to say that all cities were incapable of moving churches to accommodate railways. The church of St Simon and St Jude in Liverpool was dismantled, moved and rebuilt three times as Lime Street station was repeatedly enlarged.

The setting of Berwick-on-Tweed castle was not so much disturbed as destroyed by the railway. Built originally in the twelfth century by Scottish King David I, it became of strategic importance in this disputed border territory and changed hands many times. Successive improvements turned it into one of the most important fortified towns in Europe. But one onslaught it could not withstand was that of the North British Railway in 1843. They demolished the Great Hall and various other parts of the structure, to create a site for their station. To add insult to injury, they used some of the stone from the demolition to build a pseudo-Gothic station and train shed on the site. Where King Edward I once got Scottish nobles to swear allegiance in 1296, modern commuters now swear whenever their train is late.

Shrewsbury, which Pevsner called 'England's finest Tudor town', also had a Norman castle (in their case to keep out the marauding Welsh) and other architectural treasures, and this time the railway chose to build their railway station immediately beneath the castle. This arrangement may have found favour with the authorities because a number of the properties it displaced were ramshackle, and included some houses of ill repute. Biddle describes the impact of the station on this location:

> In building it there, a railway viaduct was required which ruined the highly praised view of Shrewsbury alongside the river. Even greater visual damage was caused by the station's proximity to the adjacent castle, and to the sixteenth-century Shrewsbury School (now the library) nearby.

> (Biddle, p. 312)

In the interest of balance, Biddle at least acknowledges the efforts of the Victorian railway architect to try and blend in with the school by providing a neo-Tudor station building (if one can conceive of what a Tudor railway station might have looked like), but he goes on to say: 'Unfortunately, such care did not extend to the retaining wall below the castle mound, which was built in glaring red brick.' (Ibid.)

But the railway was not the first source of damage to this historic town. Shortly before they got there, Thomas Telford destroyed much of the abbey precincts when his London–Holyhead road ploughed through them.

As Shrewsbury shows, the wrong choice of materials can be fatal in some locations. In the granite city of Aberdeen, the railways chose to build their station in an incongruous pale buff sandstone, chosen because it was easier to work. Simmons' verdict: 'The design is restrained, and the proportions are right, but the colour is a disaster; remediable only over the years as a merciful pollution descends, to cover the building with a neutral grime.' (Simmons (1999), p. 171)

Just to add to the city's architectural cohesion, the Guild Street goods station, immediately opposite, was built in red brick.

Newcastle has had a castle (from which it takes its name) since Roman times. It was rebuilt by the Normans and the parts that survive today are the keep (dating from 1172–77) and the Black Gate (1247–50). They now sit incongruously, and separated from each other, as islands surrounded by a sea of railway tracks. Part of the castle walls, plus a good bit of the medieval town (involving the displacement of some 800 families), had to be demolished to accommodate the station, but the geography of the place made it difficult to thread the railway into the urban fabric without something getting knocked down. Pevsner was less generous: 'Owing to the ruthlessness of the Victorian railway company, Newcastle's chief mediaeval monument ... can be appreciated as a castle only with effort.'

That said, the station and the High Level Bridge across the Tyne are at least striking examples of Victorian railway architecture.

A story with a slightly happier ending is that of Berkhamsted Castle. This eleventh-century motte-and-bailey castle was built and occupied by William the Conqueror's half brother, Robert de Mortain, and was once in the ownership of Thomas à Becket. Today it is thought of as one of the finest surviving examples of its kind and is a Scheduled Ancient Monument. But in 1833 the preferred route for the London & Birmingham Railway ran straight through the middle of it. There was local opposition to this, including from the landowners, the Bridgewater Estate, who did not want a steam railway spoiling their view. The castle earned the distinction of becoming the first building ever to receive statutory protection from the government. But even the revised route the government imposed upon the railway involved the demolition of the castle gatehouse and some of the earthworks.

Happier still was the outcome at Fort William in the Scottish Highlands. The fort from which it takes its name dates from 1690. It was used for controlling the rebellious Highlanders and was the place where the order for the notorious Glencoe massacre was signed in 1692, so the locals may have viewed this part of their heritage as something of a mixed blessing. By 1889 it was disused and empty when the railway from the Clyde to Fort William was proposed to come straight through the middle of it. The landowner had no objections (particularly to the compensation he would receive). For once, the railway company dealt with the matter sensitively. The best parts of the fort were retained and the gatehouse (which had to come down) was dismantled and reassembled nearby. The railway has since won a place in local hearts by becoming an important part of their tourist industry.

At Conway the railway company were required by government to protect the environs of the thirteenth-century castle by building the bridge which ran alongside it in a style which was in keeping with it. It also ran alongside Telford's 1826 suspension bridge into the town for road traffic. Robert Stephenson was entrusted with this challenging task. The battlemented stone towers with circular turrets at either end of the bridge may have been a reasonable response to the brief (the jury is divided on the matter, but apparently they were wished upon Stephenson by the city fathers), but how the two 400-foot rectangular iron tubes that connect the two towers and house the railway fit into the medieval vernacular may be a subject for even greater debate.

One castle whose demise cannot be blamed on the railways is Northampton. True, its station now stands on what was once a 'massive and important castle'. Parliament used to meet there, it was King John's favourite castle and the Royal Treasury was based there from 1205. However, it was in decline by the time of the Black Death (1349–50) and was described as 'ruinous' by 1593. Not ruinous enough for Charles II, however, for in 1662 he ordered it to be further slighted, as punishment for the town's support for the Parliamentary cause in the Civil War. Much of the town's historic centre was destroyed in a great fire in 1675, and the site was further robbed for building materials by the local people. In 1861 the castle site was sold to a Samuel Walker, who dug for treasure in it before selling it to the London & North Western Railway. They finally levelled the site (assuming they could find anything left to level) for the station.

Victorian railway promoters were generally no respecters of ancient monuments, even those with religious associations. Lewes Priory was the first Cluniac monastery in Britain and one of the country's largest monastic houses. It was founded in 1081 and, like every other such establishment, was closed down by Henry VIII. The locals thereafter helped themselves to most of the useful building materials. The process of destruction was helped along in 1844 by the London, Brighton & Hastings Railway driving their railway line through the middle of the site, destroying much archaeological evidence as they went. The outrage that this provoked was instrumental in establishing the Sussex Archaeological Society (in overall national terms, however, it may be argued that archaeology has gained at least as much as it has lost from the railways, when evidence destroyed by railway building is weighed against the number of archaeological investigations railway building has occasioned).

But it did not require the desecration of a national monument for railway building to cause a scandal. When a railway ploughed through old St Pancras churchyard, the contractor, Joseph Firbank, was asked to keep a lookout, as he unearthed bodies, for the bones of a French bishop who had been buried there as a refugee from the revolution. Firbank, a man not noted for his love of foreigners, simply gave the authorities the darkest set of bones he could find, working on the assumption that all foreigners were swarthy, right down to their bones. An apprentice architect was employed thereafter to oversee the exhumations more closely. This was one Thomas Hardy, a man later better known as a writer, and he immortalised the event in his poem 'The Levelled Churchyard'.

Another valued local amenity was the Stray at Harrogate, a public common where medicinal springs had been discovered in 1571. Its use as a public common had been protected by law since 1770, and when proposals came forward in 1862 to take a new railway line into Harrogate across it, the line was made to go into cutting, so as not to offend the sensibilities of users of the common.

Sutton Park near Birmingham is a huge (2,400 acres) area of heathland, wetland and marsh. There is some evidence of Roman occupation and it was a royal forest in Anglo-Saxon times. Henry VIII gave it to the local community in 1528. It was in 1879 that a railway was proposed, running through the park. It met with considerable local opposition, which the railway tried to buy off with the promise of cheap coal supplies for local people, and the scheme was finally approved. The park even got its own station, complete with a separate platform for the excursion trains that ran there on a daily basis. Again, at least part of the line was built in cutting to try and reduce its impact, though the flood of additional visitors it brought to the area was probably more disturbing to seekers of tranquillity.

Sometimes it was not the building of the railway so much as its use of steam traction that was considered vandalism. As we saw, the Liverpool & Manchester Railway's steam locomotives were not originally allowed to enter the precincts of either town, other than on their permitted tracks. It was alleged that steam engines would stop cows grazing, hens laying, and would kill passing birds, make horses extinct and massacre passengers on an industrial scale with their exploding boilers. The Newcastle & Carlisle Railway originally disarmed opposition of this kind by proposing to operate the entire length of their 60-mile railway by horse, which was scarcely more intrusive than a road (and would have allowed the use of cheaper rails, had it been their genuine intention). Having got their parliamentary Act, they negotiated use of steam traction with each individual landowner along their length of the track. This was eventually (though not without difficulty) secured, making their two breaches of Hadrian's Wall seem child's play by comparison.

Even more outrageous than the schemes which went ahead were some of those that were either refused or were permitted but did not go ahead for other reasons. Epping Forest was only saved from the encroachment of a railway in the 1860s after a twenty-year battle. In 1882/83, Norwich was confronted by a proposal that would have driven a line through the lower close of the cathedral and across Mousehold Heath, a valued local nature reserve, much painted by artists and with historical associations going back to the Peasants' Revolt of 1381 and beyond. The year 1883 also saw proposals for a new London–Bristol line that would have marched across Salisbury Plain and carved through the avenue at Stonehenge. This was rejected, but not on the grounds of its impact on a monument of world importance. Rather, the proposers failed to make the case in railway terms. Leicester Castle faced demolition from an 1890 scheme of the Manchester, Sheffield & Lincolnshire Railway, but was able to get an alternative route agreed that missed the castle.

Some would-be mistakes were on a truly heroic scale. Aysgarth Force (or Falls) in Wensleydale is regarded today as one of the wonders of the north of England. It is described as 'an awesome sight (and sound) when the river is in spate' and may be familiar to readers as the setting for one of the scenes in the film *Robin Hood, Prince of Thieves*. In their day, Ruskin and Wordsworth rhapsodised about its beauty and J. M. W. Turner sketched it in 1816, later turning the sketches into a watercolour. In 1884, a railway company decided that the very thing that was needed to frame the scene was an 80-foot-high brick viaduct. Fortunately, the powers that be thought otherwise. London was less fortunate when the London, Chatham & Dover Railway proposed a river crossing at Blackfriars, running northwards and providing a station on the site of the derelict Fleet prison, as well as the promise of rejuvenating one of the most impoverished parts of the city – Farringdon Without. It was approved, and what it also did was to ruin the setting of St Pauls, as seen from Fleet Street, as J. M. Wilson complained at the time: 'That viaduct has utterly spoiled one of the finest street views in the metropolis, and is one of the most unsightly objects ever constructed, in any such situation, anywhere in the world.' (J. M. Wilson, *The Imperial Gazetteer of England and Wales* (1869))

This environmental crime was only remedied in 1991, when the bridge was replaced by a tunnel. One that would surely have at least equalled it in ugliness was the 1864 proposal by the Thames Railway to build a railway on an iron viaduct running down the middle of the Thames in London, a scheme that was fortunately thrown out. As for one that was not rejected: 'We stare impudently down upon the glorious old church of St Saviour, lying in the pit which we have made for it.' (A. L. Munby on the elevated railway track running past Southwark Cathedral (1865))

Another scheme that got approval was the Midland Railway's 1863 proposal for a 333-foot-long, 78-foot-high viaduct (the Headstone Viaduct) crossing the spectacularly beautiful Monsal Dale in the Peak District. It was bitterly condemned at the time. Ruskin wrote of it:

> There was a rocky valley between Buxton and Bakewell, once upon a time, divine as the valley of Tempe ... You enterprised a railroad through the valley – you blasted the rocks away, heaped thousands of tons of shale into its lovely stream. The valley is gone and the Gods with it.

Today, the viaduct is considered an elegant structure, one that blends perfectly into its grandiose surroundings. No longer used as a railway, latter-day conservationists campaigned against its demolition and it is now protected as a listed structure.

Prehistoric sites were little understood in the nineteenth century and were relatively easy meat for the railway builder. A round barrow near Cheltenham was destroyed in 1846 when a station was built on it. Spetisbury Rings, an Iron-Age hill fort near Blandford Forum, got its own railway when the Somerset & Dorset Railway bisected it in 1857. The railway builders uncovered a mass grave of some 120 people, thought to date from the time of the Roman invasion. Similar fates were suffered by a stone circle at Shap, which fell victim to a high railway embankment in 1848, and Grim's Dyke near Hatch End. One that was saved by local protest (this time from two railways' predations) was Maumbury Rings near Dorchester, a Neolithic henge dating from 2,500 BC, which had also been a Civil War fortification and used in 1685 as a site for mass executions by Hanging Judge Jeffries. It may not have been destroyed by railways but by 1847 it was virtually enclosed by them.

But we should perhaps try to end what has sometimes appeared like a catalogue of destruction on a more positive note. Starting at the most neutral, Clapham argues that we have at least got used to the impact that the railways made: 'In most places the railway had sunk into the landscape, like the road and canal before it. All that it brought in sight and sound had become established, and as familiar as the uninterrupted spreading of the mutter of the towns.' (Clapham, ii, p. 489)

Robbins goes further, and argues first that the English landscape has not unambiguously been ruined by the railways:

At certain places there may be two views about particular pieces of line: at Dawlish, where the Great Western runs between the town and the sea; on Ludgate Hill, where a bridge is set in the foreground of the view of St Paul's Cathedral from the west, though it does not block the view from Fleet Street; on the Thames at Charing Cross; near Southwark Cathedral; at Conway, where the castle is shaved by the Chester & Holyhead line; or in Edinburgh, where the approach from the north and west to the best-sited station in the two kingdoms runs at the foot of Princes Street gardens.

(Robbins, quoted in Morgan, pages 219–20)

As we have seen, others would consider that there are not two views about the impact on, say, Ludgate Hill. However, Robbins goes further:

The railway has taken its place in the landscape with all the other artificial elements that man has put there: fields, hedges, farms, roads, canals. It has taken its place because it fits in – it rarely dominates any view – and because, unlike the airfield which must obliterate existing features to create its shaven emptiness, the railway etches in fresh detail to the scene. It rarely jars and usually pleases.

(Ibid., p. 222)

Even better, what if the railway buildings were felt to be such an adornment that the rest of the place had some catching up to do? It actually happened, in Blackburn, when they got their new station in the mid-nineteenth century: 'The design is far too superb for a station in that part of the town; and, under the circumstances, years will have to pass over before suitable buildings will be erected to correspond with it.' (P. A. Whittle, *Blackburn As It Is* (1852))

Similarly, in Folkestone, Pevsner no less (often the railways' most trenchant critic) described the Foord viaduct, which towers over the town, as 'without any doubt the most exciting piece of architecture in the town'.

Pevsner also waxed lyrical in Stoke, where the North Staffordshire Railway undertook a major piece of town planning in Winton Square. This square was designed to show off its spectacular station building, an elaborate affair in the Jacobean style with a giant bay window thought to be modelled on the one at Charlton House, near Malmesbury in Wiltshire. Pevsner called it the finest piece of axial planning in the county, and thought it was probably the only focal point in the Stoke part of the Six Towns. Pevsner also called Worcester Shrub Hill station 'a remarkably good building', despite subsequent corporate vandalism.

Leaping forward a century, the new railway station in war-damaged Coventry, finished in 1962 to be ready for the opening of Coventry Cathedral, has stood the test of time well. It still retains an elegant simplicity and freshness after fifty years and is a suitably uplifting note on which to end a chapter on railway vandalism.

CHAPTER 12

The Railways and a Share-Owning Public

At private risk for public service.

(The motto of the Stockton & Darlington Railway)

There are three roads to ruin: gambling, women ... and engineers. The first two are more pleasant, but the last is the most certain.

(Lord Rothschild, quoted in Odlyzko)

The railways, and in particular the railway manias of 1835–37 and 1844–47, when much of the network got approved (though not in every case built), attracted huge amounts of public investment from people who had not previously been share buyers, but who were eager to share in the bonanza that rail shares were seen as being. But was this mass share ownership a new phenomenon that the railways gave us, or part of a longer-standing tradition?

There were several earlier precedents for the kind of collective madness that was railway share mania. One of the first, centred in seventeenth-century Holland, involved the recently introduced tulip bulb. Prices for these soared to unimaginable levels as a growing merchant class used tulips to advertise their newly earned wealth. At the height of tulip mania, in March 1637, a single bulb of a particularly rare variety could fetch more than ten times the annual wage of a skilled craftsman. A form of futures market for the bulbs developed, with prospective purchasers having to pay very little of the cost up front when contracting to buy a supply.

These purchasers (like many railway share owners after them) would hope to sell on these contracts at a profit before they took delivery of the bulbs. At the peak of the mania, some bulbs could be changing hands up to ten times a day. But then the market collapsed, possibly brought on by the distraction of an outbreak of bubonic plague in Holland. By this time, the entire nation appeared to have become tulip speculators, with even the dregs of society selling such meagre possessions as they had to finance their trading. Inevitably, it was often these who were ruined when they ran out of 'bigger fools' to pay ever higher prices for the bulbs. They were left holding contracts at ten times the now-deflated market price for the bulbs, and no means of honouring the payment due on them.

The Dutch parliament, with a generosity not shown by their nineteenth-century British counterparts, decreed that these contracts should be treated as gambling debts, and thus not enforceable under Dutch law. Anyone wishing to void their contract to purchase bulbs could do so by paying 10 per cent of the outstanding sum. Some modern scholars question whether this price inflation was as great as the limited data of the time suggests, and whether it even constituted a bubble.

Another period of wild speculation came with the launching of the South Sea Company in 1711 – the so-called South Sea Bubble. This was a public/private partnership, whose main asset was said to be a monopoly to trade with the countries of South America. However, Britain was at that time at war with Spain, who controlled southern America, making any prospect of trade vanishingly remote, and most of what income the company made came from illegal insider dealing in government debt. The company continued trading until 1720, with share prices being driven ever higher as more and more of the public tried to get in on the act. Vendors even sold stocks on the street. When the collapse came, many of those who had borrowed money to buy shares found themselves bankrupted.

The initial success of the South Sea Company brought a lot of other stockholding opportunities onto the market. Some were genuine businesses, albeit some with what were then novel prospectuses, such as funding the establishment of insurance companies. Others had no basis in law or in some cases links with reality, or they used any funds they attracted for entirely different purposes to those listed in their prospectus. There were schemes for trading in hair, for developing perpetual motion and for making iron out of coal. But first prize has to go to the stocks that were marketed in 'a company for carrying out an undertaking of great advantage, but nobody to know what it is'.

One consequence of the South Sea Bubble was the Bubble Act 1720 (which lasted until 1825 – just as the railway age was dawning) which forbad companies to raise funding for an enterprise from more than five partners without a government charter, and limiting them to the purposes set out in that charter.

Another bubble with a South American flavour was launched by a confidence trickster named Gregor McGregor in the 1820s. This promoted investment in the territory of Poyais (capital St Joseph) on the Mosquito Coast. The prospectus spoke very highly of the territory which, potential investors were told, had its own civil service, bank, gold and silver mines almost overflowing with precious metals, an army, democratic government and an eager workforce. The truth was very different; its sole assets were four rundown buildings, a good deal of uninhabitable jungle and (as its name suggests) an inexhaustible supply of mosquitoes. But this did not stop McGregor selling bonds in the territory, land, officer places in the imaginary army, concessions to sell to, or serve, the fictitious population and even an invented local currency. Such was the demand for these items that McGregor was a multimillionaire by 1823. Two boatloads of settlers even set off for this new nirvana in 1822 and 1823 but such were its amenities, of the 240 who set out, only fifty survived to make the return trip, by which time McGregor had fled to France and launched a new market for shares – in the territory of Poyais.

But the bubble with the closest parallels to railway mania was the canal mania that seized Britain in the 1790s, buoyed up by the commercial success of the Bridgewater Canal and other pioneers. It was also helped by a series of good harvests, creating a quantity of disposable income which people were looking to invest profitably. Not all of these investors speculated wisely. The difference with canals, compared to tulips or South Sea bubbles, is that they involved engineering works of a cost which tended to be beyond the means of most individuals. Even the wealthy Duke of Bridgewater was heavily in debt by the time his canal was finished. The economist Adam Smith recognised in 1775 that 'navigable cuts and canals are of great and general utility; while at the same time they frequently require a greater expense than suits the fortunes of private people'.

So the ability to sell shares to fund them was important to their success. Between 1790 and 1797 some fifty-three new canals won parliamentary approval and investors fought with each other for the chance to underwrite them – the Rochdale Canal raised the entire £60,000 needed to finance it in an hour. In 1793 alone, canals attracted investment of £2,824,700 (or around £281 million in current values). Subscription meetings were organised with the minimum possible publicity, in order that the promoters could keep a good thing to themselves. When someone made the mistake of advertising a shareholder meeting for the proposed Bristol–Taunton Canal in the local newspaper, the promoters went around buying up every copy of the newspaper they could find, in order to keep it secret. Elsewhere, false details of the timing and venue of such meetings were circulated, to throw outsiders off the scent. Would-be investors would turn up at what they expected to be a canal fund-raising meeting, only to find themselves gatecrashing a hunt dinner.

The number of new schemes coming forward meant that there were shortages of engineers and even of navvies to dig them, leading to calls from some quarters to promote more Irish immigration. Inevitably, the economy went into reverse, making money harder to come by, just at a time when a number of schemes started to overrun their original cost estimates. For some, the answer would be that many of the branches or extensions that they had proposed to their canals were not really necessary, or that some could be replaced by less expensive tramways. Other schemes were more severely delayed or did not proceed at all, and yet others were completed but never made a penny in profits for their shareholders. Once again, as with most bubbles, many of those who were last to buy into the scheme – often using borrowed money – found themselves financially ruined, as share prices started to go down, rather than up, just as they invested.

Railway Mania

Faith argues that the railways were the biggest capital projects ever undertaken in Britain, and that the pre-railway financial markets were feeble affairs, unable to generate the level of funding the railways would need. In his view, the railways not only transformed the financial markets, they also conjured up what he called 'new breeds of men' – the promoters and financiers who found the money.

The first, more minor, of the two great railway manias occurred between 1835 and 1837, during which time fifty new lines, with a total mileage of around 1,600 miles, won parliamentary approval. During a single year of the second major mania (1846) no less than 4,540 miles of track were approved – as much as had been built in all the years since 1820. If the railway manias had characteristics in common with canal mania, they were vastly different in scale. Canal mania ran from 1790 to 1797. Over that eight-year period some fifty-three canal schemes received government approval, involving a total capital authorisation of around £7,749,000. A single railway line – Brunel's Great Western between London and Bristol – alone cost £6,500,000, almost as much the whole of the investment in canal mania. Taken in the round, the scale of railway mania was even more striking: 'In January 1846 the Prime Minister, Peel, stated cautiously that plans for 815 new railways had been legally lodged before Parliament, at a prospective cost of £350 million – or well over six times the entire expenditure of the nation in that year.' (Simmons (1975), p. 54)

By no means all of these were eventually approved or built but, by 1850, the paid-up share capital of railways in Britain still came to £187 million. Vast new sources of share capital had to be assembled to feed the demand. It revolutionised the London stock market and led to the creation of stock exchanges in the main provincial towns and cities.

A number of factors contributed to railway mania. There were a number of years of good harvests, generating a surplus; the burgeoning Industrial Revolution was creating a growing middle class with cash to invest (which they could now do more easily with the repeal of the Bubble Act), as well as themselves providing an ever-bigger market for the transport of goods and people; the first railways had come into being, and were proving a great commercial success; and the bank rate had gone down, making investment in government stocks less attractive as an alternative.

In just three years of the 1840s railway mania (1843–45) a total of 179 Railway Acts were passed. Forty-eight out of the sixty-six schemes submitted to the 1844 session of Parliament were approved and in 1845 alone Parliament was asked to consider no fewer than 220 Railway Bills, of which ninety-one were passed. Had they all been approved, they would have been unfundable, as well as being undeliverable in terms of the manpower required to build them. London alone had nineteen proposals for urban lines and termini, which together would have obliterated much of the centre of the city. Seventeen of them were rejected by Parliament, but the idea of wholesale remodelling of the urban fabric was perhaps not such a fanciful one. Haussmann's grandiose rebuilding of Paris for Napoleon III had involved knocking down half the existing city, but was widely admired in Victorian Britain. Outside the metropolis, the London–Brighton route alone had had six competing proposals in 1836–7. Nationwide, it is estimated that, had all the railways proposed been built, the network would have reached something like double its actual peak size.

Investment in a railway was risky, and the earlier in the life of a scheme the investment was made, the greater the risk. A scheme might not even attract enough investor interest to get it to the parliamentary stage; it might well founder in Parliament in the face of competition or opposition from other interested parties; construction costs, and construction timetables, could run way over estimates (a doubling of the estimated cost was by no means unheard of); a scheme might be hit by a change in the national economic climate, or the completed railway might have higher than expected operating costs, or might fail to live up to the forecast level of traffic and income generation. But, correspondingly, the value of shares was likely to increase as the railway cleared each of these potential hurdles and the early investor had the option of selling them on at a profit, provided this happened.

Also in the shareholder's favour was the fact that the money for railway shares was only called up in stages. When first launched, a shareholding interest in a railway could be had for very little financial outlay. Even as it was going through Parliament, no more than 10 or 15 per cent of the shares' face value might be called upon. So railway shares could be acquired by people who were quite unable to meet their full cost, in the hope (or expectation) that they could be sold on profitably before the balance of the share price was called upon.

But in the feverish climate of railway mania these arrangements tended to encourage the advancement of schemes that were to varying degrees speculative, half-baked or downright fraudulent. Parliament tried in 1837 to control this speculation by insisting that a half of the capital needed for a railway should be subscribed before it was laid before Parliament, but this encountered widespread opposition. They reverted back to the old system in 1842, just in time for the next outbreak of railway mania.

As with the canals before them, there was no thought of the government developing a coherent national network. For a brief while, the Board of Trade's new Railways Department attempted to carry out a thorough evaluation of new schemes, but this was abandoned by July 1845, leaving the door wide open to ill-informed speculation. All was left to private initiative and whereas many of the pioneering railways were built on a solid business case, the same could not be said of all those that followed. Sometimes the grander the name of the enterprise, the wobblier was the business case that underpinned it. Thus, Ransom suggests, the Great North Eastern & South Western Connecting Railway and the Grand Hibernian Central Junction Railway were not quite the glittering investment opportunities their names would imply, while the Great Eastern & Western Railway made possible that vital direct link between Yarmouth and Swansea. The less discerning of the great and the good had no problem with lending their name to add legitimacy to a railway proposal without them having the slightest knowledge of the scheme or those connected with it. Their name might even be found on two competing lines. The Scottish judge Lord Cockburn lamented the railway mania in his part of the United Kingdom in 1845:

From Edinburgh to Inverness the whole people are mad about railways. The country is an asylum of railway lunatics. The Inverness patients, not content with a railway to their hospital from Aberdeen, insist on having one by the highland road from Perth. They admit that there are no towns, or even villages, no population and no chance of many passengers. But then they will despatch such flocks of sheep and such droves of nowt!

(Ransom, p. 83)

Some went even further, and took the view that all the potentially profitable lines had already been built. One critic described what is now the East Coast route into Scotland as 'this most barren of projects, the desert line by Berwick', and went on:

A line of railway by the [East] coast seems almost ludicrous, and one cannot conceive for what other reason it can have been thought of, except that the passengers by the railway, if any, might have the amusement of looking at the steamers on the sea, and reciprocally the passengers by sea might see the railway carriages.

(Acworth, quoted in Morgan, p. 78)

The Atheneum in May 1843 produced a critique of the railway schemes that had already been duplicated and the amount of wasted investment associated with them. They concluded that a more rational basis for choosing lines might have produced millions of pounds of savings: 'The whole traffic at present existing might have been concentrated on the remaining lines by a judicious selection, so that they would have been rendered more profitable to the country, while these six millions would have remained for investment.'

Another publication, *The Artisan*, went on to point out that the more actively state-controlled model, as practised in Belgium, had advantages not just in economy but also in safety. This may have been true but, according to Gash, was simply not a realistic possibility in the Britain of the 1830s. The government did not have the money, the men or the administrative skills needed to undertake state enterprise on that scale. It had to be private enterprise or face huge delays.

Evidence to support this comes from a comparison of Britain with its Continental neighbours, where the state was more interventionist. According to Simmons, in 1849 Britain had three times as much railway open as France, ten times as much as Belgium, and more than the whole of the rest of Europe put together. The process may have been untidy and wasteful, but it worked.

In too many cases, railway mania proposals were built on the false business case that railways were a licence to print money; they tended either to duplicate existing lines, or had other shortcomings that militated against their success. It became clear that not all of these schemes were going to get off the ground and even fewer would make their forecast profits. This led the government to pass the Rail Abandonment Act (1850). Under this, the Rail Commissioners could (at the shareholders' request) declare previously approved railway works to be abandoned. In the end, around 2,000 miles of the lines approved between 1845 and 1847 were written off in this way and never got built.

Gullible investors cannot say that they were not warned. In 1845 *Blackwood's Edinburgh Magazine* ran a satire detailing the fraudulent launch of the fictitious Glenmutchkin Railway, linking the most obscure and depopulated parts of the Celtic fringe, and novelist W. M. Thackeray followed a similar theme in *Punch* with his 'Diary of C. Jeames de la Pluche' (and which of us would not place our trust in investment advice from a company named Flimsy, Diddler & Flash?). The mass hysteria over railway shares came to a rather sudden halt on 16 October 1845, when the Bank of England raised Bank Rate to 3 per cent. A slump in the price of speculative shares followed, which also affected some of the more established railways. Speculators found themselves landed with unsaleable shares, leading to bankruptcies, imprisonments for debt, family break-ups and even suicides. As with previous manias, the insanity had spread to every corner of society:

> A return called for by the House of Commons of the dealers in railway undertakings, forms a very remarkable blue book. The noble, who in the pride of blood and birth had ever held traffic in contempt, was there blazoned as a trader. The priest who at his desk prayed to be delivered from the mammon of unrighteousness, was there revealed as seeking in the city to sell his script at a premium. The lawyer who, madly risking his money, sold the property of his client to meet his losses; the physician who periled the savings of a life and the well-being of a family; the chemist who forsook his laboratory for a new form of the philosopher's stone; the banker who in the city and the senate denounced all speculation as illegitimate; the deacon of the meeting house; the Jew, the Quaker, the saint, the sinner were all down in that huge condemning volume … there was scarcely a family in England which was not directly or indirectly interested in the fortunes of the rail.
>
> (Francis, quoted in Morgan, pages 96–7)

Punch ran a cartoon in 1845, showing Queen Victoria asking Prince Albert whether he had any railway shares.

But even as the crash gained momentum, promoters still queued to propose further additions to the network. The year 1846 saw 270 railway bills passed, which would have added 4,540 miles to the railway network at a cost of over £131 million, while the total for 1847 added 189 new schemes to the network – approved, if not yet built (1,414 miles, costed at over £34 million). But by this time, raising the investment was proving an even bigger barrier to construction than the parliamentary process. By 1856, only 5,597 of the 9,792 miles of track approved between 1844 and 1850 had been built. By this time, even a laissez-faire Parliament was trying to put an embargo on further railway schemes coming forward, at a time when there were other, urgent calls upon the nation's finances – like the Crimean War and the ending of the Italian Mutiny. But with over 100 MPs now representing the railway lobby, any such embargo was a forlorn hope. They need not have worried; the mania ran out of steam of its own accord. By the 1850 session of Parliament the additions proposed came to just 6¾ miles.

By the end of 1854 Parliament had authorised railway promoters to raise a total of £368,106,336. As a basis for comparison, the United Kingdom government's entire average annual income between 1851 and 1855 was £58,320,000. As we saw, the Great Western Railway alone cost £6,500,000 at 1840 prices, more than twice the original estimate. The cost of simply getting parliamentary approval for a scheme was daunting. According to government statistics, 160 railway companies laid out a total of £14,086,110, 14s 5½d before laying a brick or digging a turf (another forty-five companies did not bother even making a return for inclusion in those statistics). There was a further, smaller outbreak of railway mania in the 1860s, much of which had to do with duplicating existing broad gauge routes to get round the inconvenience of the break in gauge.

This wasteful and inefficient method of planning the railways (along with the time-consuming and costly parliamentary process) made them expensive, and this too invited unfavourable comparisons with the likes of Belgium, where the state planned and ran the network between the major towns and cities. There, the average cost of building a railway was £17,120 per mile, compared with £32,360 in Britain (free-market apologists found various reasons to explain this, such as the fact that Belgium was much flatter than Britain and therefore needed less engineering).

In 1850, Britain's railway network extended to just over 6,000 miles. This grew to over 9,000 by 1860, 15,500 by 1870, and over 17,000 in 1890. By this time many market towns of any size had not one but two railway lines serving them. Many of these would fall victim to Beeching and other reviews in the following century.

One early attempt to regulate the railways that did reach the statute book was the 1844 Railway Act, William Gladstone's response to the disastrous accident at Sonning. While his select committee was meeting to consider the legislation, Gladstone received a delegation representing some nineteen major railways, led by George Hudson and some leading lawyers of the day. Among the regulatory powers being proposed was the radical one that the government should have the right, under certain circumstances, to acquire railways after twenty years in operation. Gladstone's committee in 1844 even heard evidence calling for the complete nationalisation of the rail network, but this was judged to be a step too far by the committee. Gladstone's Bill was badly mauled by them, and he later complained in Parliament about agents who 'knew how to get up an opposition' in Parliament, and who made 'gross misstatements' about his Bill. Of the Bill's original forty-eight clauses, half were abandoned entirely and others modified as the Bill became the Railway Regulation Act 1844.

The Collapse of Railway Mania

By the end of 1845 the febrile speculation was over, but the foundations had been laid, however inefficiently and at the cost of untold personal grief, for a national rail network:

> The small speculator trembles with despair in the possession of a hundred shares, upon the obtaining of which he has so much congratulated himself. The aforesaid shares, at £25 each, amounting to more than he ever even hoped to possess; he only intended to turn a pound or two. They now hang like a lodestone around his neck, and must eventually sink him, by slow and torturing degrees, in the shape of frequent calls; for those who can pay must...
>
> All rule and order are upset by the general epidemic, as in the plague of London, where all ties of blood, honour or friendship were cast away; and man grew callous to the suffering of his fellow man and only looked to his own welfare and safety in the calamity, and as to how far he could best secure himself from the general ruin.
>
> (*Illustrated London News*, 18 November 1845)

CHAPTER 13

The Railways and Literature

The railways captured the world's imagination, and that included those of writers, poets and artists. They gave them new locations in which to set their dramas, new twists to their plots and added what had previously been an unimaginable dimension of speed and mobility to their characters. In this chapter, we will look at a small selection of how different aspects of life in the railway age were portrayed in literature, poetry and the theatre.

Railways feature in poetry from their earliest days; Tennyson and Wordsworth wrote of them from the 1830s, not always in the most complimentary of terms. Tennyson first travelled by train from Liverpool to Manchester in the year of its opening (1830). He boarded the train in the dark, in the midst of a crowd, and never actually got to see the wheels and workings of the railway. This would explain why, in his poem 'Locksley Hall' (written in 1835 and published in 1842), Tennyson betrays how little he understood of the mechanics of a railway, when he implied that railway wheels ran in grooves: 'Let the great world spin forever down the ringing grooves of change.'

This did not create a fundamental problem for the poem, which was about change more generally, of which railways were just one symbol. As for Wordsworth, one of his first involvements with the railways was, as we saw, his campaign in 1844 against the Kendal & Windemere Railway. This would, he felt, despoil his beloved Lake District and fill it with vulgar tourists. His campaign was conducted partly in verse, including the sonnet 'On the Projected Kendal and Windemere Railway', quoted in the opening chapter.

His campaign was unavailing, the railway opening in 1847, but it prompted one of the contracting engineers, George Heald, to pen his own riposte in verse to the great man. In it, he praised the democratising impact of the railways and their cultural and social benefits:

Why give each town-cramped soul the sight so grand
To view the peaks that decorate our land?
Speak! – answer why! – or crumble into sand
The rail and Barge both glory in the deed,
And to the impeachment gladly Guilty plead.

Heald even dares to suggest that, if more people can get to see the landscapes that inspired them, it would do no harm to the sales of Wordsworth's poems:

And for the Bard – (as Off'ring for our crimes)
We'll give the world to appreciate his rhymes,
The mind will surely place his duties higher
When read 'mid scenes that did the thoughts inspire.

Charles Dickens was perhaps the best-known novelist during the early days of rail, and railways featured heavily in his real life. His extensive recital tours in Britain and the United States would not have been possible without them. But he was a product of the old world, the stagecoach world that was reflected in his early novels from *Pickwick Papers* (1836) to *Barnaby Rudge* (1841).

Railways feature in various parts of Dickens' later writing, in particular *Dombey and Son*, written in 1846 at the height of the railway mania and at the time of George Hudson's spectacular fall from grace. In the book one of the villains, James Carker, dies under the wheels of a train and 'an early chapter gives an unforgettable description of the building of the (London & Birmingham) railway – a kind of "earthquake" that has hit Camden Town'. (*The Guardian*, 23 September 2011)

Part of that description is reproduced elsewhere in this book. *Dombey and Son* reflects Dickens' concerns about railways, in that they created employment and prosperity, but encouraged speculation and the breakdown of the older ways of living, with which he had grown up. The railways also play an important, if more background, role in his book *Hard Times* (1854), serving almost as a metaphor for the heartlessness of the new industrial world that was being created. Elsewhere, in *Bleak House* (chapter 55) he records the coming of the railway to Lincolnshire, while in *The Uncommercial Traveller* he bemoans the impact of the railways on the Rochester of his childhood (recast as Dullborough).

But Dickens also creates some memorable images of the new world of the railways. He likens the relentless nodding up and down of the steam engine's piston to the 'head of an elephant in a state of melancholy madness'. The telegraph wires 'ruled a colossal strip of music paper out of the evening sky', while the criss-crossing of railway lines is 'like a congress of iron vipers', and the pointsman in his elevated signal box 'was constantly going through the motions of drawing immense quantities of beer at a public house bar'.

Dickens hated the railways in real life, and his phobia was not helped by his involvement in the Staplehurst rail crash of 1865, as he was travelling back from Paris. Dickens himself was unhurt, though ten passengers were killed and over forty injured. He was travelling with his secret mistress, Ellen Ternan, and her mother and the trauma of the crash must have been compounded by the fear of his liaison becoming public knowledge through it. Nonetheless, Dickens rescued the Ternans from their carriage, precariously balanced among the wreckage, and spent the next three hours trying to help the wounded (and watching some of them die).

Dickens was traumatised by it all. He lost his voice for a fortnight and thereafter became very nervous of train travel – wherever possible, he would take a slow train or find some alternative mode of travel. He died five years to the day after the crash, and his son said he never really recovered from it. The crash itself has found its own place in literature, featuring in R. F. Delderfield's book *God Is an Englishman*, Dan Simmons' 2009 novel *Drood* and the 2013 film *The Invisible Woman*, in which Ellen Ternan is the central character.

Shortly after Staplehurst, Dickens wrote two further railway-related pieces – 'Mugby Junction', a thinly disguised satire of the notoriously awful refreshment facilities at Rugby, at which Dickens had been badly served, and 'The Signal Man', a short ghost story in which the appearances of the phantom forewarn of a tragic event on the signalman's stretch of line. This latter appears to have been inspired by the Clayton Tunnel crash of 1861, with which most contemporary readers would have been familiar.

The novelist Anthony Trollope (1815–82) was also a great traveller and it is unsurprising that railways feature prominently in his writing. One of his novels, *The Way We Live Now* (1875), draws upon the financial scandals of the early 1870s and concerns the funding of a major railway project. One of the central characters, Member of Parliament and swindler Augustus Melmotte, is thought by some to have been modelled on real-life railway swindler George Hudson. One of his Barsetshire novels, *Dr Thorne* (1858), features another anti-hero railway builder, Sir Roger Scratcherd. On another occasion, Trollope's fire was even directed at that perpetual butt of humour, the railway sandwich:

> The real disgrace of England is the railway sandwich – that whitened sepulchre, fair enough outside, but so meagre, poor and spiritless within, such a thing of shreds and parings, with a dab of food, telling us that the poor bone whence it was scraped had been made utterly bare before it was sent to the kitchen for the soup pot.
>
> *(He Knew He Was Right, 1868)*

A railway disaster always offers good scope for a writer, be it as a plot device in fiction or the commemoration of a real-life event. The sublimely awful Scottish poet William McGonagall was inspired to verse (if inspired be the right word) by the tragic collapse of the Tay railway bridge in 1879. I will quote just the first verse, though readers may rest assured that the remaining three are just as good:

> Beautiful Railway Bridge of the Silv'ry Tay!
> Alas! I am very sorry to say
> That ninety lives have been taken away,
> On the last Sabbath day of 1879
> Which will be remember'd for a very long time

A train crash (possibly also drawing on events at Staplehurst) features centrally in Robert Louis Stevenson's black comedy *The Wrong Box*. Stevenson was not born until well into the railway age (1850) and the story was published in 1889. In it, two elderly brothers were the last surviving members of a tontine (an arrangement by which a group of people pool a sum of money, which is invested and eventually all goes to the last surviving member of the group). One of the brothers is being kept alive (for purely financial reasons) by his two sons, until the three of them are caught up in a major train crash. The sons survive, assume the father has been killed and eventually find what they take to be his body. They decide to take the body and keep his death a secret, so that their father (or, rather, they) can inherit the money. The plot revolves around their attempts to conceal the body (which, of course, turns out to be the wrong body).

Stevenson's other famous use of the railway was in a poem, 'From a Railway Carriage', which appeared in his book *A Child's Garden of Verses* (published in 1885). Generations of children will have been familiar with the opening lines of this:

Faster than fairies, faster than witches,
Bridges and houses, hedges and ditches;
And charging along like troops in a battle,
All through the meadows the horses and cattle

From the earliest days of the railway, people were intoxicated by the unprecedented sensation of speed it gave them and the parallel with the imagined sensation of flight was one that was often conjured up. Dickens gives us an effective and extended image of that sensation in *Dombey and Son*, in part of which he speaks of the train going 'away with a shriek, and a roar, and a rattle, and no trace to leave behind but dust and vapour; like as in the track of the remorseless monster, Death!'

By contrast, another of the most famous railway poems captures a moment of utter stillness. On the afternoon of 23 June 1914 a train from Oxford to Worcester made an unscheduled stop at a small village station, in the heart of the beautiful Gloucestershire countryside. No one got on or off, but a young man travelling on the train enjoyed a moment of perfect peace on a summer's day. The peace was symbolic, for the carnage and madness of the Great War was just weeks away. The young man was the poet Edward Thomas, the village was called Adlestrop, and the poem that the moment produced was to be one of his masterpieces. It was published in 1917, though he did not live to see it in print, for a shell blast claimed him that same year at the Battle of Arras:

Yes, I remember Adlestrop –
The name, because one afternoon
Of heat the express-train drew up there
Unwontedly. It was late June.

The steam hissed. Someone cleared his throat.
No one left and no one came
On the bare platform. What I saw
Was Adlestrop – only the name...

All that talk about no one getting on or off may have been too provocative for Dr Beeching, for in 1966 he closed the station at Adlestrop. All that remains of it today is the bench which formerly stood on the platform, and which now sits in the village bus shelter with a commemorative plaque.

Another First World War poet, Wilfred Owen, captures the frightening image of young recruits embarking on a rail journey to the front. 'The Send Off' was written at the huge Army camp at Ripon, and conjures up the picture of garlanded troops, fresh from their sending-off ceremony, entraining on their way to as yet unimagined and unimaginable horrors. The flowers they wear are the colour of death, for few of them will return:

> Down the close, darkening lanes they sang their way
> To the siding shed
> And lined the trains with faces grimly gay.
> Their breasts were stuck all white with wreath and spray
> As men's are, dead.

If railways can unite people over long distances, they can also separate them. Thomas Hardy (who set several of his poems in trains or on stations) paints a characteristically gloomy picture of one such station farewell in 'On the Departure Platform':

> We kissed at the barrier, and passing through
> She left me, and by the moment got
> Smaller and smaller, until to my view
> She was but a spot

If Dickens' view of the railways is generally hostile, that of Lewis Carroll in *Alice Through the Looking Glass* (1871) is positively unhinged, with passengers (including a goat, a beetle and a horse) all brandishing tickets the size of people. Alice, naturally, does not have a ticket and is variously told that she will have to travel as luggage, by post, as a telegraph message or pull the train herself. No reliable conclusions as to what the railways did for us can be drawn from it.

William Thackeray, who was not averse to knocking the railways, immortalised the get-rich-quick world of railway mania in his poem 'The Speculators'. In it:

> Two gents of dismal mien,
> And dank and greasy rags,
> Came out of a shop for gin,
> Swaggering over the flags;

As the poet listens to their conversation, it revolves around nothing but railway shares, and how fortunes are to be made and lost with them. The poem ends:

> 'Bless railways everywhere,'
> I said 'and the world's advance;
> Bless every railroad share
> In Italy, Ireland, France;
> For never a beggar need now despair,
> And every rogue has a chance'

W. H. Auden was one of the leading British poets of the twentieth century, and his venture into the subject matter of railways became part of the soundtrack (Benjamin Britten provided the musical part of it) to one of the most acclaimed British documentaries of the pre-war period. *Night Mail* (1936) tells how the overnight mail train carried the post from London to Aberdeen, and all points in between. It was made by the Post Office Film Unit, in the days when they could still afford such a thing. Auden's verse, which had to be cut to fit with the visual images, authentically captured the relentless driving rhythms of the train.

It seems that even Dr Beeching and his closures could be the muse that inspired railway literature. Peter Ling's poem 'Harviston End' refers (as far as I can establish) to a fictional station, but is representative of those whose passing was mourned under the Beeching closures, where 'the platform bell will ring no more'.

Perhaps the most famous children's book based on railways is Edith Nesbit's novel *The Railway Children*. It was published (as a book, having previously been serialised) in 1906 and concerns a family who move to the countryside after the father is wrongly imprisoned for spying. Their new home is near a railway, and much of the dramatic action is set on or around it. Needless to say, the father is ultimately reunited with the family. The espionage plot is thought to have been inspired by the notorious Dreyfus affair in France a few years previously, and two Russian émigré characters may have been modelled on real-life Russian dissidents Sergius Stepniak and Peter Kropotkin, who were friends of the author. The book has not been out of print since its first publication, though the story may be better known these days for its film and television versions.

In modern times, the Hogwarts Express has played an important, if incidental, part in the Harry Potter stories, carrying the trainee wizards between platform 9¾ at King's Cross and Hogsmeade station. The film version excites the anger of some rail enthusiasts by sacrilegiously repainting a Great Western Hall class locomotive red!

While on the subject of films, it should be noted that railways have been a favourite theme since the birth of cinema. One of the first true moving pictures to be exhibited was Louis Lumière's *Arrival of a Train at La Ciotat Station* in 1896. It consisted of a single fifty-second shot of a train approaching the camera. Popular legend has it that the realism of this new medium had the audience either screaming and fleeing from the oncoming juggernaut or hiding behind their seats, but this is now thought to be an urban myth. As we saw in the chapter on crime, just about the first narrative film (and certainly a huge (for the day) early box office hit) was Edwin S. Porter's *Great Train Robbery*, a twelve-minute western from 1903. It was important and technically innovative, and has since been conserved by the Library of Congress.

CHAPTER 14

The Railways and Political Change

The Railways and the Anti-Corn Law League

The harvest of 1837 was poor and the winter that followed saw the onset of a depression. One of the factors that added to the hardships faced by ordinary people was the tax on imported grain, designed to protect domestic farming interests. It drove up the cost of corn, making bread less of a staple diet for the poor and more like a luxury foodstuff. The Importation Act of 1815, which imposed this tax, reflected the balance of power between the landowning class (for a long time the most influential vested interest in Parliament), the manufacturers and industrialists (a rising force in the land, but still a minority in 1815) and the majority of the working people (at that that time virtually unrepresented in government). The farmers wanted high wheat prices (so no cheap imports) in order to maximise their income; the manufacturers wanted cheap wheat, so that they could pay their workers less and be more competitive in world markets, for high food prices meant higher wage demands. The working people simply wanted to be able to feed their families.

Under this law, foreign corn could not be imported unless domestic corn reached a price of 80s a quarter. Despite some disastrous harvests in the years that followed, domestic corn never once reached that price level between 1815 and 1848. To make the problem worse, when corn prices decreased the Conservative government of the day passed a law to keep them artificially high. Various reformers in Parliament tried over the years to amend or repeal the corn law, but without success. One of these, the Liberal Whig MP Charles Pelham Villiers addressed a meeting of 'working-class men' on the subject, in Manchester in

1838. Some 5,000 of them turned up, demonstrating the strength of public feeling on the matter. That same year, the Anti-Corn Law League was set up to seek its repeal.

The significance of this, for our purposes, is that the Anti-Corn Law League became a model for all successful modern pressure groups, and that this model was heavily dependent upon the railways. The *Anti-Bread-Tax Circular*, what the League described as their 'well-known organ', described how these were organised:

> Deputations from the League have visited eighteen counties, in which twenty-two meetings have been held...
>
> The course pursued in calling these meetings has, we believe, been invariably the same. From a fortnight to three weeks' notice has been given throughout the county, by advertisements in the local papers, by placards posted in all the towns and villages within 20 miles of the place of meeting and by handbills distributed to all the farmers visiting the principal markets. Hustings have been erected in the most convenient public place sufficiently spacious to accommodate all who desired to take part in the proceedings, and the most influential landowner present has always been preferred for chairman. With a view to giving the widest and most correct publicity to the proceedings, able reporters have invariably accompanied the deputation from London, who have taken down the speeches verbatim, which have been printed and systematically distributed by the agents of the League throughout every parish in the county.
>
> (The *Anti-Bread-Tax Circular*, 2 September 1843)

This nationwide blanket coverage, with travelling speakers and reporters, and a positive blitz of advertising, leaflets, newsletters and placards across a wide area, would scarcely have been possible without a rapidly growing network of railways to deliver it. And it was to have its success in 1846, when the infamous law was repealed. As one contemporary observer commented:

> The Anti-Corn Law agitation was wonderfully forwarded by quick railway travelling and the penny postage. Even in 1830 the railways promoted the cause of reform; and people thought that something like this achievement in constructive and mechanical science might be effected in political science.
>
> (Prentice, quoted in Robbins, p. 38)

Closely involved in the running of the Anti-Corn Law League's campaign was Edward (later Sir Edward) Watkin, who would become one of the most important figures in the development of the railways in the second half of the nineteenth century.

Running in parallel to the Anti-Corn Law League and seeking political reform were the Chartists. They have been described as the first political party of the working class and, being active at a time when revolution was a live issue across Europe, they were feared more by the ruling elite. They, too, used the railways to transport their speakers to meetings around the country. But, by the same token, the government could use its powers to get the railways to ferry troops to wherever they thought Chartist activity might get out of hand. Large barracks were built at Weedon (in Northamptonshire, near what became the West Coast Main Line) and elsewhere for this purpose.

Parliament, the Labour Party and the Railways

While Parliament exercised its – sometimes haphazard – influence over the first railways, the railways soon came to exercise their influence over Parliament: 'The railways were the biggest business Britain had yet seen. Almost a quarter of the expansion of British national income between 1840 and 1865 was attributable to railway development.' (Evans, p. 118)

If the railways were not the start of a new type of share-owning democracy, they had their impact on democracy in another way – as an important pressure group influencing Parliament and other parts of the democratic process. In 1837, there were only seven railway directors in the Commons, but by 1847 the number had risen to eighty. At its peak, in 1873, Parliament contained no fewer than 132 MPs and fifty-four members of the House of Lords who were directors of railway companies. With such a powerful lobby, it is small wonder that they were able to see off threats of nationalisation and other more radical controls over their operations. More generally, the railway lobby played no small part in the shift of power that took place within the Victorian Parliament, away from traditional landed interests and towards a dominant urban, industrial class. This appears to have been part of a very deliberate policy on the part of the railway companies:

> We have but to look back a few years and mark the unanimity with which companies adopted the policy of getting themselves represented in the Legislature, to see that the furtherance of their respective interests – especially in cases of

competition – was the incentive. How well this policy is understood among the initiated may be judged from the fact that gentlemen are now sometimes elected on boards simply because they are members of Parliament.

(H. Spencer, 'Railway Morals and Railway Policy', *Edinburgh Review* Volume
25, 1856)

The railways – or, more specifically, the railway unions – can also claim at least part of the credit for the creation of the Labour Party, which was to change the class structure of Parliament further. The Amalgamated Society of Railway Servants, forerunners to the National Union of Railwaymen, was established in 1871 to defend railway workers against the railway owners. It was a Doncaster member of the society, Thomas Steels, who in 1899 proposed bringing together a number of left-wing organisations to sponsor working-class parliamentary candidates. Labour, acting on its own, had so far failed to gain a foothold in Parliament. The society's general secretary, Richard Bell, helped to make this proposal a reality.

At the 1900 General Election the new organisation, the Labour Representation Committee, got its first two MPs, one of whom was Keir Hardie, elected. During that Parliament, it was also a rail dispute, the Taff Vale Case of 1901, that secured greatly increased support for the Labour movement. This case rendered strikes effectively illegal (or at least prohibitively expensive) for the union movement, by making them liable for any losses incurred by the employers as a result of industrial action. In the 1906 election Labour parliamentary representation increased to twenty-nine members and the party was on its way to becoming a force in the land.

Pressure groups such as the Anti-Corn Law League were quick to see the potential of the railways as a campaigning tool. Politicians took a little longer. The idea of the train-based 'whistle-stop tour' for politicians seeking election had its origin in the rather more far-flung constituencies of America, but was first used in this country by William Gladstone in his so-called 'Midlothian Campaign' of 1878–80. This has been described as the first modern political campaign, and was one in which Gladstone took full advantage of the growing railway network to speak on foreign policy issues up and down the country, in the run-up to the 1880 General Election. It produced a Liberal victory, with Gladstone as Prime Minister, and introduced railway stations as a new venue for political meetings. Not all politicians were immediately attuned to the time constraints this new way of campaigning imposed. At one meeting at Lockerbie station the speech of welcome from a local dignitary was so long that Gladstone's train had to pull out before the great man had a chance to say a word!

The Railways and Democracy

It can be argued that the railways played their part in furthering the cause of democracy, by increasing public awareness of the inequalities that existed in early Victorian England. Part of the lack of awareness stemmed from the geography of the growing industrial towns and cities. This is Friedrich Engels, describing Manchester in 1844:

> Owing to the curious layout of the town it is quite possible for someone to live for years in Manchester and to travel daily to and from his work without ever seeing a working-class quarter or coming into contact with an artisan. He who visits Manchester simply on business or for pleasure need never see the slums, mainly because the working-class districts and the middle-class districts are quite distinct ... plutocrats can travel from their houses to their places of business in the centre of town by the shortest routes, which run entirely through working-class districts, without even realising how close they are to the misery and filth which lie on both sides of the road. This is because the main streets which run from the Exchange in all directions out of the town are occupied almost uninterruptedly on both sides by shops, which are kept by members of the lower middle classes ... Even the less pretentious shops adequately serve their purpose of hiding from the eyes of wealthy ladies and gentlemen with strong stomachs and weak nerves the misery and squalor which are part and parcel of their own riches and luxury.
>
> (Henderson (ed.), pages 26–27)

As we saw in the chapter on the railways as town planners, the railway builders were drawn to the poorest areas of the towns and cities, simply because they were where the cost of land and property was cheapest. While they obliterated large areas of slum housing, they also opened up the remainder to the scrutiny of the travelling public in a way which other journeys from the suburbs to the centre did not. There is a famous and striking picture by Gustav Doré and Blanchard Jerrold, 'Over London by Rail' (1872), showing the squalor of an area of Victorian inner London slums. Cutting a swathe through it are railway viaducts, affording passengers a stark and unavoidable view of what life was like for the poorest in society.

The railway journey between Liverpool and Manchester uncovered another dimension of inequality. At the time the first railways opened, only about 435,000 (by some counts as few as 366,000) out of a nationwide population of some 14 million had the vote, and the spread of seats was very unequal. A rapidly growing town like Manchester, which had a population of some 182,000 by 1831, had not had a Member of Parliament since the time of Oliver Cromwell. But 276 of the seats in the Commons were controlled by landed patrons and had little or no electorate. They were known as rotten or pocket boroughs. Thomas Paine had railed against these in his book *The Rights of Man* as long ago as 1791: 'The town of Old Sarum, which contains not three houses, sends two members: and the town of Manchester, which contains upwards of 60,000 souls, is not admitted to send any. Is there any principle in these things?'

The railway dimension to this is that the line from Liverpool to Manchester went through one of Parliament's more notorious pocket boroughs, Newton. It had been a pocket borough since its establishment in 1558, with the lord of the manor dictating who represented it in Parliament (and, from time to time, selling the privilege). By 1831, this right was the property of the Legh family, who, you will be surprised to learn, consistently selected as one of their MPs one Thomas Legh. In 1831 Newton (unlike Old Sarum) was not entirely deserted; it had 285 houses and a population of 2,139. But of these, only an estimated fifty-two were eligible to vote, and given (a) that it was not a secret ballot and (b) that lords of the manor could evict any tenant voting the wrong way, the votes of their tenants could usually be relied upon. One Manchester man foresaw the impact the opening of the railway would have on public opinion:

> Parliamentary reform must follow soon after the opening of this [rail] road. A million of persons will pass over it in the course of this year, and see that hitherto unseen village of Newton; and they must be convinced of the absurdity of its sending two Members to Parliament, whilst Manchester sends none.
>
> (Prentice, quoted in Hylton (2007), p. 192)

Sure enough, the 1832 Reform Act swept away parliamentary representation to Newton and fifty-five other pocket and rotten boroughs, and gave it instead to Manchester and other major centres of industrial growth. Of course, these reforms would have happened without the opening of the railway, but at the very least the railway increased public awareness of the iniquity of the old system.

CHAPTER 15

The Railways and London

Going Underground

A subterranean railway under London was awfully suggestive of dark noisome tunnels, buried many fathoms deep, beyond the reach of light or life; passages inhabited by rats, soaked with sewer drippings, and poisoned by the escape of gas mains. It seemed an insult to common sense to suppose that people who could travel as cheaply to the city on the outside of a Paddington 'bus would prefer, as a merely quicker medium, to be driven amid palpable darkness through the foul subsoil of London.

(The Times, 30 November 1861)

We knew [Charles Pearson] well and ... have often smiled at the earnestness with which he advocated his project for girdling London round with one long drain-like tunnel, and sending people like so many parcels in a pneumatic tube, from one end of the metropolis to the other.

(Henry Mayhew, *The Shops and Companies of London* (1845), p. 145)

By 1850 London already had seven major railway termini dotted around the fringes of the city centre. This was the result of a conscious decision on the part of a Royal Commission in 1846, to protect the historic core of the city by not allowing the railways into it. (Another consideration, from the railways' point of view, was the ruinously high cost of the land needed to get right into the heart of London or any other major city.) But it meant that passengers could only transfer from one line to another through streets that were even more congested and slow-moving than they are today. An 1807 cartoon by Rowlandson, entitled 'Miseries of London', vividly portrayed this chaos above the caption: 'In going out to dinner (already too late) your carriage delayed by a jam of coaches which choke up the whole street and allow you at least an hour or more than you require to sharpen your wits for table talk.' (Quoted in Taylor, p. 29)

The idea of an underground railway first emerged in the 1830s, but it was 1854 before the Metropolitan Railway got permission to build a £1-million line. But the Crimean War had just started and funding proved to be elusive; it was 1860 before construction could begin.

The first section of line was to run from Bishop's Road, Paddington, where it could connect up with the Great Western, to Farringdon Street (serving the termini of King's Cross and Euston on the way). It broadly followed the route George Shillibeer's pioneering omnibus service had taken in 1829. Most of the route was built by the 'cut and cover' method, during the course of which thousands of (mostly poor) residents were displaced. That said, the City Corporation's slum clearance had already created something of a wasteland around the Farringdon Road part of the route, providing a blank canvas for the railway builders to work on in that area. The line – the world's first underground railway – opened on 10 January 1863 and was an immediate success, carrying 38,000 passengers on its first day and 9.5 million in the first year (50,000 actually tried to buy a ticket on the first day but not all could be accommodated on the trains).

This prompted a rash of 259 applications for other underground railways that would have involved demolishing a large part of the city. A House of Lords Select Committee extended the earlier city centre cordon sanitaire for overground railways, despite the fact that the earlier one had already been breached by a number of parliamentary consents.

Within that area, any railways had to be underground and the Committee decided that one of the priorities should be 'an inner circuit of railway that should abut, if not actually join, nearly all of the principal railway termini in the metropolis'. This was to be the Circle Line, but unfortunately different parts of the route were in the hands of bitter rivals, for whom cooperation was unthinkable. It took James Staats Forbes and Edward Watkin twenty years to complete the Circle Line, due to bickering. Once the line was eventually completed, one rival ran the clockwise services and the other the anti-clockwise and they would not sell or honour each other's tickets. Their rival stations were poorly connected or even duplicated unnecessarily and when the Circle Line was electrified in 1905, they installed incompatible electrification systems (overhead on one, third rail on the other) on their respective lines.

'Pearson's main problem was finding an engine suitable for use underground. The users' problem was managing to breathe.' (Trench and Hillman, p. 132)

The question of how the trains were to be hauled was indeed a problem, for the smoke and fumes associated with steam engines did not commend themselves to the confined spaces of the Underground. John Fowler, the engineer to the Metropolitan, came up with the idea of a fireless locomotive, using a long cylinder of hot bricks to make the steam. The only problem with it was that it did not work; 'Fowler's Ghosts', as they came to be known, never saw service. Instead, the Great Western, who initially operated the railway, supplied tank engines with condensers that were supposed to trap all the smoke and steam. As one means of minimising smoke they tried running the engines on coke, rather than coal, until they discovered that the fumes from coke, albeit less smoky, were more toxic than those from coal.

The steam Underground soon came to be known for its foul atmosphere; one civil servant (who had served in the Sudan and therefore knew about these things) likened it to 'the breath of a crocodile', and a chemist near a Tube station did a roaring trade in Metropolitan Mixture, a patent medicine to relieve the poisonous effects of railway air.

But the railway company was having none of it. They called the atmosphere 'invigorating' and likened it to 'a sort of health resort for people who suffered with asthma'. They even claimed some asthmatics were taking regular trips on the Circle Line, purely for the benefits to their health. Health-giving or not, the railway company nonetheless tried to do at least something about the atmosphere, by banning smoking on the trains. But this resulted in an objection from H. B. Sheridan, a Member of Parliament, which meant them having to provide a smoking carriage on every train. A total ban on smoking in the Underground had to wait until 1987, after the King's Cross fire had taken thirty-one lives. An American journalist gave his view of Victorian underground railway travel:

I got into the underground railway at Baker Street ... It was very warm – for London at least. The compartment in which I sat was filled with passengers who were smoking pipes, as is the British habit, and as the smoke and sulphur from the engine fill the tunnel, all the windows have to be closed. The atmosphere was a mixture of sulphur, coal dust and foul fumes from the oil lamp above; so that by the time we reached Moorgate Street I was near dead of asphyxiation and heat.

(Diary of R. D. Blumenfeld, 21 June 1887, quoted in White, p. 97)

But, even if the atmosphere inside the Underground was foul, commuters could be compensated by being able to live further out in the cleaner air of the suburbs. Other early lines looked at the possibility of cable haulage or atmospheric traction (the latter the system tried so unsuccessfully by Brunel in Devon), but neither proved to be a viable proposition. Even electric haulage did not get off to an entirely smooth start. The powerful locomotives that drew the first electric trains caused excessive vibration at the surface, and it was only when the trains' carriages were converted to individually powered multiple units that a workable system was arrived it (multiple units had the further advantage that they did not have to be turned around at the end of the line).

Like the overground railways, the Underground provided cheap early-day workmen's services that changed the geography of London. New, more affordable suburbs came within the reach of those working in the centre, perhaps meaning that the family could live in two rooms, rather than one. Precisely how affordable these opportunities were, and to whom, was a matter for debate, one pursued elsewhere in this book. One thing that was certain was that the resident population of the City of London, which had been roughly stable since the first census in 1801, peaked at 129,000 in 1851 and fell by more than a half, to 51,000, in 1881.

Why did the early overground railways not take fuller advantage of the potential suburban traffic? The first reason was that not much of the suburbs existed. Early to mid-Victorian London was still a relatively compact city, with green fields within a couple of miles of the centre. It was the Underground lines pushing outwards, in search of additional custom to make their expensive central lines viable, that provided the stimulus for much of the suburban growth. Secondly, many early overground railways saw themselves as strategic, long-distance carriers, to which the stop-start of suburban traffic would prove a hindrance.

Early workmen's trains had been a part of railway operation since the 1844 Act, but in 1861 the Metropolitan line were actually required to provide them, as a condition of their extension to Moorgate. The workmen's tickets provided on the London, Chatham & Dover line had all sorts of conditions attached, seemingly designed to be as obstructive as possible to the customer. Only weekly season tickets were available and these had to state the traveller's name and address and that of his employer. The journey could not be varied and travellers could not carry any luggage, other than tools not weighing more than 28 lbs. No such conditions applied on the Metropolitan's workmen's trains, and by 1898 *Railway* magazine was able to publish a picture of the 'workers' leaving a workmen's train, most of them dressed not as rough artisans, but in the silk hats and morning coats associated with clerical and managerial occupations.

Metroland

> It is very difficult to say nowadays where the suburbs of London come to an end and where the country begins. The railways, instead of enabling Londoners to live in the country, have turned the countryside into a city. London will soon assume the shape of a great starfish.
>
> (Anthony Trollope, *The Three Clerks* (1857))

> The Metropolitan Railway to Watford is likely to have a much greater effect on the development of the town than is at present realised. Just as trade follows the flag, so population follows the railway.
>
> (*Watford Observer*, 2 November 1925)

Metro-land (as it was originally written) was arguably one of the most important creations of the railways as town planners, giving London a whole string of new suburbs, based on commuting by rail. The head of the Metropolitan Railway, Sir Edward Watkin, was a frustrated builder of strategic railway lines who harboured ambitions to link the Metropolitan line to places like Worcester and Manchester, in one direction, and down to Dover (and eventually to Paris, via his planned Channel Tunnel) in the other. When these schemes came to naught, other means were needed of maximising the railway's income. Well patronised though the city centre lines were, the high cost of building underground lines was difficult to recoup. Extending the lines beyond the confines of the city's then built-up area had its appeal, not least that the lines could run at surface level and therefore cost about a fifth of the price of an underground route to build. By the end of the nineteenth century, the line had extended out as far as Aylesbury (today it terminates at Amersham), and branch lines to Uxbridge and Watford were added later.

One slight problem was that they were extending out into areas with very little in the way of population to provide a potential customer base. When Hammersmith got its station in 1864 it was just a village, best known for supplying spinach and strawberries; Earls Court was a market garden with a few houses when its station opened in 1871; while Burnt Oak station was initially surrounded by fields and served no population whatsoever. At first, these new lines were promoted as gateways to leisure for Londoners. Improbable as it may now seem, places like Neasden and Kilburn were marketed as rural idylls:

Neasden: The district about Kingsbury and Neasden is intersected by flowering hawthorn hedges, while the River Brent meanders through them.

Kilburn: Amongst the charms of Kilburn is its proximity to the country. Within half an hour's walk the pedestrian is among trees and fields and pleasant places.

Harrow: The whole neighbourhood is more rural than any part of the country within the same distance from the interminable brick and mortar wilderness of London.

Pinner and Rickmansworth: Opened up a new and delightful countryside to the advantage of picturesque seekers; ancient houses and old world ways. Within fifty minutes from Baker Street and for the cost of less than a florin [10p], if the visitor can be economically disposed, he can enjoy a feast of good things, noble parks, stately homes, magnificent trees and sylvan streams.

(Quoted in Wolmar (2004, 2012), p. 96)

But the only way these areas were going to realise their full potential for the railway's balance sheet was if they were developed for commuter housing. The Metropolitan had an unusual advantage in that, unlike most railway companies, it was not required to sell off all its surplus land. These landholdings could thus be developed for housing. The Metropolitan's holdings could be quite extensive, since landowners often preferred to sell their entire holding, rather than just the narrow strip needed for the railway. From 1919 the railway's sister company, the Metropolitan Railway Country Estates Limited (set up because the Railway was advised that it had powers to own land, but not to develop it), took on the development. Their marketing people conjured up a beguiling – if schizophrenic – picture of an unspoilt arcadia, just ripe for ruination by development, and from 1915 they gave it the name of Metro-land:

A rare opportunity for small capitalists and speculators. Yet only a few minutes away is a charming landscape … tiny hills and hollows … pools of water, brambly wildernesses, where in spring nightingales sing and the air is sweet with the scent of violets, primroses and hawthorn, and in autumn the district is rich with crimson and gold leaves and hedges.

(Edwards and Pigram, p. 26)

But before the building of Metro-land really got under way, a number of the actual garden suburbs can be said to owe their existence – or at least the timing of their development – to the railway. The very first garden suburb – Bedford Park, which pre-dated Letchworth by twenty-five years – was prompted by the District Line extension to Turnham Green, and made much in its marketing of its convenient Underground links to the city. The scheme's original designer was the eminent architect Norman Shaw. Hampstead Garden Suburb was started soon after the Hampstead line opened in 1907, and Harrow Garden Village was another Metropolitan creation.

The development of Metro-land itself started with Cecil Park in Pinner and Wembley Park, at the beginning of the twentieth century. Each extension of the railway was followed by a rash of development radiating out from the stations along the way. A separate company – the British Freehold Land Company – was set up, specialising in buying up large areas of land and selling off building plots. Some of their intended purchasers were on the margins of being able to afford home ownership, as their advertising material seems to imply: 'Try to own a suburban home; it will make you a better citizen and help your family. The suburbs have fresh air, sunlight, roomy houses, green lawns and social advantages.' (Quoted in Wolmar (2004, 2012), p. 237)

What these particular suburbs also had was a good number of half-built shanties, as marginal purchasers struggled with the financial burdens of becoming a homeowner and paying for a daily commute. Fearful that they too could become a shanty town, Ruislip-Northwood Council laid down standards for their area in the country's first town plan, prepared jointly with the main landowner. This aimed to ensure that houses were at least brick-built and had access to mains services and a properly made-up road. The town's aspiration to become a garden suburb was entrusted to a company – Ruislip Manor Limited, which aimed at 'introducing all classes into the community' but not 'to indiscriminately mix all classes and sizes of housing together'. The builder E. S. Reid was certainly not prepared to entertain any riff-raff lowering the tone of his developments, promising would-be purchasers that 'you will not have a nasty cheap mass-production house anywhere near you to lower the value of your property'. The plan was approved by the Local Government Board in 1914, just in time for the war to provide a major distraction.

The suburbanisation of London produced some sizeable shifts in population. Between 1901 and 1937 the population of inner London fell by almost 800,000, while the suburbs increased by some 2,500,000. Individual suburbs grew even more dramatically, as small existing settlements were overwhelmed by the volume of newcomers. The population of Harrow Weald rose from 1,500 to 11,000 and that of Pinner from 3,000 to 20,000 between 1900 and 1930, while Morden grew from a village of 1,000 in 1926 to 12,600 in just five years.

Eventually development destroyed the illusion of a rural idyll that had been a central part of Metroland's marketing strategy, and growth began to slow. In 1933, the Metropolitan Railway was absorbed into London Transport, whose core business was transport rather than housing development, and investment from that quarter came to a halt. Some private sector activity continued, until the Second World War and post-war green belt legislation brought it to a complete stop.

Surbiton, not least by its name, can claim a special place in suburbia (in fact, the name is nothing to do with 'suburban', but is a contraction of South Barton, an old name for the area felt to be more suitable than an earlier rebranding effort – Kingston-upon-Railway). In fact, it can lay claim to be the oldest suburb in Europe, and one that owes its being – as the earlier name suggests – to the railway. It started life in 1838, as a failed speculative housing estate between the London & South Western Railway and the town of Kingston-upon-Thames. The bank foreclosed on the original speculator and their replacement, Philip Hardwicke, created a substantial and successful area of development. By 1855, it could declare its independence from Kingston, which had sought to take the fledgling community into its clutches, and established local government under a body of improvement commissioners. Before long, they could provide enough custom to keep sixty trains a day into London busy and enough clout to negotiate reductions in their season ticket prices.

The Metropolitan Railway can also be said to have made a contribution to the property-owning democracy. At the start of the twentieth century, only about 10 per cent of households were owner-occupiers, but the company's policy of disposing of freeholds added significantly to their numbers.

CHAPTER 16

The Railways and Integrated Transport

Why not make it longer, and have a steamboat go from Bristol to New York and call it the Great Western.

(Brunel's proposed extension to the Great Western Railway, October 1835)

If you've got time to spare, go by air.

(Slogan coined by railway companies to highlight the unreliability of rival air services)

Throughout their history, there have been attempts to link the railways to other modes of transport, to provide – as nearly as possible – a door-to-door service. It should not be forgotten that the first modern railway – the Liverpool & Manchester – started out as one link in an intercontinental chain of transport, carrying cotton from the fields in America to the mills of Manchester. And when the first railways effectively put the long-distance stagecoaches out of business, they responded by setting up feeder services, linking the railway stations more closely to their hinterlands. Brunel's other career, as a steamship designer, was one of the earliest and most ambitious attempts to develop an integrated international transport service.

International rail travel from Britain began early in the railway age. Day trips by railway to the Continent became a reality from 1843, when the South Eastern Railway opened its service to Folkestone Harbour (which it had purchased). They announced their intention to tie this service in to a steam ferry, serving Calais and Boulogne. On board this inaugural service were 'several Members of Parliament, and other distinguished persons who take a warm interest in the promotion of science'. The visit appears to have had little to do with the advancement of science, however, and much more to do with banqueting and exchanging toasts with their French hosts. The company anticipated that the scheduled service should give day-trippers five or six hours to sample all the promotion of science that France had to offer. More to the point, many of the 'nicer' class of British tourists saw the new service as an alternative to the 'roaringly plebeian' character many British seaside resorts appeared to be adopting:

> The seaside towns along the Belgian and north French coasts were discovered to be morally bearable as well as picturesque, and a good deal cheaper than the English resorts offering the desired combination of safe sea bathing, rustic hinterland, and security from the gaze or, worse, conversational approaches of the vulgar.
>
> (Best, p. 228)

The South Eastern Railway's timetable for 1857 offered travellers from Reading a through ticket that would enable the traveller to leave that town in the morning and arrive by the evening in Paris. Meanwhile, in 1850, the next step towards integration had been taken when the world's first public train ferry was introduced. It crossed the Firth of Forth between Granton and Burntisland, carrying a first-class carriage and up to twenty wagons. A similar service was provided across the Firth of Tay the following year, and in 1870 proposals were brought forward for a cross-Channel rail ferry. Detailed plans were drawn up for the design of the boats carrying the trains, the ferry termini and the route. The latter proved a problem:

> On the French coast, much consideration has been given to the locality for the harbour, and great reluctance was felt in being compelled to adopt any place except either Calais or Boulogne. Calais is, however, so exposed from all winds from west to east, and so choked with sand, that it could not possibly comply with the indispensable conditions of the proposed harbour.
>
> (*Illustrated London News*, 12 March 1870)

Similar objections were raised to Boulogne, and a place called Andrecelles, near Cape Grisnez, was chosen. In the event, no Anglo-Continental train ferry was provided until 1924, when a service carrying goods wagons between Harwich and Zeebrugge was opened.

From 1936 a sleeping car service was introduced between London (Victoria) and Paris. The process of loose coupling the sleeping cars, shunting them onto the ferry and chaining them to the deck (a process to be reversed on the other side of the Channel) sounds bumpy, noisy and disruptive, and not conducive to a good night's sleep. But the service was apparently popular. It was one of nine cross-Channel routes served by the Southern Railway in the 1930s.

Before even that, railway interests were behind the first serious attempt to construct a Channel Tunnel, as the *Illustrated London News* reported in March 1882. The very first, short-lived proposal for a Channel Tunnel dated back, surprisingly, to a brief lull in the long-running war between Britain and France in 1802. It was revived as a railway project in the 1860s under the guidance of Sir Edward Watkin, chairman of the South Eastern Railway Company and the Metropolitan Railway, and presiding director of the Submarine Continental Railway Company. A substantial start was made on a pilot tunnel (there was, at roughly the same time, a proposal for a fixed bridge across the Channel, but the obvious objections to this from shipping trying to navigate the Channel prevented it becoming a serious proposition).

Interestingly, it was not a London-centred project. The aim was to link Manchester and the metropolitan north to the Continent by a southward extension of the Manchester, Sheffield & Lincolnshire Railway.

According to the contemporary reports, two compressed air boring machines set out from opposite sides of the Channel, advancing at a stately rate of almost an inch a minute. They hoped to complete the task in three and a half years. The same compressed air that powered the boring machines would provide ventilation in the tunnels. Compressed air locomotives, of a type already being tried on the North Metropolitan Tramways, would be used to haul the trains. They would be loaded with 1,200 cubic feet of air at seventy times atmospheric pressure, which was estimated to be sufficient to draw a 150-ton train across the Channel. The compressed air it discharged along the way would give the passengers plenty to breathe. Should an engine for any reason run out, a back-up pipe of compressed air running the length of the tunnel would provide a reserve supply.

One aspect of the 1882 design that did not feature so strongly in its modern counterpart was the arrangements for defending the tunnel from foreign attack. More space was given over to these in the *Illustrated London News* coverage of the day than was devoted to its construction and peacetime operation. Despite the fact that we had not been at war with France for sixty-seven years, the guns of Dover fort and naval guns from the Channel were to be ready to repel invaders and there were arrangements to flood the tunnel in the event of hostilities. There were even contingency plans against any foreign power trying to smuggle in a surprise party of 2,000 invading troops, disguised as innocent visitors. A Colonel Beaumont explained:

> They cannot come by train; as, irrespective of any suspicions by the booking clerks, special train arrangements would have to be made to carry so large a number; they cannot march, as they would be run over by the trains, running, as they would do, at intervals of ten minutes or oftener, without cessation, day or night.

Invasion by stealth could also be addressed by the compressed air pumping engines being able to redirect their smoke into the tunnel, creating an atmosphere in which no living creature could survive. Some other fairly fanciful ideas were proposed to overcome the military's security objections to the scheme, including a giant lift, by which entire trains would be lowered into or raised out of the tunnel. But the military's opposition was implacable, as the Adjutant-General, Lieutenant General Sir Garnet Wolseley, told a parliamentary committee: 'The proposal to make a tunnel under the Channel … will be to place her under the unfortunate condition of having neighbours possessing great standing armies.'

Two and a half miles of the tunnel were dug before it was abandoned. Ten years later, Sir Edward Watkin was still battling, without success, to secure Board of Trade approval for the project.

Fly By Rail

By the 1920s aviation was the coming mode of travel and in 1929 the big four railway companies were given powers by Parliament to run passenger and freight air services. Five years later, they got together with Imperial Airways to form Railway Air Services Limited. This provided a network of domestic airmail and passenger services around the country, the most important being that between London (Croydon) airport and Scotland. It also provided Imperial Airways with a series of feeder services to their Continental flights. Part of the service included special bus services connecting railway stations and airports.

Despite the fact that the aircraft were little faster than the speediest rail services of the day, their ability to travel in a straight line meant they achieved dramatic time savings on some routes. The rail service between Cardiff and Plymouth took some five hours, whereas it could be done by air (including bus connections) in 1 hour 55 minutes. The original aircraft on this service was a six-seater Westland Wessex, painted in GWR colours and fitted out like a GWR first-class railway carriage. The flights were small-scale and generally unprofitable.

The service was also relatively short-lived. At the start of the Second World War civil aviation was severely restricted and part of the RAS fleet came under government control. At first they flew communications flights, but by 1940 the RAF had taken these over and they were left to fly 'routes of national importance'. In practice this meant carrying mail and government VIPs. The railway-run service resumed early in 1946, using ex-RAF Douglas Dakotas and Avro Ansons, as well as (briefly) some ex-Luftwaffe Junkers Ju 52 trimotors.

During the war years, the railway companies had developed some big ideas for their post-war aviation business. Their Rail Air Plan saw them leading the development of European air services that would deliver 20 million miles of flying per year. But the government had other ideas. At the start of August 1946 the Railway Air Services got caught up in the nationalisation of British airline services generally that led to the establishment of British European Airways as a publicly owned monopoly. RAS ceased operating on 31 January 1947.

CHAPTER 17

Railways and Closures

Oh, Doctor Beeching, what have you done?
There once were lots of trains to catch, but soon there will be none!
I'll have to buy a bike, 'cause I can't afford a car.
Oh, Doctor Beeching, what a naughty man you are!

(Theme song to the television series *Oh Doctor Beeching*)

Beeching … was sardonically amused by what he regarded as a noticeable lack of enthusiasm on the part of some of those who had accepted his report, to support closures in their constituencies with an election pending.

(Hardy, p. 87)

This inhuman plan … is like cutting off the nation's feet to save the cost of shoe leather.

With no station and no trains we might as well be dead.

(1960s protesters' laments)

We have seen a variety of ways in which the historic growth of the railways transformed the fortunes of cities, towns and villages up and down the country. More recently, the trend has been in the opposite direction, with the railways contracting rather than expanding. Did their closure produce the kinds of dire social and economic consequences that some of the prophets of doom, opposing the closures, forecast? Did the railway closures give us ghost towns?

As we have seen, successive nineteenth-century governments failed to take a strategic overview of the growth of the railway network. Lines were allowed to duplicate each other in a wasteful and haphazard manner until, by the First World War, the nation had a network totalling 23,440 miles. The heavy cost of building and maintaining a railway line meant that they were always going to be potentially vulnerable to road-based competition, for whom the cost of providing the trackbed (i.e. a road network) fell largely on the public purse, rather than directly on the users.

This competition began to manifest itself in a serious way immediately after the First World War, as large numbers of Army surplus lorries found their way onto the market. Enterprising individuals started trading as hauliers, in competition with the railways' freight business. Others converted lorries into buses of a kind (some of the conversions were very basic indeed, like fixing garden seats into the back of open lorries). Their economic model was different to the railways; for all their slowness and discomfort, they could often provide a more frequent service, with better penetration into the rural communities they served (urban areas had been getting horse-drawn bus services since the early nineteenth century, when John Greenwood introduced horse-bus services in Manchester and George Shillibeer in London, and there had been electric trams in some of the larger towns and cities since late Victorian times). Railway closures began in earnest in the 1920s and between 1923 and 1939 some 1,300 miles of passenger lines were closed.

A serious programme of closures continued as the railways were nationalised in 1948 and a further 3,000 miles disappeared by 1960. By this time, there was already an established opposition to closures, led by the Railway Development Association (of which poet John Betjeman was a leading member). However, they were more than matched by a powerful roads lobby, which was growing as fast as the traffic on the highway network. It was epitomised in 1959 by the government's choice as Minister of Transport – Ernest Marples, the self-made head of a road construction firm, and it also had its champions within Whitehall. In 1955, Brigadier Thomas Lloyd, Deputy Engineer-in-Chief at the War Office, wrote a report recommending that the nation's entire rail network be converted into roads. He even founded the Railway Conversion League to pursue this aim, one which was later taken up by the Centre for Policy Studies in the Thatcher years.

It was in 1960 that the government of the day brought in a businessman from outside the railway industry, Dr Richard Beeching, to review its future. The railways were by then part way through the fifteen-year modernisation programme introduced in 1955, but this had substantial cost implications (£1.24 billion at 1955 prices), was based on some questionable assumptions about future levels of business and had some serious flaws in its implementation (such as the over-hasty introduction of unreliable diesel traction at the same time as they were still building some of the steam trains that the diesels were supposed to be replacing). Meanwhile, competition from road transport and a combination of out-of-date working practices, strikes and overmanning, for which management and unions could share the blame, were driving the railways' losses ever upwards. Beeching's brief was to look for ways to make the railways pay for themselves.

To some extent Beeching's work can be seen as part of a wider government attempt to prioritise its public spending. Within the sphere of transport, this boiled down to a contest between the rapidly growing demand for more investment in road capacity and a rail network whose recent history had been characterised by decline, spiralling debt and failure.

Beeching's first report, *The Reshaping of British Railways*, appeared in March 1963. It found that one-third of the route mileage carried just 1 per cent of passengers. To give just one example of this, the line from Thetford to Swaffham in East Anglia ran five trains in each direction every weekday, each one carrying an average of nine passengers, whose fares covered just 10 per cent of the line's operating costs. Similarly with stations, they found that one half of passenger stations produced less than 2 per cent of total passenger receipts while, at the other extreme, just thirty-four stations (less than 1 per cent of the total), brought in 26 per cent of the fare income. In fairness, it should be noted that critics of Beeching complain that his statistics were based on a survey conducted in a single week, 17–23 April 1961. This would have missed out things like seasonal holiday traffic, though it would need to have been a severely abnormal week to explain away fully such a dramatic shortfall in revenue.

Beeching recommended that 6,000 miles of the nation's remaining 18,000 miles of railway be closed entirely, along with 2,363 stations and the scrapping of a third of a million freight wagons. Some of the remaining lines would be for freight only. He also proposed that freight services should concentrate on containerised traffic and minerals, rather than traditional wagonloads. Most of Beeching's initial proposals for closure were accepted by the governments of the day (though some were saved by powerful local lobby groups, others by the fact that they served marginal constituencies or by technical arguments about the ability of the local road network to cope with the additional traffic. Some, like the proposed closure of the line serving the Prime Minister's constituency, were also not as politically sensitive as they might have been). The closures had been facilitated in advance by the Transport Act 1962, which made it much easier for railways to be closed without the case for closure needing to be heard in detail. Before that, the local Transport Users' Consultative Committee had a powerful input to any closure debate, and one that deterred rail managers from cutting any but the worst-performing lines. The 1962 Act seriously limited the Committees' input to the decision-making process.

A number of points should be made about the Beeching report. First, it should have preceded, not followed, the 1955 Modernisation Plan for the railways. Second, it was by no means all negative. For example, it recommended important modernisation of the freight service, and many of the proposals in the Modernisation Plan were implemented at the same time as the cuts. Third, Beeching did not disregard the social costs of railway closure. At one point the report says: 'It might pay to run railways at a loss in order to prevent the incidence of an even greater cost which would arise elsewhere if the railways were closed.' (Quoted in Simmons (1975), p. 136)

However, this was seen as a judgement that politicians, rather than a group with their commercial brief, needed to make. As the British Railways Board later acknowledged, a 'necessary railway' could only be defined as part of a government national transport policy.

As we have seen, the contraction of the rail network by no means started with Beeching. In the twelve years leading up to his first report, lines were already being closed at an average rate of 258 miles a year; in the first eleven post-Beeching years the average rate was 369 miles a year – an increase but by no means a quantum leap. Nor was Beeching intended as the last word in railway closures, and some lines he had not earmarked for closure have subsequently been shut down, such as the Woodhead route between Manchester and Sheffield and much of the 'Varsity Line' between Oxford and Cambridge.

Beeching produced a second report in February 1965, *The Development of the Major Railway Trunk Routes*. This said that of the 7,500 miles of trunk railway, just 3,000 should be selected for future development and investment. This would involve traffic being routed along just nine lines and large parts of Great Britain (such as most of Wales, Scotland and East Anglia) becoming railway-free zones. This proved to be a cut too far for the incoming Labour government, who rejected the report. Beeching resigned (some say was sacked) as chairman of the British Railways Board three months later and returned to private industry.

Criticisms of Beeching

> To annihilate the unprofitable, but extremely safe, railway system by increasing the lethal propensities of our ridiculous and costly road system will transfer the price to be paid in money to an account which will be paid for in blood.
>
> (The Mayor of Chard, quoted in the House of Lords, 2 May 1963)

Beeching (and Marples) were naturally demonised, then and to this day, and not only by railway supporters but by many others. An effigy of Marples was burned at Cirencester railway station and demonstrators staged a sit-down demonstration in front of the last train out of Silloth station. The criticisms made of Beeching include:

That he failed to make any recommendations about the land made surplus to railway requirements by his closures. This left British Rail free to dispose of this land for development in a haphazard manner, without any regard for the consequences (such as the potential for reopening the line if demand revived, or developing the trackbed for other uses, like pipeline routes or even improvements to the rural road network);

That his proposals failed to make the inroads promised to the railways' losses. The 1962 deficit of £159 million had only fallen to £151 million by 1968, after more than 5,000 miles of route closures. What did become clear by the late 1960s was that no amount of closures (short of shutting down the network entirely) would bring the railways out of deficit;

That the 'bustitution' policy to replace the railway service with buses often failed. His survey evidence certainly seemed to overstate the extent and quality of existing rural bus coverage, which in many areas could be infrequent almost to the point of uselessness. Most of the bus replacement schemes lasted less than two years before they were withdrawn due to lack of patronage, leaving the communities with no public transport at all. (Again, Beeching also made proposals for greatly improved bus services, which the government failed to act upon);

That Beeching largely disregarded the potential for cost-saving or additional income generation measures to make marginal lines more viable (though, again, was this part of his brief, or his expertise?);

That Beeching made some incorrect assumptions about the contribution branch lines made to the wider network by feeding customers into it. He overestimated car owners' willingness to drive to the nearest surviving railhead and continue their journeys by train, rather than complete their journeys by car. Similarly with the idea that freight customers would take their goods by lorry to and from the nearest points on the rail network, involving the additional cost and delay of two transhipment points, rather than make a seamless delivery by road;

That Beeching failed to factor in the costs associated with shifting more traffic onto the roads, in terms of the need for highway improvements, congestion costs and the cost of road traffic accidents (again, properly a part of a national transport policy). Labour peer Lord Stoneham told the House of Lords on 2 May 1963 that the net subsidy to road transport from the public purse came to roughly four times the railway deficit.

But not all the usual suspects queued up to criticise Beeching. The then general secretary of ASLEF, the train drivers' union, said in a press release: 'The Beeching plan [is] an entirely honest attempt to rationalise the railway system of this country. Many would consider it ruthless but the fact cannot be escaped that had it been less ruthless, it would also have been less honest.' (Hardy, p. 91)

That said, the ASLEF Executive promptly repudiated his release, and normal (i.e. hostile) service was resumed.

Did Beeching achieve the kind of cost savings that were expected of him? The simple answer seems to be that the savings from closure are almost impossible to calculate. As we saw, the overall deficit seemed little changed between the early and late 1960s. According to another estimate, by closing almost a third of the network, Beeching made a saving of just £30 million, at a time when the railway's losses were running at over £100 million a year. For their part, the Ministry of Transport estimated the saving in rail operating costs at over £100 million, although much of it was subsequently offset against improved wages. Others sought to argue that the closure of branch lines cost the railway a lot of traffic that fed passengers into the core network, though over 90 per cent of the railway's 1960 traffic was carried on lines that were still open ten years later.

Life after the Railway

So what became of the communities that were stripped of their railway services? Are there deserted ghost towns? I looked at a sample of the settlements that lost their railway to Beeching, concentrating on smaller, more isolated places in the rural fringes of Britain (as being the ones most likely to have suffered). Nowhere did I find any evidence of a community going into long-term decline. Most appeared to be flourishing. Taking at random just three of the examples I looked at:

If asked to locate Hemyock in Devon, locals might say it was 5 miles from Wellington (which would leave most of the world none the wiser). It had a population of around 1,000 when it got its own branch railway line in 1876. The line was poorly patronised and loss-making until a milk depot was opened in the village and this became the railway's main traffic. Beeching closed the line to passengers in 1963 (without even a replacement bus service being laid on) and the goods traffic to the milk depot ceased in 1975. The village suffered the further blow of the closure of the milk depot in the 1990s. If any community might have suffered as a result of the railway closure, this would seem a reasonable candidate. However, it remains a viable village with a full range of community facilities and a population which has now risen to around 2,000. At the time of writing this the facilities include not one but four local bus services.

Barnoldswick sits in the foothills of the Pennines, in Lancashire. It was for a long time a small village until the coming of the canal and then the railway prompted its growth into a cotton town. It currently has a population of around 10,000 and has the dubious distinction of being the largest town in the British Isles without an A road to its name. The railway was closed in 1965. This, and its economic roots in the now nearly extinct cotton industry, suggests it could have been another candidate for decline after the railway closure. But the town still supports a range of manufacturing industries, including stoves, beds, parts for mountain bikes and even Rolls-Royce jet engines. It also promotes itself as a tourist centre, 'where Brontë country meets the Yorkshire Dales', and boasts a town centre that (against national trends) has grown in the last five to ten years and is 'bursting with bustling shops' (including the highest proportion of independent traders in the country). Again, no sign that Beeching dealt the town a mortal blow.

Llanymynech straddles the border between England and Wales – literally. The boundary runs down the high street and a former pub had two bars in England and one in Wales (subject to different licensing laws). This divided responsibility might have been a reason for neglect and decline. Its history recedes back into the mists of time and its limestone and mineral deposits made it an early transport hub for the canals and the railways. Various railways came there from the 1860s onwards, and began closing from 1933 onwards (including the 1965 Beeching closure). It is rather more coy than Barnoldswick in promoting itself, but the fact that it can support five hotels, a golf club, holiday cottages and a range of community activity suggests that, again, the community was not mortally injured by Beeching. Although it is currently not connected to the railway network, there are proposals by two heritage railways to re-establish that connection.

In fact, what was striking was the number of Beeching closures that were now centres of activity for railway preservation groups. This prompted the question of whether Beeching was the unwitting godfather of preserved steam railways, both by providing a focus for opposition to their closure and creating the opportunities for preservation? Certainly, we seem to have developed a greater enthusiasm for them than almost anywhere else; Great Britain and Ireland currently have 102 passenger-carrying preserved railways. The whole of the rest of Europe can only boast 117 between them. Doctor Beeching, the champion of steam railways? Now, there's a thought!

CHAPTER 18

And Another Thing…

This final chapter gives an opportunity to bring together topics that did not fit naturally into any of the previous ones.

Cattle on the Platform and Other Food Issues

> In the grey mists of the morning, in the atmosphere of a hundred conflicting smells, and by the light of faintly burning gas, we see a large proportion of the supply of the great London markets rapidly disgorged by these night trains: Fish, flesh and food, Aylesbury butter and dairy-fed pork, apples, cabbages and cucumbers, alarming supplies of cats' meat, cartloads of water cresses and we know not what else, for the daily consumption of the metropolis.
>
> (*The Railway News*, 1864)

One of the undoubted benefits of the early railways was the improvement it made to the diet of the average city dweller, through the importing of fresh food. Acworth cites some further examples of this:

> New trades were springing up on all sides. One day it is recorded in a Liverpool paper that a Cheshire farmer has ceased to make cheese, and is supplying the Liverpool market with fresh milk, 'conveying this nutritious article from a distance of over 43 miles and delivering the same by half past eight in the morning'. Another day readers are startled to learn that wet fish from the east coast ports can be delivered fresh in Birmingham or Derby. A tenant on the Holkham estate bears witness to the advantage of a railway to the Norfolk

farmers. His fat cattle, so he said, used to be driven up to London by road. They were a fortnight in the journey, and when they reached Smithfield had lost three guineas in value, beside all the cost out of pocket. As soon as the eastern Counties line was opened he would send his cattle through by train in twelve hours.

(Acworth, quoted in Morgan, p. 91)

Food markets had rapidly become much more national, courtesy of the railways, producing winners and losers among both suppliers and shoppers:

During the past month (November 1843) vast numbers of sheep had been slaughtered by the Darlington butchers and have been sent per railway to London ... The Butter Wives frequenting Barnard Castle market were not a little surprised on Wednesday ... to discover that, through the facilities offered by the railways, a London dealer had been induced to buy butter in their market for the supply of the Cockneys, and in consequence the price went up 2*d* per pound immediately. This rise, however, did not deter the agent from purchasing, and 2,000 pounds of butter were quickly bought, sold and packed off for the great metropolis ... the railway had greatly affected prices in the cattle market at Southall, and had occasioned much discontent among the farmers, who complained that, in consequence of the facility that it afforded for the rapid transfer of stock from one county to another, they had been deprived of the advantages which they formerly possessed from their proximity to London. Five hundred head of sheep and a hundred head of cattle had on more than one occasion been suddenly introduced into the market from the west of England, and prices had been proportionately forced down.

(Ibid.)

Fresh fish suddenly became a part of the diet of those living well away from the sea. By 1848 the Eastern Counties Railway was bringing in 70 tons of fresh fish a week to London from Yarmouth and Lowestoft, from where it could also be rapidly distributed to the provinces by rail.

Surprisingly, London was self-sufficient in milk – of a sort – before the railways. Urban cows were kept in all sorts of odd corners, often under unsavoury conditions. But in 1865 there was a major outbreak of cattle plague and the authorities ordered every cow in London to be destroyed:

Within a week there was not a cow left legally alive within the boundaries of London and the inner home counties. And the capital faced a milk famine ... An enterprising dairyman, George Barham, took the opportunity to bring in supplies of milk by rail from round London, emphasising its freshness by calling his company – which still supplies London with much of its milk – Express Dairies.

(Quoted in Faith, p. 263)

For a long time, the milk was transported in churns – the Southern Railway alone owned over a million of these in the 1920s. Only in 1927 did they start to be superseded by stainless steel tank cars.

One thing the railways did not initially get right was the segregation of livestock and their human passengers on arrival in London. A picture from the *Illustrated London News* of 15 December 1849 showed chaos on the platform at the Euston Square railway terminus, as passengers struggled to make their way through a herd of cattle being discharged from their wagons onto the same platform.

The same publication enumerated the many dietary benefits the Great Northern Railway brought the capital:

Nearly half the tonnage of the line is in grain, consisting of corn, chiefly from Lincolnshire. Until the opening of the Great Northern Line, this corn was almost entirely conveyed coastwise, at great delay and risk of loss and damage. Now, within twenty-four hours it reaches its most distant market with the most perfect punctuality and safety by rail; and for the accommodation of this traffic the Company keep a stock of 100,000 sacks. The carriage of potatoes has reached 300 tons a week; hay, from 30 to 40 tons; and on a single market day, from the neighbourhood of Biggleswade and Sandy no less than 30 tons of cucumbers have arrived at the London stations. Vegetables can now be brought by rail from 50 to 60 miles off in as short a time, and as fresh condition, as by market cart from Barnet, Finchley, Greenwich, Hampton or any place within 8 to 12 miles of London. The rails, in short, give a radius of full 50 miles for metropolitan market gardens; and however great may be the present consumption of fruit and vegetables, there can be no doubt that it is infinitely below the wishes of the population. But the scarcity of such articles of food, in consequence of the narrow limits and high rent of the land on which they are grown, so raises the price as to place them out of the reach of the great majority of the population. And, for such extension of gardens the railway affords still further facilities by carrying down in the returning coal trucks, at a very low rate, the fresh stable manure from London – an item of traffic as yet in its infancy, but which is rapidly gaining ground.

(*Illustrated London News*, 28 May 1853)

The railways also formed part of a supply chain that reached right back to the prairies of Canada and the United States and the Argentine pampas, and contributed to a major agricultural slump across Europe.

The Railways and the Sabbath

Quiet as Marylebone on the Sabbath.

(Victorian saying, quoted in Whitehouse)

The railways played a part in undermining (or liberating us from, depending upon your point of view) the traditional British Sunday. When the railway companies started to respond to the demand for Sunday travel, they quickly fell foul of the strict Sabbatarians, who judged that more or less any activity on a Sunday (other than going to church) was sinful. There was even an Anti-Sunday Travel Union, which by 1889 could boast fifty-eight branches and 8,000 members.

The Sabbatarians would come to consider their position vindicated by the Tay Bridge disaster, when a trainload of sinners was swept away by the collapse of the bridge during a storm, one Sunday in December 1879. For years, many railway companies maintained an uneasy truce with religious interests, by observing a break in rail services during that part of Sunday (10 a.m. – 4 p.m.) when people would normally be attending church. Some railway shareholders objected even to this level of service, to the extent of refusing to accept the part of their dividend that they deemed to have been earned on Sundays. The LNWR used this unclaimed money to fund educational 'good works', and the Liverpool & Manchester Railway paid money from what it called its Sunday Travel Fund to charities.

But in some cases, the shutdown was not driven by religion but by hard-headed commerce, when patronage of Sunday services failed to live up to expectations. The suspension of services was also a useful opportunity to carry out unavoidable heavy engineering works to the track (perhaps a less obvious form of Sabbath breaking).

But when the Newcastle & Carlisle Railway announced Sunday excursions in 1841, Sabbatarians responded with predictable outrage:

A reward for Sabbath breaking
People taken safely and swiftly to Hell!
Next Lord's Day, by the Carlisle Railway, for 7*s* 6*d*
It is a pleasure trip!

The Sabbath was much more closely observed (and militantly enforced) north of the Border, where for a long time almost no Sunday services ran. On one occasion in June 1883, troops had to be despatched to Strome Ferry in the West Highlands, when religious fervour was taken to violent extremes by Sabbatarian hard-liners, trying to prevent the landing and onward delivery by train of fish being brought ashore on a Sunday. The ringleaders of the protest ended up in prison.

One of the pressures for the Sunday running of trains came from the Post Office, who needed Sunday services to ensure Monday deliveries. But the real impetus came from those godless customers who were prepared to patronise Sunday services. As Dr Grantley put it in Trollope's *Barchester Towers*: 'If you can withdraw all the passengers the company I dare say will withdraw the trains. It is merely a question of dividends.'

The Railways and Ticketing

The railways gave us the idea of having pre-printed tickets to act as permits to travel. The first ones on the Liverpool & Manchester followed the stagecoach practice and had to be bought twenty-four hours in advance. They were written onto pre-printed counterfoils in a book (hence booking a ticket). Passengers had to give their name, address, place of birth, age, occupation and reason for travelling. One of the comforting reasons for this welter of information was to make it easier for the railway to trace your next of kin, in the event that you were killed in the course of your journey. Liverpool & Manchester passengers were also warned that, should the train fail to reach its destination by nightfall, passengers were responsible for paying for their own overnight accommodation (this on a journey of 31 miles).

Others, like the Newcastle & Carlisle Railway (who presumably had more confidence in your chances of surviving to the other end) simply wrote down your number, date, time of departure and destination, while the likes of the London & Greenwich and Leicester & Swannington issued reusable metal tokens. At the other extreme, the Edinburgh & Dalkeith Railway did not bother with tickets at all. As its manager explained – rather oddly – to a parliamentary committee in 1839: 'Many people could not tell, or did not make up their minds, where they were going, which causes great confusion in issuing tickets.'

Thomas Edmondson was a cabinetmaker who came to work as a stationmaster for the Newcastle & Carlisle Railway after his idea for a combined cradle rocker and butter churn unaccountably failed to catch on (I am not making this up). He came up with the idea of pre-printed tickets in 1837. They were pre-printed with a serial number and the destination and could have the date of travel stamped onto them with a machine of his own invention. The Newcastle & Carlisle showed no interest in them, so Edmondson sold the idea – and himself – to the Manchester & Leeds Railway. For the benefit of the many illiterate members of the railway staff, the early tickets showed the destination as a thick black line of variable length. The idea caught on and became a national standard, after the Railways Clearing House was set up in 1842. It was adopted in many countries worldwide and British Rail continued to use it until March 1984. All the railways using it paid Edmondson a royalty of 50p per track mile per year and he died a wealthy man.

Credit for the season ticket must go to one William Owen, an enterprising regular traveller on the Liverpool & Manchester Railway, who asked whether he could have a discount if he bought a lot of tickets at once. He got a third off six months' travel in 1842, and the season ticket became generally available on the line from 1845. Other lines also had them; the Stockton & Darlington Railway called them freedom tickets, though they were only available to first- and second-class passengers – third class was strictly pay as you go. But for the ultimate in season tickets, see the section in the book dealing with Alderley Edge.

The Railways and the Eiffel Tower

The railways (briefly – and almost!) gave us Britain's answer to the Eiffel Tower. It was one of the many brainchildren of the ubiquitous Sir Edward Watkin of the Metropolitan Railway. He decided that what Britain was lacking was its own version of the Eiffel Tower (only it needed to be slightly larger). He chose in 1890 to locate it near his new Wembley Park railway station and the first 155-foot phase was actually built. Unfortunately, almost nobody (about 100 people a day) paid to go up it; no doubt having seen Brent and Harrow at close quarters, they decided that the additional height would not lend enchantment to the view. Watkin was eventually forced to demolish it in 1907.

In its place came the largest exhibition the world had ever seen, the Empire Exhibition of 1924–5 – what one commentator described as an imperialist Disneyland, and which the official programme claimed to reproduce in miniature the entire resources of the British Empire. Featured among its attractions were a replica Taj Mahal, the queen's doll's house and a life-size statue of the Prince of Wales made out of (what else?) butter. The centrepiece of the event was the

Empire Stadium (or, as we know it, Wembley stadium). The Exhibition was far more successful than the tower, attracting 27 million visitors to defray its £12-million cost. It featured many railway exhibits and the railways carried many of its visitors.

The Railways and the Government Finances

> They manage generally to relieve the farmers of all poor rates and parish taxes, by the heavy way in which the railways are rated. I hear in Huyton this has amounted to an absolution from all such rates by the general body and the laying of almost the whole upon the railway. This makes the railway a great benefit to the lands through which it passes.
>
> (C. P. Grenfell to the Earl of Sefton, 13 January 1845)

Did the railways single-handedly bankroll the government? Perhaps not all of it, but quite a bit, it seems. Starting with the rates, one of the railways' perennial complaints was that they paid an amount to local rates which was quite disproportionate to the demands they made on local services. As they saw it, they were providing the community with a benefit, in the form of a railway, and were being punitively taxed in return. Moreover, they got no representation as a result.

They do seem to have had a point. To take the example quoted above, in 1849 the railways occupied less than 1 per cent of the local authority area of Huyton but provided 35 per cent of its total rates income. The railways had been given their own method of assessment for rates, based on their profitability, and as a result they found themselves paying up to twenty times more per employee than other industrial or agricultural businesses. The Great Western's total rates bill came to about £1 million in 1913, and rose to £2,250,000 by 1921. The railway companies naturally became skilled at challenging their rating assessments. But the rates were not their only problem; in some areas they faced tithes and periodic payments to turnpike trusts and, from 1870, school boards made heavy demands on them to fund new school buildings. One way round this was for the railway to make more modest payments to local church schools, which would remove the need for a school board to be set up at all.

This was over and above national taxation. Taxation (and 'volunteer' labour) had been the means of providing for the upkeep (such as it was) of the road network since the sixteenth century. Carriage and stagecoach owners were taxed from the eighteenth century, but canals and those that used them somehow escaped taxation entirely. The first direct railway tax came in 1832, when they were charged a halfpenny a mile for every four passengers they carried. This tax fell equally upon all classes of rail travellers, which meant that it formed a far greater part of the fares of the poorest. After much campaigning, the 1844 Railways Regulation Act exempted everybody travelling in the parliamentary trains at a fare of a penny a mile or less. Even so, this duty became an ever-better earner for the government as the quantity of rail travel increased beyond all expectations. By 1883 it was bringing them in £810,000 a year. By then, the railways were the only means of travel still being taxed, with the proportionately heaviest burden still falling on the poorer passengers. Campaigns against the duty finally bore fruit with the Cheap Trains Act 1883, which gave railways exemptions from the duty in return for providing adequate workmen's services. The duty was only finally abolished in 1929, though even then the government ensured that the railways were no better off as a result.

The Railways and Uniformity

One of the sometimes unwelcomed effects of the railway was to help impose uniformity on the country, ironing out differences in food, the environment, clothing and social customs. People became more and more urbanised, towns grew more and more similar in appearance as mass-produced building materials became available across ever-wider areas of the country, and chain stores, selling identical brands of goods, proliferated (their management facilitated by having swift rail access between branches). The spread of literacy and of affordable newspapers to every part of the land also levelled out people's knowledge of the wider world.

The Railways and Temperance

It may be hard to believe, given the early railway navvies' notorious relationship with the demon drink, but it has been argued that the railways made a major contribution to the cause of temperance. According to Harrison, the stagecoaches that preceded the railways were notorious for the excessive drinking by drivers and passengers alike, aided and abetted by the frequent stops at coaching inns to change horses. Not least, it may have helped to ward off the worst effects of long cold journeys, exposed to the elements.

Certainly, the early days of the railway included some notable temperance campaigners, such as Edward Pease, the Quaker promoter of the Stockton &

Darlington Railway, and the leading light of railway excursions, Thomas Cook. But beyond any religious or other grounds for abstinence, the need for safety in operating the railway dictated that drunkenness could not be tolerated. The 1845 Rule Book of the London & South Western Railway is not unusual in stating: 'Any engineman or fireman found drunk whilst on duty, or on the company's premises, will be instantly discharged, and visited with the severest penalties of the law.'

In 1882 a group of railwaymen, encouraged by a much larger national temperance movement and the Church of England, formed the United Kingdom Railway Temperance Union. It had two classes of membership – A: total abstinence and B: 'other'. It had a steady, if not spectacular, growth over the years that followed, by 1908 having 300 branches with 37,947 members. The Bishop of Exeter presided over the opening of that town's branch of the Union in 1885 and, in his opening remarks, rather called into question the need for it. He called it 'a very peculiar and striking' organisation, as 'it could not be said that railwaymen as a general rule were tempted to drunkenness and were as temperate a body as could be found'.

But, to put all this into context, the years of the railways' major growth were also those when alcohol consumption nationally grew most dramatically. In 1831 Burton-on-Trent had nine breweries, producing 50,000 barrels a year. By 1888 there were thirty-one breweries with a combined output of 3,025,000 barrels and the railways helped make them available to a much wider market.

And last, but not least:

The Railways and the Village Idiot

One of their more unusual boasts is that the railways can claim at least part of the credit for helping to eradicate that figure of fun and pity, the village idiot. Before the railways, rural poor people had relatively low mobility, and one of the consequences of that was a relatively small choice of gene pool for marriage partners. This in turn encouraged inbreeding and led to the kinds of genetic problem that might be characterised as 'village idiocy'. When the railways created greater mobility for all, it widened the possibilities for marriage and thereby reduced the possibility of producing offspring that might be classed as village idiots.

Select Bibliography

Acworth, W. M., *The Railways of England* (5th edition) (John Murray 1900)

Adams, William Bridges, *Roads and Rails* (1862)

Aye, John, *Humour on the Rail* (London 1931)

Bagwell, Philip and Lyth, Peter, *Transport in Britain: From Canal Lock to Gridlock* (Hambledon and London 2002)

Beaumont, Robert, *The Railway King* (Review 2002)

Best, Geoffrey, *Mid-Victorian Britain 1851–75* (Fontana 1979)

Biddle, Gordon, *Britain's Historic Railway Buildings* (Oxford University Press 2003)

Blythe, Richard, *Danger Ahead: The Dramatic Story of Railway Signalling* (Newman Neame 1951)

Booth, Henry, *An Account of the Liverpool & Manchester Railway* (Frank Cass 1830, 1969)

Boughey, Joseph, *Hadfield's British Canals* (Sutton 1994)

Brandon, David and Brooke, Alan, *Blood on the Tracks: A History of Railway Crime in Britain* (History Press 2010)

Briggs, Asa, *A Social History of England* (Weidenfeld & Nicholson 1994)

British Railways Press Office, *Facts about British Railways in Wartime* (1943)

Bryan, Tim, *Railways in Wartime* (Shire 2011)

Carlson, Robert E., *The Liverpool & Manchester Railway Project 1821–1831* (David and Charles 1969)

Cavendish, Richard, 'The First W. H. Smith Railway Bookstall' (*History Today*, Volume 48, issue 11, 1998)

Chesney, Kellow, *The Victorian Underworld* (Penguin 1972)

Clapham, J. H., *A Concise Economic History of Modern Britain* (Volume ii, 1932)

Coleman, Terry, *The Railway Navvies* (Pelican Books 1968)

Dendy-Marshall, C. F. and Kidner, R. W., *History of the Southern Railway* (Ian Allan 1968)

Dickens, Charles, *Dombey and Son* (1848)

Disraeli, Benjamin, *Sybil* (Henry Colburn 1845)

Donaghy, Thomas J., *Liverpool and Manchester Operations 1830–45* (David & Charles 1972)

Edwards, Dennis and Pigram, Ron, *The Romance of Metroland* (Baton Transport 1986)

Evans, Eric J., *The Forging of the Modern State* (Longman 1983)

Faith, Nicholas, *The World the Railways Made* (Bodley Head 1990)

Ferneyhough, Frank, *Liverpool and Manchester Railway 1830–1980* (Book Club Associates 1980)

Foxwell, E. and Farrer, T., *Express Trains* (1889)

Francis, John, *A History of the English Railway* (Longman, Brown, Green & Longman 1851)

Frangopulo, N. J. (ed.), *Rich Inheritance* (Manchester Education Committee 1962)

Fuller, Gavin (editor), *Leaves on the Line: Letters on Trains to the* Daily Telegraph (Aurum 2012)

Gash, Norman, *The Age of Peel* (Edward Arnold 1968)

Gibbins, E. A., *Britain's Railways: The Reality* (Leisure Products 2003)

Glancey, Jonathan, *Giants of Steam* (Atlantic 2012)

Guy, Andy and Rees, Jim, *Early Railways 1569–1830* (Shire 2011)

Hall, Stanley, *Railway Milestones and Millstones* (Ian Allan 2006)

Hamilton-Ellis, C., *British Railway History 1877–1947* (Allen & Unwin 1959)

Hardy, R. H. N., *Beeching: Champion of the Railway?* (Ian Allan 1989)

Harrington, Ralph, 'Reading on the Move: A Victorian Precedent' (*The Literary Platform* 8 October 2012)

Harrison, Brian, *Drink and the Victorians* (Faber 1971)

Harrison, J. F. C., *Early Victorian Britain 1832–51* (Fontana 1988)

Henderson, W. O. (ed.), *Engels: Selected Writings* (Penguin 1967)

Holland, Julian, *Dr Beeching's Axe: Fifty Years On* (David & Charles 2013)

Hoskins, W. G., *The Making of the English Landscape* (Guild 1988)

Hylton, Stuart, *The Grand Experiment: The Birth of the Railway Age 1820–45* (Ian Allan 2007)

Hylton, Stuart, *A History of Reading* (Phillimore 2007)

Hylton, Stuart, *The Horseless Carriage: The Birth of the Motor Age* (History Press 2009)

Hylton, Stuart, *A History of Manchester* (Phillimore 2010)

Jenkins, Simon, *Landlords to London* (Constable 1975)

Johnson, Peter, *An Illustrated History of the Travelling Post Office* (Oxford Publishing Company 2009)

Jones, Robin, *Cheshire Railways* (Countryside Books 2011)

Kellett, John, *The Impact of Railways on Victorian Cities* (Routledge & Kegan Paul 1969)

Lambert, Anthony J., *Nineteenth-Century Railway History Through the* Illustrated London News (David & Charles 1984)

MacDermot, E. T. (revised C. R. Clinker), *History of the Great Western Railway* (Volume 1 1833–63) (Ian Allan 1964)

Mayhew, Henry, *London Labour and the London Poor*, Volume 4 (1862, reprinted Hamlyn 1969)

Morgan, Brian (ed.), *The Railway Lover's Companion* (Eyre & Spottiswoode 1963)

Nock, O. S., *Great Western in Colour* (Blandford Press 1978)

Odlyzko, Andrew, *The Railway Mania* (University of Minnesota 2012)

Olivier, Edith, *Without Knowing Mr Walkley* (Faber 1907)

Parkinson-Bailey, John J., *Manchester: An Architectural History* (Manchester University Press 2000)

Pendleton, John, *Our Railways* (Cassell 1894)

Phillips, Daphne, *How the Great Western Came to Berkshire* (Berkshire Books – undated)

Prentice, A., *Historical Sketches and Personal Recollections of Manchester* (1851)

Ransom, P. J. G., *The Victorian Railway and How It Evolved* (Heinemann 1990)

Richards, Jeffrey and MacKenzie, John M., *The Railway Station: A Social History* (OUP 1986)

Robbins, Michael, *The Railway Age* (Routledge and Kegan Paul 1962)

Roden, Andrew, *Great Western Railway: A History* (Aurum 2010)

Ross, David, *British Steam Railways* (Parragon 2011)

Russell, J. H., *A Pictorial Record of Great Western Coaches (Part 1)* (Oxfordshire Publishing Company 1972)

Sadlier, Michael, *Forlorn Sunset* (Pan 1965)

Sampson, Anthony, *The Changing Anatomy of Britain* (Hodder & Stoughton 1982)

Scott, Peter, *A History of the Butlin's Railways* (Peter Scott 2001)

Simmons, Jack (ed.), *Rail 150* (Eyre Methuen 1975)

Simmons, Jack, *The Railways in Town and Country 1834–1914* (David & Charles 1986)

Simmons, Jack (ed.), *Railways: An Anthology* (Collins 1991)

Simmons, Jack, *The Victorian Railway* (Thames & Hudson 1991)

Simmons, Jack and Biddle, Gordon (eds.), *The Oxford Companion to British Railway History* (OUP 1997)

Sowan, Adam, *All Change at Reading* (Two Rivers Press 2013)

Stevenson, John, *British Society 1914–45* (Penguin 1984)

Stewart, Graham, *Britannia: 100 Documents That Shaped a Nation* (Atlantic Books 2010)

Taylor, Sheila (ed.), *The Moving Metropolis* (Laurence King 2001)

Tonge, Neil and Quincey, Michael, *British Social and Economic History 1800–1900* (Macmillan 1980)

Trench, Richard and Hillman, Ellis, *London under London* (John Murray 1985)

Trinder, Barrie, *The Making of the Industrial Landscape* (Sutton 1987)

Vaughan, Adrian, *Railway Blunders* (Ian Allan 2003)

Watson, J. Steven, *The Oxford History of England: The Reign of George III* (OUP 1960)

Whitbread, J. R., *The Railway Policeman* (London 1961)

White, Jerry, *London in the Nineteenth Century* (Vintage 2008)

Whitehouse, J. H. (ed.), *Problems of Boy Life* (London 1912)

Whitehouse, Patrick and St John Thomas, David, *LNER 150* (Guild 1989)

Williams, Frederick S., *Our Iron Roads* (Ingram Cooke 1852)

Williams, Michael, *Steaming to Victory* (Preface 2013)

Wilson, A. N., *The Victorians* (Arrow 2003)

Wintle, Justin (ed.), *The Dictionary of War Quotations* (Hodder & Stoughton 1989)

Wolmar, Christian, *Engines of War* (Atlantic 2010)

Wolmar, Christian, *The Subterranean Railway* (Atlantic 2012)

Woodward, Sir Llewellyn, *The Age of Reform 1815–1870* (OUP 1961)

Wragg, David, *LNER Handbook* (Haynes 2011)

Index